Mastering RethinkDB

Master the capabilities of RethinkDB and implement them to develop efficient real-time web applications. The way to better database development is here!

Shahid Shaikh

BIRMINGHAM - MUMBAI

Mastering RethinkDB

First published: December 2016

Production reference: 1131216

Published by Packt Publishing Ltd.
Livery Place
35 Livery Street
Birmingham
B3 2PB, UK.
ISBN 978-1-78646-107-0

www.packtpub.com

About the Reviewer

Rafael Ferreira dos Santos

Ted's father, Geysla's husband, Developer/Entrepreneur/Bjj addicted, 10 years working with software developer, loves to code, specially in ASP.NET and Node.js.

Thanks to Glenn Morton and the QuizJam team for such an amazing workplace. I would like to thank God and my wife for all the support and love that they give to me. I would not be in such an amazing moment without you.

www.PacktPub.com

For support files and downloads related to your book, please visit www.PacktPub.com.

Did you know that Packt offers eBook versions of every book published, with PDF and ePub files available? You can upgrade to the eBook version at www.PacktPub.com and as a print book customer, you are entitled to a discount on the eBook copy. Get in touch with us at service@packtpub.com for more details.

At www.PacktPub.com, you can also read a collection of free technical articles, sign up for a range of free newsletters and receive exclusive discounts and offers on Packt books and eBooks.

https://www.packtpub.com/mapt

Get the most in-demand software skills with Mapt. Mapt gives you full access to all Packt books and video courses, as well as industry-leading tools to help you plan your personal development and advance your career.

Why subscribe?

- Fully searchable across every book published by Packt
- Copy and paste, print, and bookmark content
- On demand and accessible via a web browser

Table of Contents

Preface

RethinkDB is database built for real time web. It offers us variety of features over NoSQL databases already present in market such as very powerful query language, changefeed and easy scaling.

In this book, we are covering RethinkDB in deep and learning mastering level topics such as scaling, integration and deployment. We are also covering programming with RethinkDB along with step by step screenshot to help you understand the concepts easily.

What this book covers

Chapter 1, *The RethinkDB Architecture and Data Model,* covers the architecture of RethinkDB and data modeling, along with revisiting the concepts of RethinkDB.

Chapter 2, *RethinkDB Query Language,* covers RethinkDB query language, or ReQL, which is the core and essential learning curve of RethinkDB. ReQL provides various SQL-like features such as join, indexing, and foreign keys, along with document-based storage with NoSQL.

Chapter 3, *Data Exploration Using RethinkDB,* covers data extraction and loading along with example use cases using ReQL.

Chapter 4, *Performance Tuning in RethinkDB,* covers various methods and tricks to improve the performance of RethinkDB.

Chapter 5, *Administration and Troubleshooting Tasks in RethinkDB,* covers failover mechanisms along with example use cases.

Chapter 6, *RethinkDB Deployment,* covers various options available to deploy RethinkDB on production.

Chapter 7, *Extending RethinkDB.* This chapter covers the integration of RethinkDB with other products, such as ElasticSearch.

Chapter 8, *Full Stack Development with RethinkDB,* covers the implementation of full stack JavaScript application using RethinkDB.

Chapter 9, *Polyglot Persistence Using RethinkDB,* covers complex synchronization application development using RethinkDB.

Chapter 10, *Using RethinkDB and Horizon.* This chapter covers the RethinkDB-powered framework called Horizon with a demo application.

What you need for this book

A computer with at least 2 GB of RAM that can support Node.js and Java.

Who this book is for

This book caters to all the real-time application developers looking forward to master their skills using RethinkDB. A basic understanding of RethinkDB and Node.js is essential to get the most out of this book. Developers working in backend development, full stack developers and database architect will find this book useful.

Conventions

In this book, you will find a number of styles of text that distinguish between different kinds of information. Here are some examples of these styles, and an explanation of their meaning.

Code words in text, database table names, folder names, filenames, file extensions, path names, dummy URLs, user input and Twitter handles are shown as follows: "We can include other contexts through the use of the include directive. "

A block of code is set as follows:

```
var hash = md5(email);
gravatarUrl = 'http://gravatar.com/avatar/' + hash + '?d=retro';
r.table('users').get(userId).update({
gravatar: r.http(gravatarUrl, {resultFormat: 'binary'})
}).run(conn, callback)
```

When it is necessary to draw your attention to a particular part of a code block, the relevant lines or items are set in bold:

```
r.table(users).reconfigure(
{emergencyRepair: "unsafe_rollback_or_erase"}
).run(conn, callback);
```

Any command-line input or output is written as follows:

```
npm install --save express rethinkdb socket.io async body-parser
```

New terms and **important words** are shown in bold. Words that you see on the screen, in menus or dialog boxes, for example, appear in the text like this: "Clicking on the **Next** button moves you to the next screen".

Warnings or important notes appear in a box like this.

Tips and tricks appear like this.

Reader feedback

Feedback from our readers is always welcome. Let us know what you think about this book—what you liked or may have disliked. Reader feedback is important for us to develop titles that you really get the most out of.

To send us general feedback, simply send an e-mail to feedback@packtpub.com, and mention the book title via the subject of your message.

If there is a topic that you have expertise in and you are interested in either writing or contributing to a book, see our author guide on https://www.packtpub.com/books/info/packt/authors.

Customer support

Now that you are the proud owner of a Packt book, we have a number of things to help you to get the most from your purchase.

Downloading the example code

You can download the example code files for all Packt books you have purchased from your account at http://www.packtpub.com. If you purchased this book elsewhere, you can visit http://www.packtpub.com/support and register to have the files e-mailed directly to you.

You can download the code files by following these steps:

1. Log in or register to our website using your e-mail address and password.
2. Hover the mouse pointer on the **SUPPORT** tab at the top.
3. Click on **Code Downloads & Errata**.
4. Enter the name of the book in the **Search** box.
5. Select the book for which you're looking to download the code files.
6. Choose from the drop-down menu where you purchased this book from.
7. Click on **Code Download**.

Once the file is downloaded, please make sure that you unzip or extract the folder using the latest version of:

- WinRAR / 7-Zip for Windows
- Zipeg / iZip / UnRarX for Mac
- 7-Zip / PeaZip for Linux

The code bundle for the book is also hosted on GitHub at https://github.com/PacktPublishing/Mastering-RethinkDB. We also have other code bundles from our rich catalog of books and videos available at https://github.com/PacktPublishing/. Check them out!

Downloading the color images of this book

We also provide you a PDF file that has color images of the screenshots/diagrams used in this book. The color images will help you better understand the changes in the output. You can download this file from: https://www.packtpub.com/sites/default/files/downloads/MasteringRethinkDB_ColorImages.pdf.

Errata

Although we have taken every care to ensure the accuracy of our content, mistakes do happen. If you find a mistake in one of our books—maybe a mistake in the text or the code—we would be grateful if you would report this to us. By doing so, you can save other readers from frustration and help us improve subsequent versions of this book. If you find any errata, please report them by visiting http://www.packtpub.com/submit-errata, selecting your book, clicking on the errata submission form link, and entering the details of your errata. Once your errata are verified, your submission will be accepted and the errata will be uploaded on our website, or added to any list of existing errata, under the Errata section of that title. Any existing errata can be viewed by selecting your title from http://www.packtpub.com/support.

Piracy

Piracy of copyright material on the Internet is an ongoing problem across all media. At Packt, we take the protection of our copyright and licenses very seriously. If you come across any illegal copies of our works, in any form, on the Internet, please provide us with the location address or website name immediately so that we can pursue a remedy.

Please contact us at copyright@packtpub.com with a link to the suspected pirated material.

We appreciate your help in protecting our authors, and our ability to bring you valuable content.

Questions

You can contact us at questions@packtpub.com if you are having a problem with any aspect of the book, and we will do our best to address it.

1
The RethinkDB Architecture and Data Model

RethinkDB is a real-time, open source distributed database. It stores JSON documents (basically unstructured data) in an operable format with distribution (sharding and replication). It also provides the real-time push of JSON data to the server, which redefines the entire real-time web application development.

In this chapter, we will look over its architecture and key elements in order to understand how RethinkDB supports these awesome features with high performance. We will also look over data modeling along with SQL operations in NoSQL, that is, joins.

Here is the list of topics we are going to cover in this chapter:

- RethinkDB architectural components
- Sharding and replication in RethinkDB
- RethinkDB failover handling
- The RethinkDB data model
- Data modeling in RethinkDB

RethinkDB architectural components

RethinkDB's architecture consists of various components such as cluster, query execution engine, filesystem storage, push changes (real-time feed), and of course RethinkDB client drivers.

Refer to the following diagram to understand the block-level components of RethinkDB:

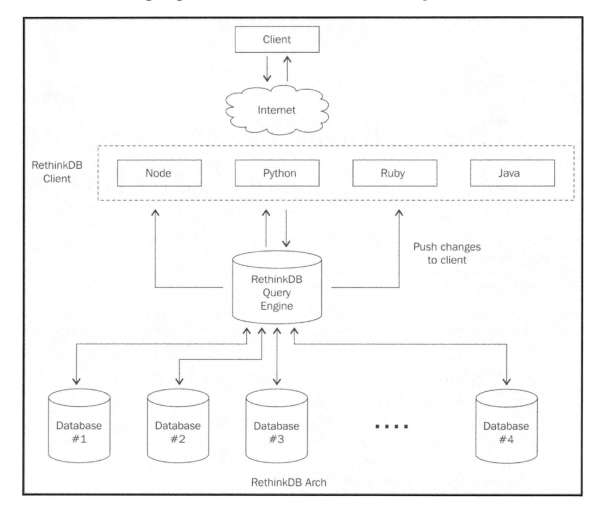

Client drivers

RethinkDB provides official client drivers for Node.js, Python, Ruby, and Java and various non official community drivers which are listed at the official website (`https://rethinkdb.com/docs/install-drivers/`). At the time of writing this book, only these languages were supported. In this book, we will refer to code examples with Node.js.

RethinkDB query engine

RethinkDB query handler, as name implies, performs query execution and returns the response to the client. It does so by performing lot of internal operations such as sorting, indexing, finding the cluster, or merging data from various clusters. All of these operations are performed by RethinkDB query handler. We will look at this in detail in the upcoming section.

RethinkDB clusters

RethinkDB is a distributed database designed for high-performance, real-time operations. RethinkDB manages distribution by clustering (sharding or replication). RethinkDB clusters are just another instance of the main process of RethinkDB and store data. We will look at sharding and replication in detail in the upcoming section.

Pushing changes to a RethinkDB client

This is a revolutionary concept introduced by RethinkDB. Consider this scenario: you are developing an application for the stock market where there are too many changes in a given amount of time. Obviously, we are storing every entry in the database and making sure that other connected nodes or clients know about these changes.

In order to do so, the conventional way is to keep looking (polling) for the data in the particular collection or table in order to find some changes. This improves the latency and turnaround time of packets, and we all know that a network call in a **wide area network** (**WAN**) is really costly. An HTTP call in a WAN is really costly.

Then came something called socket. In this, we do the polling operation but from the socket layer, not the HTTP layer. Here, the size of network requests may get reduced, but still we do the polling.

 Socket.io is one of the popular projects available for real-time web development.

RethinkDB proposes a reverse approach of this: what about the database itself tells you:

Hey, there are some changes happen in stock value and here are the new and old value.

This is exactly what RethinkDB push changes (change feed in technical terms) does. Once you subscribe to a particular table to look for its changes, RethinkDB just keeps pushing the old and new values of changes to the connected client. By "connected client," I meant a RethinkDB client and not a web application client. The difference between polling and push changes is shown here:

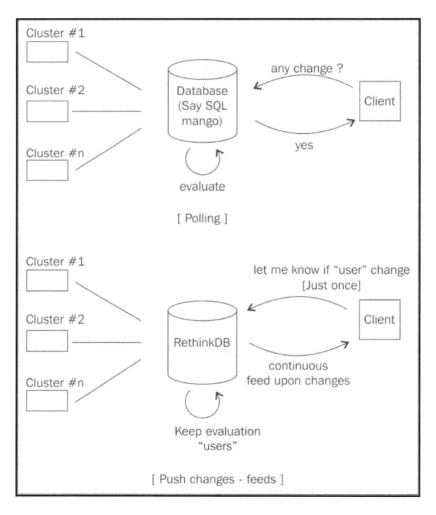

So you will get the changes in the data in one of the RethinkDB clients, say Node.js. And then you can simply broadcast it over the network, using socket probably.

But why are we using socket when RethinkDB can provide us the changes in the data? Because RethinkDB provides it to the middle layer and not the client layer, having a client layer directly talk to the client can be risky. Hence it has not been allowed yet.

But the RethinkDB team is working on another project called Horizon, which solves the issue mentioned previously, to allow clients to communicate to the database using secure layer of the middle tier. We will look at Horizon in detail in `Chapter 10`, *Using RethinkDB and Horizon*.

Query execution in RethinkDB

RethinkDB query engine is a very critical and important part of RethinkDB. RethinkDB performs various computations and internal logic operations to maintain high performance along with good throughput of the system.

Refer to the following diagram to understand query execution:

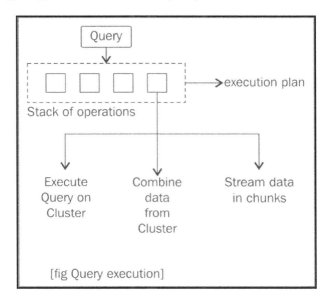

RethinkDB, upon arrival of a query, divides it into various stacks. Each stack contains various methods and internal logic to perform its operation. Each stack consists of various methods, but there are three core methods that play key roles:

- The first method decides how to execute the query or subset of the query on each server in a particular cluster
- The second method decides how to merge the data coming from various clusters in order to make sense of it
- The third method, which is very important, deals with transmission of that data in streams rather than as a whole

To speed up the process, these stacks are transported to every related server and each server begins to evaluate it in parallel to other servers. This process runs recursively in order to merge the data to stream to the client.

The stack in the node grabs the data from the stack after it and performs its own method of execution and transformation. The data from each server is then combined into a single result set and streamed to the client.

In order to speed up the process and maintain high performance, every query is completely parallelized across various relevant clusters. Thus, every cluster then performs the query execution and the data is again merged together to make a single result set.

RethinkDB query engine maintains efficiency in the process too; for example, if a client only requests a certain result that is not in a shared or replicated server, it will not execute the parallel operation and just return the result set. This process is also referred to as lazy execution.

To maintain concurrency and high performance of query execution, RethinkDB uses block-level **Multiversion Concurrency Control (MVCC)**. If one user is reading some data while other users are writing on it, there is a high chance of inconsistent data, and to avoid that we use a concurrency control algorithm. One of the simplest and commonly used methods method by SQL databases is to lock the transaction, that is, make the user wait if a write operation is being performed on the data. This slows down the system, and since big data promises fast reading time, this simply won't work.

Multiversion concurrency control takes a different approach. Here each user will see the snapshot of the data (that is, child copies of master data), and if there are some changes going on in the master copy, then the child copies or snapshot will not get updated until the change has been committed:

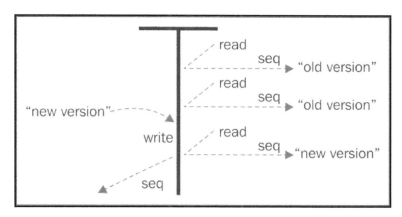

RethinkDB does use block-level MVCC and this is how it works. Whenever there is any update or write operation being performed during the read operation, RethinkDB takes a snapshot of each shard and maintains a different version of a block to make sure every read and write operation works in parallel. RethinkDB does use exclusive locks on block level in case of multiple updates happening on the same document. These locks are very short in duration because they all are cached; hence it always seems to be lock-free.

RethinkDB provides atomicity of data as per the JSON document. This is different from other NoSQL systems; most NoSQL systems provide atomicity to each small operation done on the document before the actual commit. RethinkDB does the opposite, it provides atomicity to a document no matter what combination of operations is being performed.

For example, a user may want to read some data (say, the first name from one document), change it to uppercase, append the last name coming from another JSON document, and then update the JSON document. All of these operations will be performed automatically in one update operation.

RethinkDB limits this atomicity to a few operations. For example, results coming from JavaScript code cannot be performed atomically. The result of a subquery is also not atomic. Replace cannot be performed atomically.

Filesystem and data storage

RethinkDB supports major used filesystems such as NTFS, EXT and so on. RethinkDB also supports direct I/O filesystems for efficiency and performance, but it is not enabled by default.

About direct I/O

File is stored on disk and when it's been requested by any program, the operating system first puts it into the main memory for faster reads. The operating system can read directly from disk too, but that would slow down the response time because of heavy-cost I/O operation. Hence, the operating system first puts it into the main memory for operation. This is called buffer cache.

Databases generally manage data caching at the application and they do not need the operating system to cache it for them. In such cases, the process of buffering at two places (main memory and application cache) becomes an overhead since data is first moved to the main memory and then the application cache.

This double buffering of data results in more CPU consumption and load on the memory too.

Direct I/O is a filesystem for those applications that want to avoid the buffering at the main memory and directly read files from disk. When direct I/O is used, data is transferred directly to the application buffer instead of the memory buffer, as shown in the following diagram:

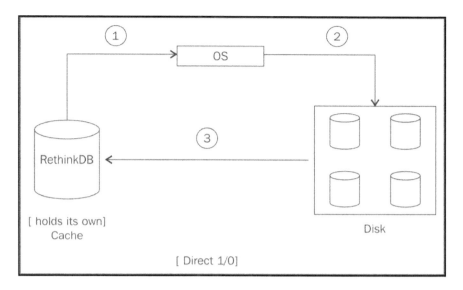

Direct I/O can be used in two ways:

- Mounting the filesystem using direct I/O (options vary from OS to OS)
- Opening the file using the O_DIRECT option specified in the open() system call

Direct I/O provides great efficiency and performance by reducing CPU consumption and the overhead of managing two buffers.

Data storage

RethinkDB uses a custom-built storage engine inspired by the **Binary tree file system by Oracle** (**BTRFS**). There is not enough information available on the RethinkDB custom filesystem right now, but we have found the following promises by it:

- Fully concurrent garbage compactor
- Low CPU overhead
- Efficient multi-core operation
- SSD optimization
- Power failure recovery
- Data consistency in case of failure
- MVCC supports

Due to these features, RethinkDB can handle large amounts of data in very little memory storage.

Sharding and replication

Sharding is partitioning where the database is split across multiple smaller databases to improve performance and reading time. In replication, we basically copy the database across multiple databases to provide a quicker look and less response time. Content delivery networks are the best examples of this.

RethinkDB, just like other NoSQL databases, also uses sharding and replication to provide fast response and greater availability. Let's look at it in detail bit by bit.

Sharding in RethinkDB

RethinkDB makes use of a range sharding algorithm to provide the sharding feature. It performs sharding on the table's primary key to partition the data. RethinkDB uses the table's primary key to perform all sharding operations and it cannot use any other keys to do so. In RethinkDB, the shard key and primary key are the same.

Upon a request to create a new shard for a particular table, RethinkDB examines the table and tries to find out the optimal breakpoint to create an even number of shards.

For example, say you have a table with 1,000 rows, the primary key ranging from 0 to 999, and you've asked RethinkDB to create two shards for you.

RethinkDB will likely find primary key 500 as the breaking point. It will store every entry ranging from 0 to 499 in shard 1, while data with primary keys 500 to 999 will be stored in shard 2. The shards will be distributed across clusters automatically.

You can specify the sharding and replication settings at the time of creation of the table or alter it later. You cannot specify the split point manually; that is RethinkDB's job to do internally. You cannot have less server than you shard.

You can always visit the RethinkDB administrative screen to increase the number of shards or replicas:

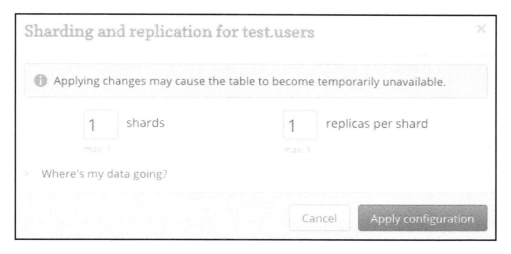

We will look at this in more detail with practical use cases in Chapter 5, *Administration and Troubleshooting Tasks in RethinkDB* totally focused on RethinkDB administration.

Let's see in more detail how range-based sharding works. Sharding can be basically done in two ways, using vertical partitioning or horizontal partitioning:

- In vertical partitioning, we store data in different tables having different documents in different databases.
- In horizontal partitioning, we store documents of the same table in separate databases. The range shard algorithm is a dynamic algorithm that determines the breaking point of the table and stores data in different shards based on the calculation.

Range-based sharding

In the range sharding algorithm, we use a service called locator to determine the entries in a particular table. The locator service finds out the data using range queries and hence it becomes faster than others. If you do not have a range or some kind of indicator to know which data belongs to which shard in which server, you will need to look over every database to find the particular document, which no doubt turns into a very slow process.

RethinkDB maintains a relevant piece of metadata, which they refer to as the directory. The directory maintains a list of node (RethinkDB instance) responsibilities for each shard. Each node is responsible for maintaining the updated version of the directory.

RethinkDB allows users to provide the location of shards. You can again go to web-based administrative screens to perform the same. However, you need to set up the RethinkDB servers manually using the command line and it cannot be done via web-based interfaces.

Replication in RethinkDB

Replication provides a copy of data in order to improve performance, availability, and failover handling. Each shard in RethinkDB can contain a configurable number of replicas. A RethinkDB instance (node) in the cluster can be used as a replication node for any shard. You can always change the replication from the RethinkDB web console.

Currently, RethinkDB does not allow more than one replica in a single RethinkDB instance due to some technical limitations. Every RethinkDB instance stores metadata of tables. In case of changes in metadata, RethinkDB sends those changes across other RethinkDB instance in the cluster in order to keep the updated metadata across every shard and replica.

Indexing in RethinkDB

RethinkDB uses the primary key by default to index a document in a table. If the user does not provide primary key information during the creation of the table, RethinkDB uses its default name ID.

The default-generated primary key contains information about the shard's location in order to directly fetch the information from the appropriate shard. The primary key of each shard is indexed using the B-Tree data structure.

One of the examples for the RethinkDB primary key is as follows:

```
D0041fcf-9a3a-460d-8450-4380b00ffac0.
```

RethinkDB also provides the secondary key and compound key (combination of keys) features. It even provides multi-index features that allow you to have arrays of values acting as keys, which again can be single compound keys.

Having system-generated keys for primary is very efficient and fast, because the query execution engine can immediately determine on which shard the data is present. Hence, there is no need for extra routing, while having a custom primary key, say an alphabet or a number, may force RethinkDB to perform more searching of data on various clusters. This slows down the performance. You can always use secondary keys of your choice to perform further indexing and searching based on your application needs.

Automatic failover handling in RethinkDB

RethinkDB provides automatic failover handling in a multi-server configuration where multiple replicas of a table are present. In case of node failure due to any reason, RethinkDB finds out the other node to divert the request and maintain the availability. However, there are some requirements that must be met before considering automatic failover handling:

- The cluster must have three or more nodes (RethinkDB servers)
- The table must be set to have three or more replicas set with the voting option
- During failover, the majority of replicas (greater than half of all replicas) for the table must be online

Every table, by default, has a primary replica created by RethinkDB. You can always change that using the `reconfigure()` command. In case of failure of the primary replica of the table, as long as more than half of the replicas with voting option are available, one of them will be internally selected as the primary replica. There will be a slight offline scenario while the selection is going on in RethinkDB, but that will be very minor and no data will be lost.

As soon as the primary replica comes online, RethinkDB automatically syncs it with the latest documents and switches control of the primary replica to it automatically.

About voting replicas

By default, every replica in RethinkDB is created as a voting replica. That means those replicas will take part in the failover process to perform the selection of the next primary replica. You can also change this option using the `reconfigure()` command.

Automatic failover requires at least three server clusters with three replicas for table. Two server clusters will not be covered under the automatic failover process and the system may go down during the failure of any RethinkDB instance.

In such cases-where RethinkDB cannot perform failover-you need to do it manually using the `reconfigure()` command, by passing the emergency repair mode key.

Upon running emergency repair mode, each of the shards is first examined and classified into three categories:If more than half of the total shards are available, it will return a healthy status

- **Repairable**: In the case of repairable, the shard is not healthy but has one replica, which can be used
- **Beyond repair**: In the case of beyond repair, the shard has no available replica and cannot be used

For each and every shard that can be repaired, RethinkDB will first change all the offline replicas into non-voting replicas. If there is no voting replica available, RethinkDB will choose one non-voting replica and forcefully convert it into a voting replica.

You can specify two options along with the emergency repair option:

- **unsafe_rollback**: This will leave those shards that are beyond repair during the failover process
- **unsafe_rollback_or_erase**: This will delete those shards that are beyond repair and create one on the available server that holds another shard for that table

Here is the command reference:

```
r.table(users).reconfigure(
{emergencyRepair: "unsafe_rollback_or_erase"}
).run(conn, callback);
```

Please note that emergency failover handling is very critical and should be done by a skilled person, or else you may end up losing all your data.

The RethinkDB data model

The RethinkDB data model consists of two main components:

- RethinkDB data types
- RethinkDB model relationship

RethinkDB data types are further classified into basic data types, dates, binary objects, and geospatial queries.

Refer to the following diagram for more details:

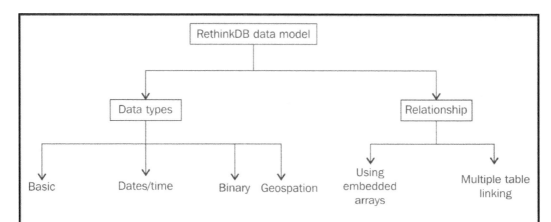

[RethinkDB data model]

Let's go over to each component in detail.

RethinkDB data types

RethinkDB provides six basic data types; they are represented in tabular format, as shown in the following table:

Data type	Description
Numbers	Numbers are stored using double-precision floating-point numbers.
Strings	Strings are stored in UTF-8 standard.
Objects	Stored as a key-value pair with standard JSON format.
Arrays	Stored as a list of elements. It supports 100,000 elements by default.
Binary	Binary objects includes files, images, and other binary data.
Date and time	RethinkDB stores date and time with millisecond precision.
Booleans	True and false values.
Null	Stores null values.

RethinkDB also provides extended data types supported by it. They are as follows:

- **Tables**: These are RethinkDB tables. You can insert and delete documents from them with proper indexing.
- **Streams**: Streams provide the transfer of large amounts of data in chunks so that the system won't reach the buffer overflow limit. They are loaded in a lazy fashion. Streams provide the navigation point to a chunk, called cursor, which you can use to traverse the result set. You can club all of them once the streams are collected using the cursor. This makes it easy to read large amounts of data. Streams are read-only operations.
- **Selections**: Selections are subsets of data, such as 10 documents out of 1,000 from a table. There are two types of selections, one with objects and one with streams. The difference between the two is that objects can be writable while streams are read-only. You can pass an object selected by, say, the `get()` command to other commands to manipulate the data.
- **Date and time**: Date and time are stored in RethinkDB with millisecond precision, along with time zones. Currently, minute-precision time offsets from UTC are supported. RethinkDB internally calculates the time zone difference; hence you don't need to do it at the client end.

You can use native date commands supported by RethinkDB drivers such as in Node.js; you can use the `Date()` object.

Binary objects

Binary objects are stored similar to BLOB in SQL databases. You can directly read and upload files, images, and so on directly into the database. Parsing and other dirty tasks will be dealt with by RethinkDB.

One of the amazing functionalities of RethinkDB is calling external APIs from RethinkDB native drivers. So, consider you want to add profile pictures of users directly into the database from Gravatar, a common place of avatars. All you need to do is call the API and convert the detail into binary. Consider the following official code snippet:

```
var hash = md5(email);
gravatarUrl = 'http://gravatar.com/avatar/' + hash + '?d=retro';
r.table('users').get(userId).update({
gravatar: r.http(gravatarUrl, {resultFormat: 'binary'})
}).run(conn, callback)
```

Assume that `conn` is the RethinkDB connection and we are passing the `email` server of the user to get the avatar. If you notice, we are calling the `gravatar` API using the `http()` function and converting `resultformat` into `binary`.

Specifying the result format is not mandatory here; if the MIME type of the calling server is set correctly, you can just call the HTTP URL and it will be converted to the default MIME type, say binary. It's better to be on the safer side though.

Geospatial queries in RethinkDB

RethinkDB provides and supports geospatial features to help you build location-based applications. By using geospatial queries, you can easily parse, convert, and perform lots of operations, such as computing the distance between two locations, finding an intersecting location, and many more. RethinkDB stores all geographical information in the GeoJSON standard format.

RethinkDB uses a geometry object to perform geographical queries. Geometry objects are derived by plotting two-dimensional objects such as lines and points on a sphere in three-dimensional space.

RethinkDB stores information in a standard geographic system, which is addressing a point on a surface in longitude and latitude. It does not support elevation yet. The range of longitudes is -180 to 180 and the range of latitudes is -90 to 90. To store the same, we use the `point()` function of RethinkDB. Here is some sample code, assuming `r` is a RethinkDB object:

```
r.table('demo').insert([
  {
   name : "Mumbai",
   location : r.point(19.0760,72.8777)
  }
])
```

Supported data types

Geospatial data types and functions are derived from three geometric object data types: points, lines, and polygons.

By using these three, RethinkDB provides various geospatial functions such as `circle()`, `intersect()`, `getNearest()`, and so on.

RethinkDB model relationships

RethinkDB, besides being a NoSQL database, provides one of the most requested features by SQL developers, that is, JOINS. RethinkDB allows you to model and structure your data in such a way that allows you to perform JOINS over it. There are two ways to model relationships in RethinkDB:

- By using embedded arrays in the document
- By linking documents stored in multiple tables

Let's see how both of them work, along with their merits and demerits.

Embedded arrays

Embedded arrays basically means using an array of objects in the table in each document. Here is a simple example:

```
{
  "id": "7644aaf2-9928-4231-aa68-4e65e31bf219",
  "name": "Shahid",
  "chapters": [
    {"title": "Chapter 01", "pages": "30+"},
    {"title": "Chapter 02", "pages": "30+"}
  ]
}
```

Here, the `"chapters"` key contains the array of objects, and each object contains the name of the chapter and the page count. In order to perform the query, here is how we do it in RethinkDB.

To display all chapters from table:

```
r.db("book").table("chapters").run()
```

To get all the chapters written by a particular author; we can do that by passing the author ID:

```
r.db("book").table("chapters").get('7644aaf2-9928-4231-
aa68-4e65e31bf219').run()
```

Here, we are passing the ID of the document, which is a system-generated primary key ID by RethinkDB. Upon passing it, we can access a single document from the table. This is a very basic way of modelling and is not recommended for production use.

Merits of embedded arrays

The following merits are as follows:

- Easy to design and query
- Updates on a single document will automatically update chapters and authors both. Hence, both pieces of data will be atomic

Demerits of embedded arrays

As soon as the size of an embedded array exceeds a certain limit, it costs too much computing power to load the entire array every time we have to perform an operation.

Document linking in multiple tables

This is similar to the foreign key relationships we make in traditional SQL databases. Here, we link two or more tables using the index. We can also query the table using functions provided by RethinkDB to perform various joins (inner, outer, and so on):

```
Authors

{
  id : "abc768332",
  name : "Shahid",
  location: "Mumbai",
  Book: "Mastering RethinkDB"
}

                                                    Chapters

                                {
                                  id : "pqrlmn765",
                                  author_id: "abc768332",
                                  ChapterName: "Chapter01",
                                },

                                {
                                  id : "lmnzc9876",
                                  author_id: "abc768332",
                                  ChapterName: "Chapter02",
                                },

[ Document linking ]
```

As shown in the preceding diagram, we have two tables with multiple documents in them. The **Authors** table will just contain documents related to authors, say name, location, and (obviously) a primary key.

The **Chapters** table will contain documents of chapters; each chapter is a separated document instead of an array. The only difference is that each document will contain an index with the same value as the primary key from the **Authors** table. This way, we link both of them together.

As you can see in the diagram, there is a key in every document in the **Chapters** table named author_id with the same value as id in the **Authors** table.

Here is how we query the tables to perform JOINS:

```
r.db("books").table("chapters").    filter({"author_id": "abc768332"}).
run()
```

This will return every chapter for the author having ID as abc768332.

You can also use RethinkDB JOINS functions such as eq_join(); we will look at the in the next section.

Merits of document linking

The following merits are:

- Data distribution and very neat design
- No need to load all of the data of chapters at once in order to perform any operation
- No matter what the size of documents in chapters table is, the performance won't be affected as in embedded arrays

Demerits of document linking

The following demerits are:

- There are no foreign key constraints, so linking of data will be complicated
- In the case of an update in one table, it won't automatically update the data in another table

Here is a list of JOIN commands provided by RethinkDB:

- eq_Join
- innerJoin
- outerJoin
- Zip

Before looking at these, let's populate some data in two tables. We have authors and chapters in the books database.

We will add author details in the authors table:

```
r.db('books').table('authors').insert({name : "Shahid", location :
"Mumbai"})
```

We will be adding chapter details in the chapters table:

```
r.db('books').table('chapters').insert({
    author_id : "521b92b1-0d83-483d-a374-b94a400cf699",
    chapterName : "Chapter 1"
})

r.db('books').table('chapters').insert({
    author_id : "521b92b1-0d83-483d-a374-b94a400cf699",
    chapterName : "Chapter 2"
})
```

Performing eq_Join

Here we are joining the chapters table with the authors table and mentioning which field we have mapped to the ID, that is, `author_id`:

```
r.db('books').table('chapters').eqJoin("author_id",r.db('books').table('aut
hors'))
```

This will return the following:

```
[
    {
        "left":{
            "author_id":"521b92b1-0d83-483d-a374-b94a400cf699",
            "chapterName":"Chapter 1",
            "id":"f0b5b2f7-1f82-41ef-a945-f5fa8259dd53"
        },
        "right":{
            "id":"521b92b1-0d83-483d-a374-b94a400cf699",
```

```
            "location":"Mumbai",
            "name":"Shahid"
        }
    },
    {
        "left":{
            "author_id":"521b92b1-0d83-483d-a374-b94a400cf699",
            "chapterName":"Chapter 2",
            "id":"f58826d4-e259-4ae4-91e4-d2e3db2d9ad3"
        },
        "right":{
            "id":"521b92b1-0d83-483d-a374-b94a400cf699",
            "location":"Mumbai",
            "name":"Shahid"
        }
    }
]
```

The left and right keys supposedly represent the tables on the left side and the right side of the query. If you map the keys and values with the ReQL query, you can easily understand.

However, this is not how we really want our data. We want processed, result-oriented data, and to do that, we need to use the `zip()` command. It basically removes all metadata information from the result and gives you only the documents of tables:

```
r.db('books').table('chapters').eqJoin("author_id",r.db('books').table('authors')).zip()
```

This returns the following:

```
[
    {
        "author_id":"521b92b1-0d83-483d-a374-b94a400cf699",
        "chapterName":"Chapter 1",
        "id":"521b92b1-0d83-483d-a374-b94a400cf699",
        "location":"Mumbai",
        "name":"Shahid"
    },
    {
        "author_id":"521b92b1-0d83-483d-a374-b94a400cf699",
        "chapterName":"Chapter 2",
        "id":"521b92b1-0d83-483d-a374-b94a400cf699",
        "location":"Mumbai",
        "name":"Shahid"
    }
]
```

Performing inner joins

An inner join, as we all know, equates two tables by comparing each row. It is very similar to working with EQJOIN, except that it compares each document in the table against the target table, while in EQJOIN, we specify which key to compare for.

Here is a simple query to perform an inner join:

```
r.db('books').table('chapters').innerJoin(r.db('books').table('authors'),fu
nction(chapters,authors) {
  return chapters
}).zip()
```

This function takes the target table as a parameter and the callback function, which contains data of both the tables in the callback argument. If you notice, for understanding, I've named the callback parameters the same as the table name. You can perform a lot of other operations such as comparison, or filtering inside the callback function and then returning the result. Since it's a JOIN, in both the variables, data will be similar-except with different table ID's.

Here is the result for the same:

```
[
    {
        "author_id":"521b92b1-0d83-483d-a374-b94a400cf699",
        "chapterName":"Chapter 1",
        "id":"521b92b1-0d83-483d-a374-b94a400cf699",
        "location":"Mumbai",
        "name":"Shahid"
    },
    {
        "author_id":"521b92b1-0d83-483d-a374-b94a400cf699",
        "chapterName":"Chapter 2",
        "id":"521b92b1-0d83-483d-a374-b94a400cf699",
        "location":"Mumbai",
        "name":"Shahid"
    }
]
```

If you observe, the result set is pretty much the same as EQJOIN (the `eq_Join()` function), except that it provides you the result of each document under the callback function. This makes it really slow, and the RethinkDB team does not recommend it for use in production.

Performing outer joins

Outer join union the result of left join and right join and returns it to the client. So, basically, the result test from both the tables will be combined and returned. Here is a sample query.

```
r.db('books').table('chapters').outerJoin(r.db('books').table('authors'),fu
nction(chapters,authors) {
  return authors
}).zip()
```

This will combine each document of `chapters` with each document of `authors` and return the result. Again, we can access each document of the query here under the callback.

It shall return the following:

```
[
    {
        "author_id":"521b92b1-0d83-483d-a374-b94a400cf699",
        "chapterName":"Chapter 1",
        "id":"521b92b1-0d83-483d-a374-b94a400cf699",
        "location":"Mumbai",
        "name":"Shahid"
    },
    {
        "author_id":"521b92b1-0d83-483d-a374-b94a400cf699",
        "chapterName":"Chapter 2",
        "id":"521b92b1-0d83-483d-a374-b94a400cf699",
        "location":"Mumbai",
        "name":"Shahid"
    }
]
```

In order to check it is working, let's just create one more author in the authors table and not create any chapter document entry for it:

```
r.db('books').table('authors').insert({name : "RandomGuy", location :
"California"})
```

Upon running the outer join query again, here is the result:

```
[
    {
        "author_id":"521b92b1-0d83-483d-a374-b94a400cf699",
        "chapterName":"Chapter 1",
        "id":"521b92b1-0d83-483d-a374-b94a400cf699",
        "location":"Mumbai",
        "name":"Shahid"
    },
```

```
{
    "author_id":"521b92b1-0d83-483d-a374-b94a400cf699",
    "chapterName":"Chapter 2",
    "id":"521b92b1-0d83-483d-a374-b94a400cf699",
    "location":"Mumbai",
    "name":"Shahid"
},
{
    "author_id":"521b92b1-0d83-483d-a374-b94a400cf699",
    "chapterName":"Chapter 1",
    "id":"78acabb5-a5b8-434b-acb1-52507b71831d",
    "location":"California",
    "name":"RandomGuy"
},
{
    "author_id":"521b92b1-0d83-483d-a374-b94a400cf699",
    "chapterName":"Chapter 2",
    "id":"78acabb5-a5b8-434b-acb1-52507b71831d",
    "location":"California",
    "name":"RandomGuy"
}
]
```

Hence we get all of the result-the union of each document of the table present in the left table (that is, authors) with each document present in the right table (that is, chapters).

Zip

This function performs the merging of left fields with right fields with a JOIN operation into a single dataset.

Constraints and limitation in RethinkDB

We have covered various architectural features and the data model of RethinkDB. Let's look over some of the constraints of RethinkDB that you need to take into account while architecting your data store.

RethinkDB divides the limitation into hard and soft limitations. The hard limitations are as follows:

- The number of databases has no hard limit
- There is a limit on shard creation, which is a maximum of 64 shards

- Creation of tables inside the database has no hard limit
- Storage size of a single document has no hard limit (however, it is recommended to keep it under 16 MB for performance reasons)
- The maximum possible size of a query is 64 MB

RethinkDB also has some memory limitation, as follows:

- An empty table will need up to 4 MB
- Each table, after population of documents, requires at least 10 MB of disk space on each server wherever it is replicated in the cluster
- Each table consumes 8 MB of RAM on each server

RethinkDB, in order to keep performance high, stores some data in the RAM. There are basically three sources of usage of RAM by RethinkDB:

- Metadata
- Page cache
- Running queries and background processes

RethinkDB stores metadata of tables in the main memory in order to ensure fast read access. Every table consumes around 8 MB per server for the metadata. RethinkDB organizes the data into blocks, with size ranging from 512 bytes to 4 KB. Out of these blocks, approximately 10 to 26 bytes per block are kept in memory.

Page cache is a very important aspect of performance. It is basically used to store very frequently accessed data in the RAM rather than reading it from disk (except in the case of direct I/O, where the page cache is in the application buffer than RAM). RethinkDB uses this formula to calculate the size of the cache:

Cache size = available memory − 1024 MB / 2

If the cache size is less than 1224 MB, then RethinkDB set the size of page cache to 100 MB. This is why it is recommended to have at least 2 GB of RAM allocated for RethinkDB processes.

You can also change the size of the page cache when you start the server or later, using configuration files.

Every database uses some memory to store the results of ongoing running queries. Since queries differ, in general, there is no exact estimate about memory usage by running queries; however, a rough estimate is between 1 MB and 20 MB, including background processes such as transferring data between nodes, voting processes, and so on.

Summary

RethinkDB is indeed a next-generation database with some amazing features and high performance. Due to these architectural advantages, it has been trusted by top-level organizations such as NASA. We covered the architecture of RethinkDB in detail in order to understand how it works and why it is great for real-time databases. We also covered disk storage, clustering, and failover handling of RethinkDB.

Along with the architecture, we also looked over data modeling in RethinkDB. We also looked over one of the most used features of SQL-JOINS working in a NoSQL database, that is, RethinkDB. There is no doubt that RethinkDB is the next big thing.

In next chapter, we are going to learn about the query language of RethinkDB, called ReQL. We will go over it with examples. We will also cover changefeeds, which is personally my favorite feature of RethinkDB.

2
RethinkDB Query Language

ReQL means RethinkDB query language. It offers a powerful and easy way to perform operations on JSON documents. It is one of the most important parts of the RethinkDB architecture. It is built on three important principles: embedding ReQL in a programming language, ReQL queries being chainable, and ReQL queries being executed on the server.

Here is a list of topics we are going to cover, along with the mentioned principles:

- Performing conditional queries
- ReQL queries are chainable
- ReQL queries are executed on a server
- Traversing over nested fields
- Performing string operations
- Performing MapReduce operations
- Calling HTTP APIs using ReQL
- Handling binary objects
- Performing JOINS
- Accessing changefeed (real-time feed) in RethinkDB
- Performing geolocation operations
- Performing administrative operations

Let us look over each one of them.

Embedding ReQL in a programming language

RethinkDB provides client drivers for various programming languages. To explain, I am going to consider Node.js, and the steps are as follows:

1. You can start the ReQL exploration journey by connecting to the database.
2. Install the RethinkDB client module and make sure you have the RethinkDB server ready and running, listening to the default port.
3. Make sure you have done npm install rethinkdb before running the following code:

```
var rethinkdb = require('rethinkdb');
var connection = null;
rethinkdb.connect({host : 'localhost', port :
                   28015},function(err,conn) {
if(err) {
throw new Error('Connection error');
  } else {
connection = conn;
  }
  });
```

The preceding simple code snippet written in Node.js is importing the rethinkdb module and connecting to the RethinkDB server on the default port. It returns the callback function with error and the connection variable, and upon getting the connection object, we are good to go!

By default, RethinkDB creates and connects to the default database named test. We can perform various operations on it such as creating a table or performing CRUD operations.

Let's begin with creating a simple table to store blog posts as follows:

```
rethinkdb.db('test').tableCreate('authors')
.run(connection, function(err, result) {
    if (err) throw err;
console.log(JSON.stringify(result));
```

Upon running the code, you should get the following on your console:

```
{
    "config_changes":[
        {
            "new_val":{
```

```
            "db":"test",
            "durability":"hard",
            "id":"a168e362-b7e7-4260-8b93-37ee43430bac",
            "indexes":[
             ],
            "name":"authors",
            "primary_key":"id",
            "shards":[
                {
                    "nonvoting_replicas":[
                     ],
                    "primary_replica":"Shahids_MacBook_Air_local_pnj",
                    "replicas":[
                       "Shahids_MacBook_Air_local_pnj"
                    ]
                }
            ],
            "write_acks":"majority"
        },
        "old_val":null
    }
  ],
  "tables_created":1
}
```

In our code, we need to check out the `tables_created` key in order to determine whether the table was created or not.

We can check whether the table was created or not in the administrative web console too. Point your browser to `http://localhost:8080` and go to the **DATABASE** section from the menu. You should be able to see something like the following:

In order to run the code in Node.js, since you get the `connection` object in callback and it's asynchronous, you need to manage the flow of the code. For now, you can just paste the code to create a table inside the closure callback of the connection and it should work fine. But when writing code for production, make sure you handle the callback flow well and do not end up being in a callback hell situation.

One of the best ways to manage it and which I use very frequently while coding Node.js programs is by using the async node module. It has a rich set of functions to properly manage and design your code. Of course, there will be no chance of callback hell and you can by far manage not to go for more than four levels of nesting (three is ideal but very tricky to reach).

We have our database up and running and we have created the table using our code. The next is to performing the very famous **CRUD (Create, read, update** and **delete)** operation on the table. This will not only cover some important functions of the RethinkDB query language but also will give a quick kick to perform basic operations, which you have probably been doing in other NoSQL and SQL databases.

Performing CRUD operations using RethinkDB and Node

Let's begin by creating a fresh new table named `users` and perform CRUD operations using ReQL queries as follows:

```
varrethinkdb = require(''rethinkdb''rethinkdb');
var connection = null;
rethinkdb.connect({host : ''localhost''localhost', port :
28015},function(err,conn) {
if(err) {
throw new Error(''Connection error''Connection error');
 } else {
connection = conn;
 }
});
```

We will use the default database to perform this operation. After getting the connection, we will create a table using the following code:

```
rethinkdb.db('test','test').tableCreate('authors','authors').run(connection
,
function(err, result) {
    if (err) throw err;
console.log(JSON.stringify(result)); });
});
```

Make sure that this piece of code is placed correctly within the else section of the connection code. Since we have created the table, we can perform the operation on it.

Creating new records

ReQL provides the `insert()` function to create new documents in the table. Here is the code to do so.:

```
rethinkdb.db('test','test').table('users','users').insert({
userId : "shahid",
password : "password123",
createdDate : new Date()
}).run(connection,function(err,response) {
if(err) {
throw new Error(err);
}
console.log(response);
});
```

Upon running the code, RethinkDB returns the following.:

```
{
deleted: 0,
errors: 0,
generated_keys: [ ''e54671a0'e54671a0-bdcc-44ab-99f3-90a44f0291f8'' ],
inserted: 1,
replaced: 0,
skipped: 0,
unchanged: 0
}
```

Providing database details is optional in the query. The key to look for in the code is `inserted`, which determines whether the document was inserted or not. Since we are not providing the primary key from our side, RethinkDB generates it automatically and you can find that in the `generated_keys`.

You can add much more complex data in the RethinkDB than you can do in any other NoSQL database. You can also store nested objects, arrays, binary objects, and so on. We will look over binary objects in the upcoming section.

Reading the document data

You can read the documents from the table using the `get()` or `getAll()` ReQL method. Here is a query to retrieve all the documents present in the table:

```
rethinkdb.table('users','users').run(connection,function(err,cursor) {
if(err) {
throw new Error(err);
}
cursor.toArray(function(err,result) {
console.log(result);
});
});
```

The preceding code performs the read operation in the table and returns you `cursor`. `Cursor` provides a batch of data in sequence instead of whole data at once. We use the `toArray()` function to read the information in the batch. It should print the following on the console:

```
[ {
createdDate: 2016-06-09T08:58:15.324Z,
id: ''e54671a0'e54671a0-bdcc-44ab-99f3-90a44f0291f8'',
password: ''password123'''password123',
userId: ''shahid'''shahid'
} ]
```

You can also read specific data based on the filter. Let's try to read the data with the uniquely generated ID the using the `get()` method as follows:

```
rethinkdb.table('users').get('e54671a0-bdcc-44ab-99f3-90a44f0291f8')
  .run(connection,function(err,data) {
if(err) {
throw new Error(err);
    }
console.log(data);
  });
```

It will return a single document from the table without the cursor. You can get the response in the callback variable.

As you may have noticed, we are directly accessing the table in the query without passing the database name because the `connection` variable contains the database information.

Updating the document

You can perform the update operation on the document using the `update()` function which accepts the object as an argument. You can at least update one key or the whole document (all keys) after fetching the document. Here is the code snippet to do so:

```
rethinkdb.table('users')
    .get('e54671a0-bdcc-44ab-99f3-90a44f0291f8')
    .update({userId : 'shahidShaikh'})
    .run(connection,function(err,response) {
if(err) {
throw new Error(err);
      }
console.log(response);
    });
```

In order to update the document, we first fetch it using the `get()` method and then running the `update()` function. We are just updating the `userId` key here but you can pass other keys as well.

It will return the following on the console:

```
{
deleted: 0,
errors: 0,
inserted: 0,
replaced: 1,
skipped: 0,
unchanged: 0
}
```

The key to look for in the code is `replaced`, which, if it returns 1, means the update operation is successfully committed; otherwise, in the case of any other value, there is an error.

You can also use `replace()` ReQL method to replace the entire document with a new document. This method generates a new document and do not preserve the same ID as the `update()` method does.

You can validate the data by either running the `get()` method again or running the following code in the web administrative console:

```
r.db('test').table('users').get('e54671a0-bdcc-44ab-99f3-90a44f0291f8')
```

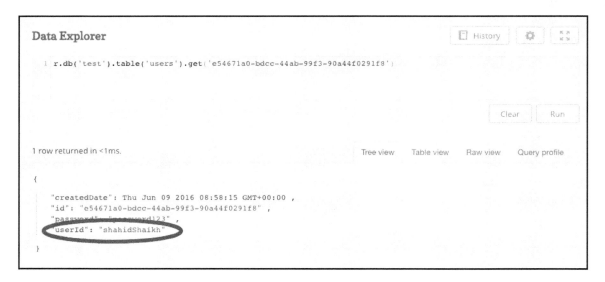

Deleting the document

We can use the delete() ReQL commands to perform a deletion. Again we need to fetch the record first and then perform the delete operation. You can perform a delete all operation as well by first fetching all documents. Here is the code to do so:

```
rethinkdb.table('users')
    .get('e54671a0-bdcc-44ab-99f3-90a44f0291f8')
    .delete()
    .run(connection, function(err, response) {
if(err) {
throw new Error(err);
    }
console.log(response);
    });
```

This should print the following on the terminal:

```
{
deleted: 1,
errors: 0,
inserted: 0,
replaced: 0,
skipped: 0,
unchanged: 0
}
```

You can check out the deleted key to know the status of the delete operation. If you want to delete all the documents from the database, you can do so by selecting all documents first and appending the delete() operation as follows:

```
rethinkdb.table('users')
    .delete()
    .run(connection, function(err, response) {
if(err) {
throw new Error(err);
    }
console.log(response);
    });
```

ReQL queries are chainable

Almost all ReQL queries are chainable. You can chain ReQL queries using the `dot` operator, just like you do with pipe in Unix. Data flows from left to right and data from one command is passed to the next one until the query gets executed. You can chain queries until your query is done.

Just like we performed some queries on the previous section, we chained the `get()` function with `update()` or `delete()` to perform the query.

Here is an example:

```
rethinkdb.table('users').delete();
rethinkdb.table('users').get('<<id>>').update({id : 10});
rethinkdb.db('test').table('users').distinct().count();
```

This way of design provides a natural way of reading and understanding queries. It's easy to learn, modify, and read.

ReQL queries are executed on a server

Queries are formed in the client but will be sent to server for execution when you run them. This makes sure there is no network round trip and bandwidth allocation. This provides efficiency in query execution.

We also mentioned in `Chapter 1`, *The RethinkDB Architecture and Data Model*, that RethinkDB executes queries in a lazy manner. It only fetches the data asked and required for the query to complete. Here is an example:

```
r.db('test').table('users').limit(5)
```

To perform this query, RethinkDB will look for only the five documents only in the `users` table. It will perform enough operations to perform the data collection requested in the query. This avoids extra computation costs and CPU cycles.

To provide the highest level of efficiency, RethinkDB automatically parallelizes the query as much as possible across the server, CPU cores, or even data centers. RethinkDB automatically processes the complex queries into stages, parallelizes them across clusters, and collects data from each one of them before returning it to the client.

Performing conditional queries

ReQL supports conditional queries using **subqueries, expressions,** and the **lambda** function. In this section, we will look at each one of them using sample code written in Node.js.

In order to perform these queries, I have populated our `users` table in the `test` database with some documents. Here is the query executed from the RethinkDB web administrative screen:

```
r.db('test').table('users').insert([{
name : "John",
age : 24
}, {
name : "Mary",
age : 32
},{
name : "Michael",
age : 28
}])
```

 In the web administrative screen, you do not need to provide the `run` function with a connection; it automatically appends and executes the query on the server.

Let us run a query to find out documents with an age greater than 30 years. We are going to execute the following code after getting a connection to the database, the same as we did in the former section:

```
rethinkdb.table('users').filter(function (user) {
return user("age").gt(30);
}).run(connection,function(err,cursor) {
if(err) {
throw new Error(err);
    }
cursor.toArray(function(err,data) {
console.log(data);
    });
});
```

Upon execution, if the data is the same as mentioned previously, you should be receive the following output:

```
[ {
age: 32,
id: 'c8e12a8c-a717-4d3a-a057-dc90caa7cfcb',
name: 'Mary'
} ]
```

Filter() can be considered a SELECT clause with the WHERE condition of SQL. It accepts a condition, matches the condition with documents, and returns the results in the case of a match. You cannot use standard comparison operators such as =, >, <, and so on. Instead, ReQL provides functions to do the same. Here is a list of common comparison operators and their substitute ReQL functions:

Comparison operators	Substitute ReQl functions
==	eq()
>	gt()
<	lt()
>=	ge()
<=	le()

Filter can also support complex queries. As we mentioned, ReQL queries are chainable; hence you can always perform these complex queries by dividing them into subtasks.

Consider an example: you need to retrieve all those users whose age is greater than 30 and name is John.

We know that we can use the lt() function to perform a check of age and eq() to check the exact name. In order to chain these two parts of the query, we will use the and() function. Here is the code to do so:

```
rethinkdb.table("users").filter(function(user) {
return user("age").lt(30).and(user("name").eq("John"))
}).run(connection,function(err,cursor) {
if(err) {
throw new Error(err);
   }
cursor.toArray(function(err,data) {
console.log(data);
   })
});
```

Upon execution, you should receive this JSON document on the console:

```
[ {
age: 24,
id: '664fced5-c7d3-4f75-8086-7d6b6171dedb',
name: 'John'
} ]
```

You can also use range queries using the between() or during() ReQL queries to solve more complex queries.

Just like comparison operators, RethinkDB also provides functions to perform math in ReQL queries. You can use them to directly perform math on values and, of course, manipulate them as well. To avail the use of math functions, you can use the expr() function as a first parameter or any number coming from the latter query. Here is an example of adding two numbers:

```
rethinkdb.expr(2).add(2).run(connection,function(err,result) {
if(err) {
throw new Error(err);
      }
console.log(result);
   });
```

On the console, you should be getting 4.

Similarly you can use the following math functions for the respective operations:

Operations	Functions
Subtracting two numbers	sub()
Multiplying two numbers	mul()
Dividing two numbers	div()
Modulus	mod()

There are of course Boolean operation functions too to perform AND/OR operations. The first chain in the query should be expr() for AND/OR Boolean operations.

To traverse over the nested fields present in the object, we need to use() operator instead of dot notation as we normally do in JavaScript. Refer to the paragraph below to get more clarity on the same.

Imagine you have a JSON document like the following:

```
{
  "id":"f6f1f0ce-32dd-4bc6-885d-97fe07310845",
  "age":24,
  "name":"John",
  "address":{
      "address1":"suite 300",
      "address2":"Broadway",
      "map":{
          "latitude":"116.4194W",
          "longitude":"38.8026N"
      },
      "state":"Navada",
      "street":"51/A"
  }
}
```

And we want to fetch the value of latitude present on the map key, which again resides in the address key. In order to do this, we will first get the document using the primary key and then traverse through the keys. Here is how you can do this:

```
rethinkdb.table("users").get('f6f1f0ce-32dd-4bc6-885d-97fe07310845')("addre
ss")("map")("latitude").run(connection,function(err,result) {
if(err) {
throw new Error(err);
}
console.log(result);
});
```

You should be able to see the value of the latitude key on the console:

Performing string operations

ReQL provides the following functions to manipulate and search strings:

- `Match()` takes a string or a regular expression as an input and performs a search over the field. If it matches, it returns the data in the `cursor`, which we can loop over to retrieve the actual data.
- For example, we have to find all the users whose name starts with J. Here is the query for the same:

```
rethinkdb.table("users").filter(function(user) {
return user("name").match("^J");
}).run(connection,function(err,cursor) {
if(err) {
throw new Error(err);
  }
 cursor.toArray(function(err,data) {
 console.log(data);
  });
});
```

- Here we are first performing a filter, and inside it, we put our `match()` condition. The filter gives every document to the `match()` function and it appends it to the `cursor`. Upon running, you should be able to view the users with names starting with J.
- `split()` takes an optional argument as a separator to filter out the string and returns an array that contains the split part of the string. If no argument is present, it is separated by a space.
- For example, you have an address stored like this: `Suite 300`. If you want to split them by space, you can do so as follows(assuming the same structure of the document as we mentioned previously):

```
rethinkdb.table("users").get('f6f1f0ce-32dd-4bc6-885d
97fe07310845')("address)
("address1").split().run(connection,function(err,result) {
if(err) {
        throw new Error(err);
      }
console.log(result);
});
```

- You should recieve the following output:

```
[ 'suite', '300' ]
[ 'suite', '300' ]
```

- Make sure your first input is a string and not an object. You can also provide any separator, say |, &, *, and so on. You can even provide an optional argument that limits the number of splits.
- The rest of the two functions will allow you to change the casing of the string. For example, if you want the name to appear in capital casing only, you can run the following query to do so:

```
rethinkdb.table("users").get('f6f1f0ce-32dd-4bc6-885d
97fe07310845'
("name").upcase().run(connection,function(err,result) {
if(err) {
        throw new Error(err);
        }
console.log(result);
});
```

You should be receiving the name in uppercase on the console. You can use `downcase()` in the same way.

Performing MapReduce operations

MapReduce is the programming model to perform operations (mainly aggregation) on distributed sets of data across various clusters in different servers. This concept was coined by Google and was used in the Google file system initially and later was adopted by the open source Hadoop project.

MapReduce works by processing the data on each server and then combine it together to form a result set. It actually divides into two operations namely Map and Reduce.

- **Map**: This performs the transformation of the elements in the group or individual sequence
- **Reduce**: This performs the aggregation and combines the results from Map into a meaningful result set

In RethinkDB, MapReduce queries operate in three steps as follows:

- **Group operation**: To process the data into groups. This step is optional
- **Map operation**: To transform the data or group of data into a sequence
- **Reduce operation**: To aggregate the sequence data to form a resultset

So mainly it is a **Group MapReduce (GMR)** operation. RethinkDB spread the MapReduce query across various clusters in order to improve efficiency. There is specific command to perform this GMR operation; however RethinkDB has already integrated them internally to some aggregate functions in order to simplify the process.

Let us perform some aggregation operations in RethinkDB.

Grouping the data

To group the data on the basis of field we can use the `group()` ReQL function. Here is a sample query on our users table to group the data on the basis of name:

```
rethinkdb.table("users").group("name").run(connection,function(err,cursor)
{
if(err) {
throw new Error(err);
  }
cursor.toArray(function(err,data) {
console.log(JSON.stringify(data));
  });
});
```

Here is the output for the same:

```
[
    {
        "group":"John",
        "reduction":[
            {
                "age":24,
                "id":"664fced5-c7d3-4f75-8086-7d6b6171dedb",
                "name":"John"
            },
            {
                "address":{
                    "address1":"suite 300",
                    "address2":"Broadway",
```

```
                    "map":{
                        "latitude":"116.4194W",
                        "longitude":"38.8026N"
                    },
                    "state":"Navada",
                    "street":"51/A"
                },
                "age":24,
                "id":"f6f1f0ce-32dd-4bc6-885d-97fe07310845",
                "name":"John"
            }
        ]
    },
    {
        "group":"Mary",
        "reduction":[
            {
                "age":32,
                "id":"c8e12a8c-a717-4d3a-a057-dc90caa7cfcb",
                "name":"Mary"
            }
        ]
    },
    {
        "group":"Michael",
        "reduction":[
            {
                "age":28,
                "id":"4228f95d-8ee4-4cbd-a4a7-a503648d2170",
                "name":"Michael"
            }
        ]
    }
]
```

If you observe the query response, data is grouped by the name and each group is associated with a document. Every matching data for the group resides under a `reduction` array. In order to work on each `reduction` array, you can use `ungroup()` ReQL function, which in turns takes grouped streams of data and converts it into an array of an object. It's useful to perform the operations such as sorting and so on, .on grouped values.

Counting the data

We can count the number of documents present in the table or a sub document of a document using the count() method. Here is a simple example:

```
rethinkdb.table("users").count().run(connection,function(err,data) {
if(err) {
throw new Error(err);
  }
console.log(data);
});
```

It should return the number of documents present in the table. You can also use it count the sub document by nesting the fields and running count() function at the end.

Sum

We can perform the addition of the sequence of data. If value is passed as an expression then sums it up else searches in the field provided in the query.

For example, to find out the total number of ages of users:

```
rethinkdb.table("users")("age").sum().run(connection,function(err,data) {
if(err) {
throw new Error(err);
  }
console.log(data);
});
```

You can of course use an expression to perform a math operation like this:

```
rethinkdb.expr([1,3,4,8]).sum().run(connection,function(err,data) {
if(err) {
throw new Error(err);
  }
console.log(data);
});
```

This should return 16.

Avg

This performs the average of the given number or searches for the value provided as field in the query. For example, look at the following code:

```
rethinkdb.expr([1,3,4,8]).avg().run(connection,function(err,data) {
if(err) {
throw new Error(err);
   }
console.log(data);
});
```

Min and Max

This finds out the maximum and minimum number provided as an expression or as field.

For example, find out the oldest users in the database we use the following code:

```
rethinkdb.table("users")("age").max().run(connection,function(err,data) {
if(err) {
throw new Error(err);
   }
console.log(data);
});
```

We use the same method to find out the youngest user:

```
rethinkdb.table("users")("age").min().run(connection,function(err,data) {
if(err) {
throw new Error(err);
   }
console.log(data);
});
```

Distinct

Distinct finds and removes the duplicate element from the sequence, just like the SQL one.

For example, in the following code we find a user with a unique name:

```
rethinkdb.table("users")("name").distinct().run(connection,function(err,data) {
if(err) {
throw new Error(err);
   }
console.log(data);
});
```

It should return an array containing the names as follows:

```
[ 'John', 'Mary', 'Michael' ]
```

Contains

Contains looks for the value in the field and if found return boolean response; true if it contains the value, false otherwise.

For example, we use the following code to find the user whose name contains John;

```
rethinkdb.table("users")("name").contains("John").run(connection,function(err,data) {
if(err) {
throw new Error(err);
   }
console.log(data);
});
```

This should return true.

Map and reduce

Aggregate functions such as count() and sum() already makes use of map and reduce internally, and if required, then group() too. You can of course use them explicitly in order to perform various functions.

Calling HTTP APIs using ReQL

RethinkDB provides support to call an external API that returns data in a JSON object, which most of the large API provider do. You can call HTTP API directly from your database hence no need of writing piece of code to just call an API and then dump into database. RethinkDB also handles it asynchronously so performance won't be affected if the API takes a longer time.

Let us try one basic API call before moving ahead with storing those in our table. We all know and use OMDb for movies review. There is a website called `http://omdbapi.com/` that provides APIs to find out the movie information present in the OMDB database. Let's call one with the following code to fetch information about the Avengers movie and see how it goes:

```
rethinkdb.http("http://www.omdbapi.com/?t=avengers&y=2015&plot=short&r=json
").run(connection,function(err,data) {
if(err) {
throw new Error(err);
   }
console.log(data);
});
```

You should be receiving the following on the console:

```
{
   Actors: 'Robert Downey Jr., Chris Hemsworth, Mark Ruffalo, Chris Evans',
   Awards: '2 wins & 37 nominations.',
   Country: 'USA',
   Director: 'Joss Whedon',
   Genre: 'Action, Adventure, Sci-Fi',
   Language: 'English',
Metascore: '66',
   Plot: 'When Tony Stark and Bruce Banner try to jump-start a dormant
peacekeeping program called Ultron, things go horribly wrong and it's up to
Earth's Mightiest Heroes to stop the villainous Ultron from enacting his
terrible plans.',
   Poster:
'http://ia.media-imdb.com/images/M/MV5BMTM4OGJmNWMtOTM4Ni00NTE3LTg3MDItZmQx
Yjc4N2JhNmUxXkEyXkFqcGdeQXVyNTgzMDMzMTg@._V1_SX300.jpg',
   Rated: 'PG-13',
   Released: '01 May 2015',
   Response: 'True',
   Runtime: '141 min',
   Title: 'Avengers: Age of Ultron',
   Type: 'movie',
   Writer: 'Joss Whedon, Stan Lee (Marvel comics), Jack Kirby (Marvel
```

```
comics)',
  Year: '2015',
imdbID: 'tt2395427',
imdbRating: '7.5',
imdbVotes: '447,454'
}
```

Well, it does work. We can now call this API to directly dump them onto our database, or maybe dump few fields. Here is a sample query to add a new document into the table using an HTTP API call. I have created another table named `movies` to add the information as follows:

```
rethinkdb.table("movies").insert(
rethinkdb.http("http://www.omdbapi.com/?t=avengers&y=2015&plot=short&r=json
")
).run(connection,function(err,data) {
if(err) {
throw new Error(err);
  }
console.log(data);
});
```

It will add a new document into our table with the information coming from the HTTP response. You can also provide dynamic URLs coming from the table to call the HTTP API.

By default, RethinkDB calls the GET http method. However, you can specify your own and, if needed, provide the data too. Here is a sample example:

```
r.http('<< URL >>', { method: POST, data: {userId : 10, name : "Shahid" }
});
```

In case you receive the response in a paginated way, RethinkDB also provides a way to solve that. You need to either provide the page or pageLimit parameter depending upon the API you are calling or which one is getting a response. RethinkDB will call the API and provide the result in streams, which we can access using the cursor API.

There are some APIs that require authentication first; you can do that too using the RethinkDB http call by passing authkey as follows:

```
r.http('<< URL >>', {
auth: {
        user: userName,
        pass: password
    }
});
```

Handling binary objects

As we have mentioned in this chapter about RethinkDB binary object support, let's look over how to use it using ReQL. The syntax to store binary objects differs from client to client. In Node.js it uses buffers to convert the stream into binary and we can use RethinkDB to insert that in a table.

Let us take an example from the preceding document. There is a key called Poster, which is the official poster of the movie in a JPEG image format. We can store the image directly in RethinkDB in a binary format.

Consider the following code:

```
rethinkdb.http("http://www.omdbapi.com/?t=avengers&y=2015&plot=short&r=json
").run(connection,function(err,data) {
if(err) {
throw new Error(err);
    }
rethinkdb.table("movies").insert({
movieName :data.Title,
posterImage :rethinkdb.http(data.Poster, {resultFormat : 'binary'})
    }).run(connection,function(err,data) {
if(err) {
```

```
throw new Error(err);
    }
console.log(data);
  });
});
```

What we are doing here is first fetching the record from OMDB and then putting `Poster` in our table using the `insert()` command. If you see the result, it looks like the following:

```
{
"id": "1890fc6f-1f95-4cbc-8b0e-c62a97884e0c" ,
"movieName": "Avengers: Age of Ultron" ,
"posterImage": <binary, 46.5KB, "ffd8ffe0 00 10...">
}
```

You can store files directly from the filesystem as well. Use the filesystem API to read the file and then provide the path to the `insert()` command. It is as simple as that, and you can also store files in raw format by passing a raw key in the `resultFormat` object.

Performing JOINS

JOINS are one of the features of NoSQL databases. RethinkDB provides the ReQL functions to perform various types of JOINS, such as inner, outer, and so on. Please refer to `Chapter 1`, *The RethinkDB Architecture and Data Model*, to study this more in detail.

Accessing changefeed (real-time feed) in RethinkDB

We had mentioned in `Chapter 1`, *The RethinkDB Architecture and Data Model*, that the real-time feature of RethinkDB is called changefeed. It is the heart of the RethinkDB real-time functionality. RethinkDB changefeed provides continuous live updates about the changes happening in the subscribed table.

In order to avail the feature of changefeed, you just need to attach your listener for the particular table, and you should receive every single minor update happening in the table such as addition, deletion, update, and so on.

Let us demonstrate this using our `users` table. Here is the piece of code that will add the listener to the table:

```
rethinkdb.table("users").changes().run(connection,function(err,cursor) {
if(err) {
throw new Error(err);
    }
cursor.each(console.log);
});
```

That's it! Run the code on a separate terminal in order to observe the behavior. Let's try to add a new document into the table and see how it works. I have added a new document using the web administrative screen of RethinkDB, and this is what it prints on the console:

```
{
new_val: {
id: '25cf3a63-f750-469a-847f-f43d827289a1', name: 'Shahid'
    },
old_val: null
}
```

Since we have performed addition, we get the `old_val` key as null. However, in case of updating and deletion, it should return the old value of the document. Let's run one update query to see the behavior of changefeed.

The following is my query from the web console:

```
r.table("users").get("4228f95d-8ee4-4cbd-a4a7-a503648d2170").update({age :
30});
```

This is the response on the terminal:

```
  {
new_val:
    {
age: 30,
id: '4228f95d-8ee4-4cbd-a4a7-a503648d2170',
name: 'Michael'
    },
old_val:
   {
age: 28,
id: '4228f95d-8ee4-4cbd-a4a7-a503648d2170',
name: 'Michael'
     }
  }
```

This is a really awesome feature. You don't just get the changes of the table; you get the old and new values in order to perform extra operations. Let's try one with deletion and see how changefeed reacts:

```
r.table("users").get("25cf3a63-f750-469a-847f-f43d827289a1").delete()
```

changefeed prints the following on the console:

```
{
new_val: null,
old_val: {
id: '25cf3a63-f750-469a-847f-f43d827289a1', name: 'Shahid'
    }
  }
```

It returns the new value as null because of deletion. That's fair enough!

You can also perform the changefeed operation over a particular or set of documents as well. All you need to do is select those documents using the get() method and append changes() after it. Have a look at following example:

```
rethinkdb.table("users").get("4228f95d-8ee4-4cbd-a4a7-a503648d2170")
.changes()
.run(connection,function(err,cursor) {
if(err) {
throw new Error(err);
    }
cursor.each(console.log);
});
```

This will return the changes happening in the document. In order to get multiple documents to find changes, you can use a filter() with it. Like we said, ReQL queries are chainable.

When we attach our listener to the table, it only provides us with the changes when there is any ReQL operation happening on the table. How about getting the initial data in order to show it to the client end and so on? You can do this too, by specifying includeInitialkey to true in the changes() function.

There might be some requirements where you want the changes in a particular way, such as without the old values. You can do this by specifying includeStateskey as true in the changes() function. It returns a type key to explain the type of change in changefeed.

You can specify the following in the type key:

- **Add**: A new value is added
- **Remove**: A value is removed
- **Change**: An value update
- **Initial**: An initial value notification
- **Uninitial**: Not an initial value
- **State**: Status information

If there are fast changes happening in the table, it is possible that one of the changes in the table will happen before the invocation of the `changes()` function. In such cases, RethinkDB will return you one object containing multiple changes.

However, if you want to receive individual changes for this special case, you can do so by specifying the squash key to false in the `changes()` function. It will buffer all the changes and return it to you; it can buffer a maximum 100,000 changes in a document.

Applications of changefeed

Since this is one of the most promising features of RethinkDB, you might be wondering where you can apply it in real time. Applications of changefeed can range from small-scale notification systems to large-scale news feeds of the application. One thing you should keep in mind regarding changefeed is that it works directly with your database, you are not doing any external or WAN `http` calls in order to know what's going on in the table; this saves lots of bandwidth and improves latency and round trip time.

You can design a real-time social media application using this or a push notification and so on. The applications of this feature are limitless and can be applied across various domains.

One limitation of changefeed is that it pushes changes to the middle layer client only. Hence you need to write some code to push this data to the client layer. I would suggest that socket will perform very best in this scenario. However, there is another project currently in beta development and probably will be available for public after launch of this book called Horizon. This project will let you access RethinkDB database from client end. Don't worry about the security; there will be a middle layer but that will be rewritten and tightly coupled with UI in order to contact database safely. We will cover this in detail in `Chapter 10`, *Using RethinkDB and Horizon*.

Performing geolocation operations

RethinkDB supports geolocation operations and you can write rich geographical data by combining geospatial queries and changefeed. Here we are going to look over some ReQL functions that we can use to perform geolocation operations.

Storing a coordinate

You can store a coordinate using `point()` ReQL API. It accepts `longitude` and `latitude` as input parameters. Here is a sample example of adding the location of `Mumbai` and `Delhi` in our table. I am using a web administrative console to execute the query as follows:

```
r.table("geo").insert([
  {
place : 'Mumbai',
location :r.point(19.0760,72.8777)
  },
  {
place : 'Delhi',
location :r.point(28.6139,77.2090)
  }])
```

Finding the distance between points

You can find out the distance between two points using the `distance()` ReQL command. Here is an example:

```
r.table('geo').get("25855d3d-70f6-4480-8472-4c7081b1874a")('location').dist
ance(r.table('geo').get("02e1f1ce-0768-460c-8ddd-9e0cf42ce887")('location')
)")('location'))
```

Here we are selecting two points and passing the location to the `distance()` function. This should return you the distance in points. You can also specify the units as kilometer, meter, and so on by passing the unit key in the distance function.

Similarly, there are ReQL functions available for finding out the nearest point, finding intersection of a point in circle, creating circle using points and lines and so on.

Performing administrative operations

RethinkDB provides administrative functions that you can use to perform various administrative tasks such as granting permission to the table or database, changing the size of a cluster or shard, re-configuring failover shards, and so on. You can perform administrative operations either by using a web console or by using ReQL commands. In the next chapter, we will look over these in detail.

Summary

We covered the basics and advanced-level queries in ReQL with the client driver (Node.js) code. We also covered performing CRUD operations using RethinkDB and handling various special cases such as calling HTTP APIs from the query and storing binary blobs in RethinkDB. We also looked over one of the most promising features of RethinkDB called changefeed in detail.

In the next chapter, we are going to look at some administrative operations such as handling permission along with configuring clusters and shard in RethinkDB. We will also look at failover and other administrative tools that you can use to manage RethinkDB in detail.

3
Data Exploration Using RethinkDB

Data exploration is the process of analyzing and refactoring structured or non-structured data and is commonly done before going onto actual data analysis. Operations such as performing a duplicate cleanup and finding whitespace data can be done at the data exploration stage.

We can keep data exploration as the pre-emptive operation before performing heavy-cost operations such as running various batches and jobs, which is quite expensive in computing, and finding irrelevant data in that stage would be painful.

Data exploration can be very useful in various scenarios. Suppose you have large dataset of DNA diversion of people living in New York or terabytes of data from NASA about Mars' temperature records. There is a huge possibility that the data is error prone. So, instead of directly uploading terabytes of data to the program written in R, we can try to make the data less error prone, which will surely process faster results.

Concepts such as those in Chapter 1, *The RethinkDB Architecture and Data Model* and Chapter 2, *RethinkDB Query Language* can be used to perform some data exploration and ad-hoc queries.

However, we will not just cover the duplicate data removal operation. In this chapter we are also going to learn how to perform data exploration using RethinkDB along with:

- Importing a large dataset in RethinkDB using the HTTP method
- Importing a large dataset from a filesystem in RethinkDB
- Performing various queries to explore the data

Along with this, we will also cover a free web service to generate lots of mock data with random values for our task. Before jumping into anything else, let's dive in and create some mock data for our exploration, say 1,000 records.

Generating mock data

We used the **mockaroo** online mock data generator to create some mock data. Unfortunately, it only allows 1,000 records for free so we were limited to that. For our case study, we have generated data for employees with some basic personal information, along with salary.

Refer to the following image to understand the schema of data:

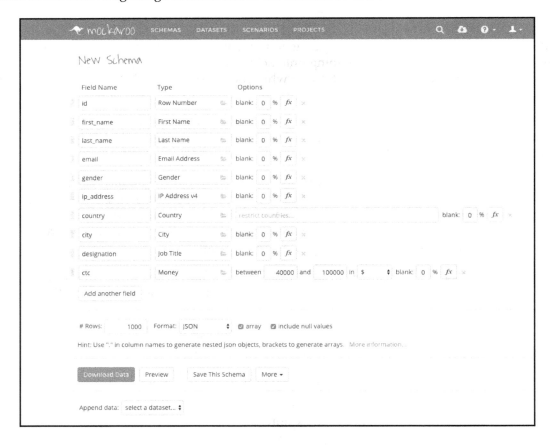

Refer to the following link: `https://www.mockaroo.com`

As you can see in the preceding image, we have chosen various keys related to employees and downloaded it as a `JSON` file. It will return the data format as 1,000 objects residing in one array; that is exactly what we need to dump the data in the RethinkDB database.

RethinkDB provides two ways in which you can import your data into the RethinkDB database for further analysis:

1. Importing data in RethinkDB using HTTP
2. Importing data via file read

In this section, we will cover both of them in detail along with uploading our dataset to RethinkDB.

Importing data in RethinkDB using HTTP

In `Chapter 2`, *RethinkDB Query Language,* we covered *Calling HTTP APIs using ReQL,* which is quite an impressive feature. Can we use the same method to import our data from an external resource? Yes, we can.

We have already generated the sample mock data using `http://mockaroo.com/` in the previous section with 1,000 JSON documents; let's upload it on an external resource. I am going to use GitHub here, but you are free to use other options.

I have uploaded the file in my repository and gotten the static file link. You can view the same on this link as well as the figure shown next:

The link is available at `https://github.com/codeforgeek/sample-mockup-data`:

We have everything in place. All we need now is our RethinkDB database and table. I am not going to use a test database this time; I am going to create one using the administrative screen. Lift up your RethinkDB Server and visit the administrative screen.

  In the case of running on local, it should be `http://localhost:8080`.

In the table section of the administrative screen, you can click on **Tables** and create a new database and table in it. I have created a database named `company`:

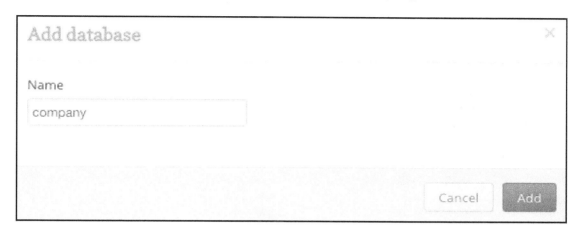

Here is my query to import our data from GitHub into our database:

```
r.db("company").table("employees")
.insert(r.http('https://raw.githubusercontent.com/codeforgeek/sample-mocku
p-data/master/employeeRecordMockup.json',
{
  timeout : 220,
  resultFormat : 'json'
}))
```

Execute the query from **Data Explorer** and sit back or go get a coffee! It will take time depending on the Internet connection and the dataset.

Here are a few points regarding the query as you can see, we have passed two extra parameters:

- The first parameter is timeout, which is going to vary from system to system. This determines that the connection stays alive to external resources if there is no activity for a particular time.
- The second parameter is very important if your response doesn't have the header set by default. In our case, we are actually calling a file. Hence, the response header is not JSON, which is what we need. So we have set the response format to JSON using resultFormat:

As you can see, it took me about 2.32 seconds to get all those records in our table. It may vary for various reasons. One of the key points is the size of the data over the HTTP connection. RethinkDB uses streams; hence, the size of data is really not an issue until there is no timeout.

This is one of the cases explained for importing data, but most of the time; you are going to have it in your filesystem. Let us look at importing data using files.

Importing data via file read

RethinkDB provides the `import` utility to read the file from the filesystem and dump it into the table. This utility comes in the Python driver at the time of writing this book. You need to install Python and then the RethinkDB driver for the same before moving ahead.

Assuming you have Python installed, the following command will install the RethinkDB driver:

```
sudo pip install rethinkdb
```

The command structure of the file import utility is as follows:

```
rethinkdb import -f FILE_PATH { parameters }
```

The following are mandatory parameters if you are importing it from a local system in one RethinkDB instance:

- `--table DB.table_name`
- `--format JSON/CSV`

The following are optional but may be mandatory in some cases:

- `-c HOST:PORT`: Connect to the given host and port
- `-p`: Password file path
- `--pkey`: Primary key
- `--shards`: Provide the number of shards
- `--replicas`: Provide the number of replicas

We will be looking at these parameters in the next chapter, covering administration in detail. Here is the command to import our file into the respective table:

```
rethinkdb import -f employeeRecordMockup.json --table
company.employees_importviafile
```

If the table is already present, apply `--force` at the end of the command. After running the previous command using force parameter because I already had a table in the database I got the following output:

Let us check the records in our RethinkDB table. For this, we are going to use `count()`.

In the ReQL method, we have to find out whether the data is inserted correctly or not. Here is the query:

```
r.db("company").table("employees_importviafile").count()
```

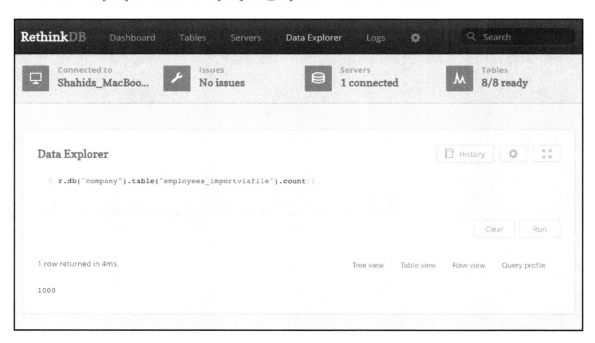

We have successfully imported the data into our RethinkDB table using the HTTP method and using the import command. Let us move ahead and perform some data exploration on the same.

Executing data exploration use cases

We have imported our database our mock data into our RethinkDB instance. Now it's time to run a use case query and make use of it. But before we do so, we need to figure out one data alteration. We have made a mistake while generating mock data (on purpose actually) we have a $ sign before `ctc`. Hence, it becomes tough to perform salary-level queries.

Before we move ahead, we need to figure out this problem, and basically get rid of the $ sign and update the `ctc` value to an `integer` instead of a `string`.

In order to do this, we need to perform the following operation:

- Traverse through each document in the database
- Split the ctc string into two parts, containing $ and the other value
- Update the `ctc` value in the document with a new data type and value

Since we require the chaining of queries, I have written a small snippet in Node.js to achieve the previous scenario as follows:

```
var rethinkdb = require('rethinkdb');
var connection = null;
rethinkdb.connect({host : 'localhost', port : 28015},function(err,conn) {
 if(err) {
   throw new Error('Connection error');
 }
 connection = conn;
 rethinkdb.db("company").table("employees")
 .run(connection,function(err,cursor) {
     if(err) {
       throw new Error(err);
     }
     cursor.each(function(err,data) {
       data.ctc = parseInt(data.ctc.split("$")[1]);
       rethinkdb.db("company").table("employees")
       .get(data.id)
       .update({ctc : data.ctc})
       .run(connection,function(err,response) {
         if(err) {
           throw new Error(err);
         }
         console.log(response);
       });
     });
   });
 });
```

As you can see in the preceding code, we first fetch all the documents and traverse them using `cursor`, one document at a time. We use the `split()` method as a $ separator and convert the outcome, which is salary, into an integer using the `parseInt()` method. We update each document at a time using the `id` value of the document:

```
polling-app-using-nodejs-rethinkDB — node rethink.js — 112×33
{ deleted: 0,
  errors: 0,
  inserted: 0,
  replaced: 1,
  skipped: 0,
  unchanged: 0 }
{ deleted: 0,
  errors: 0,
  inserted: 0,
  replaced: 1,
  skipped: 0,
  unchanged: 0 }
{ deleted: 0,
  errors: 0,
  inserted: 0,
  replaced: 1,
  skipped: 0,
  unchanged: 0 }
{ deleted: 0,
  errors: 0,
  inserted: 0,
  replaced: 1,
  skipped: 0,
  unchanged: 0 }
{ deleted: 0,
  errors: 0,
  inserted: 0,
  replaced: 1,
  skipped: 0,
  unchanged: 0 }
{ deleted: 0,
  errors: 0,
  inserted: 0,
```

After selecting all the documents again, we can see an updated `ctc` value as an integer, as shown in the following figure:

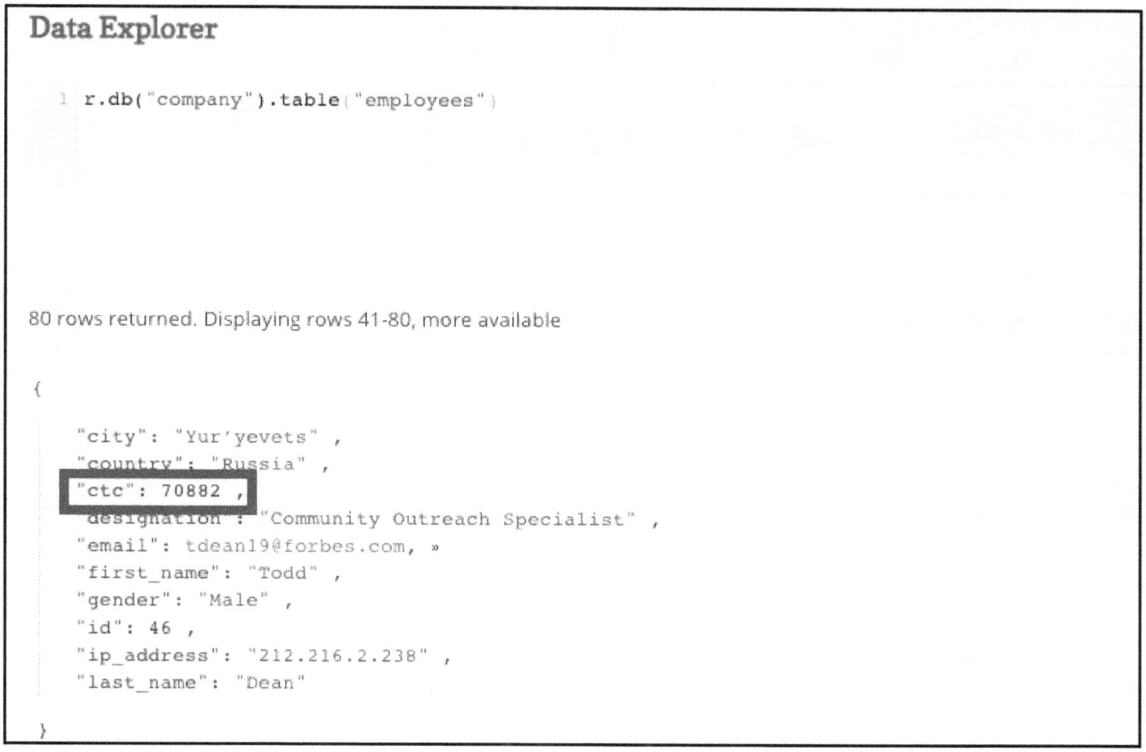

```
Data Explorer

1  r.db("company").table("employees")




80 rows returned. Displaying rows 41-80, more available


{

    "city": "Yur'yevets" ,
    "country": "Russia" ,
    "ctc": 70882 ,
    "designation": "Community Outreach Specialist" ,
    "email": tdean19@forbes.com, »
    "first_name": "Todd" ,
    "gender": "Male" ,
    "id": 46 ,
    "ip_address": "212.216.2.238" ,
    "last_name": "Dean"

}
```

This is one of the practical examples where we perform some data manipulation before moving ahead with complex queries. Similarly, you can look for errors such as blank spaces in a specific field or duplicate elements in your record.

Finding duplicate elements

We can use `distinct()` to find out whether there is any duplicate element present in the table. Say you have 1,000 rows and there are 10 duplicates. In order to determine that, we just need to find out the unique rows (of course excluding the ID key, as that's unique by nature).

Here is the query for the same:

```
r.db("company").table('employees').without('id').distinct().count()
```

As shown in the following screenshot, this query returns the count of unique rows, which should be 1,000 if there are no duplicates:

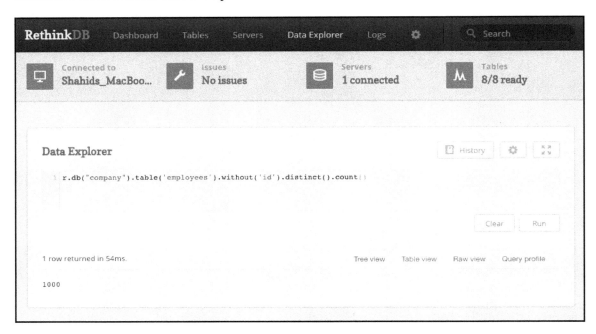

This implies that our records contain no duplicate documents.

Finding the list of countries

We can write a query to find all the countries we have in our record and also use `distinct` again by just selecting the `country` field. Here is the query:

```
r.db("company").table('employees')("country").distinct()
```

As shown in this image, we have 124 countries in our records:

```
Data Explorer                                    History      ⚙      ⤢

1  r.db("company").table('employees')("country").distinct()


                                                    Clear        Run


124 rows returned in 21ms.          Tree view   Table view   Raw view   Query profile

[

   "Afghanistan" ,
   "Albania" ,
   "Anguilla" ,
   "Argentina" ,
   "Armenia" ,
   "Bahrain" ,
   "Bangladesh" ,
   "Belarus" ,
   "Benin" ,
   "Bolivia" ,
   "Bosnia and Herzegovina" ,
   "Brazil" ,
   "Bulgaria" ,
   "Burkina Faso" ,
   "Burundi" ,
   "Cameroon" ,
   "Canada" ,
   "Chad" ,
   "Chile" ,
   "China" ,
   "Colombia" ,
   "Costa Rica" ,
```

Finding the top 10 employees with the highest salary

In this use case, we need to evaluate all the records and find the top 10 employees with the highest to lowest pay. Here is the query for the same:

```
r.db("company").table("employees").orderBy(r.desc("ctc")).limit(10)
```

Here we are using `orderBy`, which by default orders the record in ascending order. To get the highest pay at the first document, we need to use descending ordering; we did it using the `desc()` ReQL command.

As shown in the following image, the query returns 10 rows:

You can modify the same query by just by limiting the number of users to one to get the highest-paid employee.

Displaying employee records with a specific name and location

To extract such records from our table, we need to again perform a filter on the "first_name" and "country" fields. Here is the query to return those records:

```
r.db("company").table('employees').filter({"first_name" : "John","country"
: "Sweden"})
```

We are just performing a basic filter and comparing both fields. ReQL queries are really easy for solving such queries due to their chaining feature. After executing the preceding query, we show the following output:

```
2 rows returned. Displaying rows 1-2                    Tree view    Table view    Raw view    Query profile

{

    "city": "Bollstabruk" ,
    "country": "Sweden" ,
    "ctc": 96262 ,
    "designation": "Junior Executive" ,
    "email": jwellsqe@ow.ly, »
    "first_name": "John" ,
    "gender": "Male" ,
    "id": 951 ,
    "ip_address": "40.99.91.205" ,
    "ip_decimal": 677600205 ,
    "last_name": "Wells"

}

{

    "city": "Lysekil" ,
    "country": "Sweden" ,
    "ctc": 67505 ,
    "designation": "Physical Therapy Assistant" ,
    "email": jolson2r@uiuc.edu, »
    "first_name": "John" ,
    "gender": "Male" ,
    "id": 100 ,
    "ip_address": "245.195.234.14" ,
    "ip_decimal": 4123257358 ,
    "last_name": "Olson"

}
```

Finding employees living in Russia with a salary less than 50,000 dollars

We need to traverse through each document and filter on the basis of the ctc and country fields. Here is the query for the same:

```
r.db("company").table('employees').filter(r.row('ctc').lt(50000).and(r.row(
'country').eq("Russia")))")))
```

We are using the and ReQL command, which is equivalent to the `boolean` operator. Here is the output for the previous query:

Finding employees with a constant contact e-mail address

Constant contact is a popular e-mail service for mass mailers. In our randomly generated mock data, there are some employees' e-mails ending with a constant contact address. In this use case, we are going to use a regular expression to filter out employees with a constant contact e-mail. Here is the query for the same:

```
r.db("company").table('employees').filter(r.row('email').match("constantcon
tact.com$"))
```

The following are the e-mail addresses that end with the `constant` string; hence, we had put a `$` sign at the end of the expression in the `match` ReQL method:

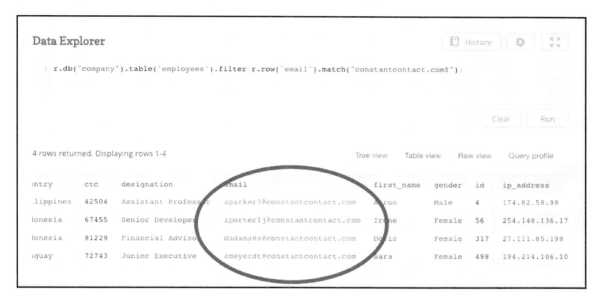

Finding employees who use class a C IP address

This is one of the more complicated use cases that we are going to deal with. As you noticed in the mock data, we have randomly generated IP addresses that lie in classes B, C, D, and so on. Here we need to find out the employees who are using a class C IP address, that is, address ranging between `192.0.1.1` and `223.255.254.254`.

Although it seems easy to find the difference between these numbers, technically it is quite difficult. As you can see, an IP address consists of four digits separated by a `dot` operator. IP addresses are written using a base `256` encoding.

In order to efficiently find the IP addresses ranging between the class C IP range, we need to convert the IP from base `256` to decimal, that is, base 10.

To convert it, we need to use following formula. Consider `192.168.1.1` as the IP:

192 * (256)^3 + 168 * (256)^2 + 1 * (256)^1 + 1 * 256^0 = decimal value of IP

Upon getting the data decimal value of the IP, we can easily use the between ReQL method to find the documents ranging in class C.

Since we don't have the decimal value of IP in our documents, we first need to calculate and create a new field in each document containing the decimal value of IP.

Here is how we do it in Node.js:

```
var rethinkdb = require('rethinkdb');
var connection = null;
rethinkdb.connect({host : 'localhost', port : 28015},function(err,conn) {
  if(err) {
   throw new Error('Connection error');
  }
  connection = conn;
rethinkdb.db("company").table("employees").run(connection,function(err,curs
or) {
    if(err) {
      throw new Error(err);
    }
    cursor.each(function(err,data) {
      let ip = data.ip_address.split(".");
      let decimalIp = 0;
      for(let ipCounter = 0; ipCounter < ip.length; ipCounter++) {
        let power = 3 - ipCounter;
        let ipElement = parseInt(ip[ipCounter]);
        decimalIp += ipElement * Math.pow(256,power);
      }
      data.ip_decimal = decimalIp;
      // updating the document
      rethinkdb.db("company").table("employees")
      .get(data.id)
      .run(connection,function(err,response) {
        if(err) { console.log(
      .update(data)
 err);}
        console.log(response);
      });
    });
  });
});
```

In the preceding code, we traverse over each document and convert the IP address into a decimal format. After that, we create a new field and update the document.

Here is the updated document in the employees table:

```
Data Explorer                                    [ History    ⚙    [ ]

  1  r.db("company").table('employees')

                                                      Clear        Run

  40 rows returned. Displaying rows 1-40, more available      Tree view    Table view    Raw view    Query profile

  {
      "city": "Selorejo" ,
      "country": "Indonesia" ,
      "ctc": 49304 ,
      "designation": "Dental Hygienist" ,
      "email": preyesj@plala.or.jp, »
      "first_name": "Paula" ,
      "gender": "Female" ,
      "id": 20 ,
      "ip_address": "1.90.125.195" ,
      "ip_decimal": 22707651 ,
      "last_name": "Reyes"
  }

  {
      "city": "Reina Mercedes" ,
      "country": "Philippines" ,
      "ctc": 42504 ,
      "designation": "Assistant Professor" ,
      "email": aparker3@constantcontact.com, »
      "first_name": "Aaron" ,
      "gender": "Male" ,
      "id": 4 ,
```

We have the data in place. Before making a query, we need to create this field as an index because the between method of ReQL works on indexes only. That's no big deal! Here is a query to do so:.

```
r.db("company").table('employees').indexCreate('ip_decimal')
```

 Note that we will learn more about Indexes in the next chapter.

Once the index is created, we can query the table to return us, employees using the class C address. I have converted the starting and ending addresses of Class C into decimal using the same preceding formula:

Base 256 IP address	Base 10 (decimal) IP address
192.0.1.1	3221225729
223.255.254.254	3758096126

Here is the query to fetch the employees using the IP in that range:

```
r.db("company").table('employees').between(3221225729,3758096126,{index :
'ip_decimal'})
```

In the next image, we pass the start and end IP addresses and use the `ip_decimal` field as an index:

Here is the last record for the same, containing the last IP address:

```
{
    "city": "Medveditskiy" ,
    "country": "Russia" ,
    "ctc": 63240 ,
    "designation": "Structural Engineer" ,
    "email": rmurrayv@washington.edu, »
    "first_name": "Randy" ,
    "gender": "Male" ,
    "id": 33
    "ip_address": "223.241.192.206" ,
    "ip_decimal" 3751102702 ,
    "last_name": "Murray"

}
```

You may get the same result by plucking the first element of the IP address and checking whether it's between 192 and 223, but to demonstrate the conversion and filtration, I have used the decimal technique.

Summary

In this chapter, we covered the use of the RethinkDB query language to perform data exploration queries. Apart from that, we also looked over some use cases where we need to perform some alteration and filtering of records in order to meet our exploration task, such as stripping the $ sign from ctc, or converting base 256 ip addresses into base 10 values and performing a query on them. We also covered some general uses cases in order to get a practical feel of ReQL.

In the next chapter, we are going to study performance tuning in RethinkDB. As we have mentioned in Chapter 1, *The RethinkDB Architecture and Data Model*, RethinkDB comes up with an easy-to-use administrative screen to perform sharding, replication, and so on. We will also look over clustering and running queries in a cluster. Then we will cover query optimization in RethinkDB and tools that can help us to identify query execution time, waiting time, and so on.

4
Performance Tuning in RethinkDB

As the size of your database grows and stores and processes million rows of records daily, so comes the challenge along with it, that is, performance. Query response time decreases as the size of data grows, most frequently accessed data puts a lot of load on the system. As we know, RethinkDB is a distributed database and it can store, index, and process data from multiple databases running independently. To the user end, it seems that the result comes from one database, but actually it doesn't.

This chapter is all about improving performance of RethinkDB by setting up clusters, replicating tables, and sharding data to improve the query time. We will also learn about the RethinkDB query profiler, which could be of great help for recognizing query performance issues.

In this chapter, we will cover the following topics:

- Creating and handling a RethinkDB cluster
- Securing a RethinkDB cluster
- Executing ReQL queries in a cluster
- Performing replication of a table in RethinkDB
- Sharding the table to scale the database
- Running a RethinkDB proxy node
- Optimizing query performance

Before jumping to clustering in RethinkDB, let's have a brief study of clustering in general just to revisit the concept so that we can understand and implement the same.

Clustering

Consider the following scenario: say you have developed a system that handles video encoding and transmission using **User Datagram protocol** (**UDP**). You have a single machine running as a server and it is acting quite well. Suddenly the view increases (say someone found a rare Pokémon and posted a video) and your server crashes. This is not the ideal situation where any programmer would want to be, so what can we do about it?

Clustering is one way to solve it. What we do is create different servers running on the same operating system, operating on the same database, and connect them together to work as a single machine. It seems like a single machine to the outside world, but in reality there is a set of machines working to serve requests.

 The **User Datagram Protocol (UDP)** is a transport layer protocol defined for use with the IP network layer protocol to give fast delivery with no ordering and guarantee of payload.

So, in general, clustering is a process of creating a network of loosely or tightly coupled machines that work together in order to perform efficiently. Each node or server machine in a cluster performs the same operation, controlled and managed by the program.

Generally, servers in clusters are connected via a fast local area network in order to reduce the network trip around time. Clusters are made to improve operational time and availability. If any cluster goes down, the working of the complete system won't be affected; instead, traffic will be diverted to a nearby cluster or low-traffic cluster depending on the algorithm and design decision.

In database clustering, we create and configure multiple machines running on the same database software with the same database to provide:

- Load balancing
- Data availability and scalability
- Fault tolerance

Database cluster provides load balancing by routing the incoming query to a different server within the cluster, which in turn reduces the load on a single server. The program to find out where to route the query depending upon the status of the clusters is called a load balancer.

If any instance in a cluster goes down, then another live instance takes its position and serves the request. In the meantime, if the instance comes up again, routing is again divided to the old instance, hence providing data availability at most. In terms of scalability, clusters provide us the way to solve large volumes of data in multiple instances of servers instead of one to scale the database on the go. When we figure out that we have a lot of requests coming up, we can set up a new machine and add it to the cluster. When the requests go down (say during Christmas vacations), we can take down a few instances to cut down the computation cost. So it affects the budget too.

Creating and handling a RethinkDB cluster

We have done enough of theory; let's deal with clustering in RethinkDB. Till now we have covered what clustering really is in terms of computing and what it provides us. In this section, we are going to learn how we can perform clustering in RethinkDB, which by nature is a distributed database.

We will also learn how to add new machines into our existing cluster, manage them from the RethinkDB administrative screen, and monitor them for any errors.

We have two ways to perform RethinkDB clustering:

- In the same machine with a different RethinkDB instance
- In a different machine with a different RethinkDB instance

Creating a RethinkDB cluster in the same machine

We can create a RethinkDB cluster in the same machine using the simple command under a minute. Yes you heard it right, in a minute (assuming you have RethinkDB installed). Let's do this.

Lift up the default RethinkDB server using the following command in the terminal:

```
rethinkdb
```

It should lift the RethinkDB server on the default port and you should be able to see the console as shown here:

```
Shahids-MacBook-Air:~ UnixRoot$ rethinkdb
Running rethinkdb 2.3.1 (CLANG 7.3.0 (clang-703.0.29))...
Running on Darwin 15.4.0 x86_64
Loading data from directory /Users/UnixRoot/rethinkdb_data
Migrating cluster metadata to v2.3
warn: Cache size does not leave much memory for server and query overhe
ad (available memory: 497 MB).
warn: Cache size is very low and may impact performance.
Listening for intracluster connections on port 29015
Listening for client driver connections on port 28015
Listening for administrative HTTP connections on port 8080
Listening on cluster addresses: 127.0.0.1, ::1
Listening on driver addresses: 127.0.0.1, ::1
Listening on http addresses: 127.0.0.1, ::1
To fully expose RethinkDB on the network, bind to all addresses by runn
ing rethinkdb with the `--bind all` command line option.
Server ready, "Shahids_MacBook_Air_local_h7u" 37dc230b-16ac-48f1-84f4-5
35261fa86d7
A newer version of the RethinkDB server is available: 2.3.4. You can re
ad the changelog at <https://github.com/rethinkdb/rethinkdb/releases>.
Connected to server "Shahids_MacBook_Air_local_z5o" eaa803e1-7c6d-4d59-
82ae-89c19427fbb3
Connected to server "Shahids_MacBook_Air_local_gqv" e11904bb-7136-4a2d-
b106-91f12d55dcc6
```

Now open a new terminal, and run the following command:

```
rethinkdb --port-offset 1 --directory rethinkdb_data2 --join
localhost:29015
```

You should be able to see a new RethinkDB instance lifting up, as shown here:

```
Shahids-MacBook-Air:~ UnixRoot$ rethinkdb --port-offset 1 --directory rethinkdb_data
2 --join localhost:29015
Recursively removing directory /Users/UnixRoot/rethinkdb_data2/tmp
Initializing directory /Users/UnixRoot/rethinkdb_data2
Running rethinkdb 2.3.1 (CLANG 7.3.0 (clang-703.0.29))...
Running on Darwin 15.4.0 x86_64
Loading data from directory /Users/UnixRoot/rethinkdb_data2
warn: Cache size does not leave much memory for server and query overhead (available
 memory: 490 MB).
warn: Cache size is very low and may impact performance.
Listening for intracluster connections on port 29016
Connected to server "Shahids_MacBook_Air_local_h7u" 37dc230b-16ac-48f1-84f4-535261fa
86d7
Listening for client driver connections on port 28016
Listening for administrative HTTP connections on port 8081
Listening on cluster addresses: 127.0.0.1, ::1
Listening on driver addresses: 127.0.0.1, ::1
Listening on http addresses: 127.0.0.1, ::1
To fully expose RethinkDB on the network, bind to all addresses by running rethinkdb
 with the --bind all command line option.
Server ready, "Shahids_MacBook_Air_local_z5o" eaa803e1-7c6d-4d59-82ae-89c19427fbb3
A newer version of the RethinkDB server is available: 2.3.4. You can read the change
log at <https://github.com/rethinkdb/rethinkdb/releases>.
Connected to server "Shahids_MacBook_Air_local_gqv" e11904bb-7136-4a2d-b106-91f12d55
dcc6
Disconnected from server "Shahids_MacBook_Air_local_gqv" e11904bb-7136-4a2d-b106-91f
12d55dcc6
```

That is it. We have our first RethinkDB cluster running. Let's verify this, visit the administrative console and you should be seeing the **2 servers connected** in **Servers** section, as shown in the following figure:

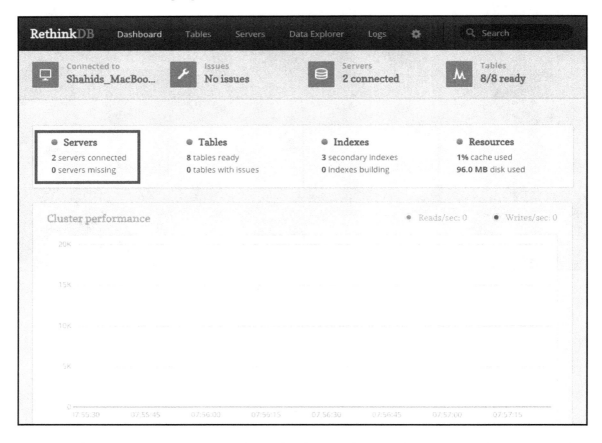

Yes it works! Try to execute a query from the data explorer and you should be receiving the same result regardless of having the cluster, because no matter which instance you use, RethinkDB will automatically route the query to the appropriate node.

Let us look at the command that we executed previously:

- `--port-offset`: This makes sure that no two nodes use the same port by incrementing them by 1
- `--directory`: This tells RethinkDB to use a different directory in order to maintain consistency and avoid read/write issues

- `--join`: This tells RethinkDB to connect to the existing seed node
- **Instance of RethinkDB to create a cluster**: In our command, it was 29015, which is the default port of RethinkDB

I would like to point out an important key here regarding failover. If you are creating a cluster in the same machine, you won't be able to achieve full failover because if a RethinkDB instance is down, it will manage it, but if your machine (which is running RethinkDB) goes down, your complete cluster will go down altogether. So, for learning purposes, this is OK, but not for production.

You can add new RethinkDB instances to the existing cluster using the same command, but make sure you use a different port offset and directory. Let's create RethinkDB using different machines.

Creating a RethinkDB cluster using different machines

We have seen how easy it is to create a RethinkDB cluster in the same machine. Let's see how we can create it using different machines. Actually, this is much easier than creating a cluster on the same machine, because you really don't need to worry about the port and directory usage.

Let's say you have two servers, one running on 104.121.23.24 and another one running on 104.121.23.25 respectively. We need to first install RethinkDB in each machine. You can find a detailed description about installing RethinkDB in the Mac, Linux or Windows machines at the official website of RethinkDB (https://www.rethinkdb.com/docs/install/).

Assuming you have RethinkDB installed on both machines, log in to the machine with the `104.121.23.24` IP address and lift the RethinkDB Server using the following command:

```
rethinkdb --bind all
```

Please note that the `--bind all` parameter allows RethinkDB to accept connections from any machine. If you don't provide this, it will restrict access to the localhost only; hence, a machine with a different IP will not be able to communicate.

RethinkDB will initiate itself, and you should be able to see the following on the terminal:

```
Shahids-MacBook-Air:Desktop UnixRoot$ rethinkdb --bind all
Running rethinkdb 2.3.1 (CLANG 7.3.0 (clang-703.0.29))...
Running on Darwin 15.4.0 x86_64
Loading data from directory /Users/UnixRoot/Desktop/rethinkdb_data
warn: Cache size does not leave much memory for server and query overhe
ad (available memory: 408 MB).
warn: Cache size is very low and may impact performance.
Listening for intracluster connections on port 29015
Listening for client driver connections on port 28015
Listening for administrative HTTP connections on port 8080
Listening on cluster addresses: 127.0.0.1, 192.168.1.4, ::1, fe80::1%1,
 fe80::ac8a:daff:fe2e:11a%7, fe80::ca69:cdff:feb7:7054%4
Listening on driver addresses: 127.0.0.1, 192.168.1.4, ::1, fe80::1%1,
fe80::ac8a:daff:fe2e:11a%7, fe80::ca69:cdff:feb7:7054%4
Listening on http addresses: 127.0.0.1, 192.168.1.4, ::1, fe80::1%1, fe
80::ac8a:daff:fe2e:11a%7, fe80::ca69:cdff:feb7:7054%4
Server ready, "Shahids_MacBook_Air_local_pnj" e2fef3ab-eb5c-4f8e-afda-a
73fb0cee8eb
A newer version of the RethinkDB server is available: 2.3.4. You can re
ad the changelog at <https://github.com/rethinkdb/rethinkdb/releases>.
```

Now log in to the machine with the `104.121.23.25` IP address and lift the RethinkDB server using the following command:

```
rethinkdb --join 104.121.23.24:29015 --bind all
```

Upon running this command, you should be seeing the two servers on the administrative screen of RethinkDB. There is our cluster.

As you may notice, this is really easy to do, but is this sustainable? What I mean by sustainable here is: will it run on production? Let's find out.

Since we have performed cluster creation using the command line, what if one of the servers requires a reboot? Will it create the same cluster automatically? Well, no. Since we have a different machine running on the Internet, is it secure enough to run on production with so many hackers trying to intercept our data? Well No!

So why did we do this in the first place? To simply learn the concept. I always believe that everyone (including me) is looking for shortcuts to get the end result. Since we have covered the shortcut part and seen why it is not good for production, let's learn to optimize this and run our cluster in production mode. That's what this book is all about Mastering RethinkDB.

Creating a RethinkDB cluster in production

We are going to consider a separate machine as an instance for a cluster in production. Considering you have a two-server machine with IPs `104.121.23.24` and `104.121.23.25` respectively. We need to define which server will act as the starting point (SEED server) for other machines to enter the cluster; for instance, say `104.121.23.24` machine is the SEED server.

Log in to the machine with the `104.121.23.24` IP address and open up the RethinkDB configuration file. Assuming it's Ubuntu, the `config` file can be located at `/etc/rethinkdb/instances.d/default.conf`. If it is not present, you need to manually create it.

If it's already present, then you can uncomment some of the code lines shown here or simply write them.

First set up the instance name as follows. For the instance, the name is `rethink_main`:

```
server-name = rethink_main
```

The next setting we need to alter or create is to allows the RethinkDB instance running on a different machine to connect to this server in order to create a cluster.

If the `config` file is already there, you may find this code:

```
# bind=127.0.0.1
```

Change it to:

```
bind = all
```

Later, save and close the file. You will need to restart RethinkDB to let change take effect. You can do this in the following ways:

- By executing the `rethinkdb` command as follows:

  sudo /etc/init.d/rethinkdb restart

- By using the `service` command as follwos:

  sudo service rethinkdb restart

- By using the `systemctl` command as follows:

  sudo systemctl rethinkdb restart

Once the restart is done, we can move ahead to configure our next machine. We need to ensure one thing before this; it's the startup script. In case we need to reboot the server (which happens at regular maintenance by the service provider), our RethinkDB Server should be started on boot.

By default, RethinkDB automatically creates the init.d script, which a Unix-based system reads on boot to start the services. As we have our configuration file in place, it will automatically start the service on boot.

This is our administrative screen after restarting the RethinkDB server:

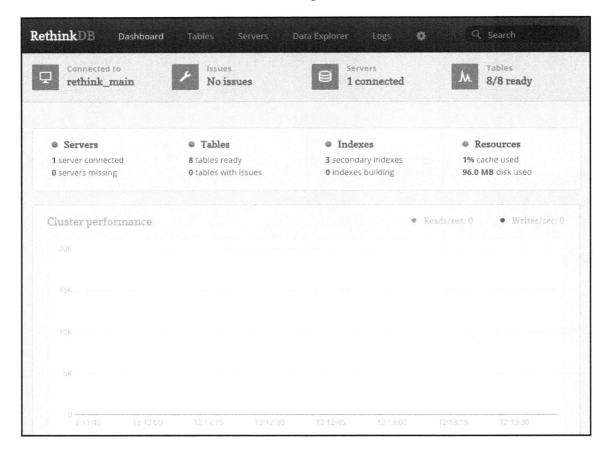

If you have a Mac- or Windows-based server, you need to install the respective packages available for them to perform the startup execution. We are covering Linux-based systems as the majority of servers are based on them.

Now let's configure our second machine and form our cluster. Log in to the machine with the `104.121.23.25` IP address and open up the configuration file using your favorite editor by the following command:

```
sudo vi /etc/rethinkdb/instances.d/default.conf
```

Change the name of the server by setting the following key:

```
server-name=rethink_child
```

Again, change the bind key and allow it to connect to other RethinkDB instances:

```
bind=all
```

Now, to add this machine to a cluster, we need to add the following `join` command. This command will join our machine to the first machine and we will have our cluster ready:

```
join=104.121.23.24:29015
```

Save and close the editor. To make the setting effective, we need to restart the server:

```
sudo /etc/init.d/rethinkdb restart
```

Once the reboot is successful, we can check whether we have our cluster formed successfully or not. Visit the administrative screen and you should be able to see a similar screen to that shown here:

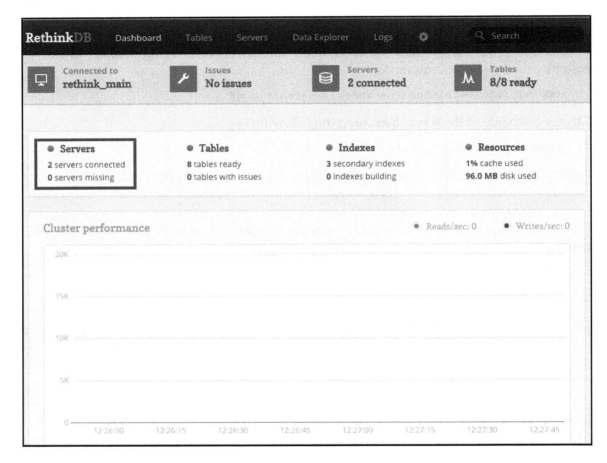

As we can see, we have two servers connected and running as one cluster. Congratulations! We have a production-ready cluster with us.

 You can learn more about the configuration files of RethinkDB at their official docs website (https://rethinkdb.com/docs/config-file/)

However, there is still a little work left to do on the security of the cluster. As you may have noticed, we are setting `bind=all` in our configuration, which simply means any machine can make an attempt to connect to our cluster. We need to add some security layers in order to have some prevention.

In the next section, we are going to learn how we can secure our cluster.

Securing our RethinkDB cluster

In order to create a cluster, we need to allow the incoming connections from other machines. Hence, we added `bind=all` in our configuration. That meant literally any machine from the Internet can attempt a connection to our server which is prone to **Distributed Denial of Service (DDOS)** attack.

To protect the RethinkDB cluster, the best thing to do is to use put the entire RethinkDB machine into one protected network by using a firewall to prevent any such connection. However, this is not optimal and possible for every infrastructure for budget or maintenance reasons.

We can protect RethinkDB in the following ways:

- Using transport layer security (successor of SSL)
- Binding the web port

Let's look over each of them in detail.

Using transport layer security

RethinkDB allows us to secure our connection between servers or between clients and servers using TLS encryption. You can either generate TLS certificates by self-signing with the host or buy a certificate from an official provider.

 You can buy SSL certificates from many sources. However, I will recommend comodo security provider (`https://ssl.comodo.com/`). Comodo also provides free SSL certificate, learn more about it by visiting this link (`https://ssl.comodo.com/free-ssl-certificate.php`)

You need to generate a key and a certificate file and send it to the security provider (if you are buying it) for verification. Here is a sample command to generate a key and a certificate file using `openssl`.

Generate a key as follows:

```
openssl genrsa -out key.pem 2048
```

Now, generate a certificate file as follows:

```
openssl req -new -x509 -key key.pem -out cert.pem -days 365
```

You need to answer a few questions in the setup wizard, but make sure that the common name matches the domain name of your server.

Once we have the key and certificate file with us, we can integrate them in RethinkDB using either the command line or a configuration file. I will go with the configuration file option. Open up the configuration file using your favorite editor as follows:

```
sudo vi /etc/rethinkdb/instances.d/default.conf
```

And add the following keys:

```
http-tls-key=/path of the key file
http-tls-cert=/path of the certificate file
```

Make sure the path is accessible by the user account.

Now to make sure that our client driver also uses the certificate to make the connection to RethinkDB, we need to start RethinkDB with the following options:

```
rethinkdb --driver-tls-key key.pem --driver-tls-cert cert.pem
```

Now, in client driver code, in the `connect()` function, pass the SSL key as shown in the following code:

```
ssl: {
     ca: /path of certificate file.
```

Note that we pass only the certificate to the client driver, not the key. Now, in order to have TLS encryption between the machines in the cluster, we need to pass the following parameter:

```
rethindb --cluster-tls-key key.pem --cluster-tls-cert cert.pem --cluster-tls-ca ca.pem
```

Here we are passing a CA certificate, which is the certificate used to sign another certificate. Servers can connect to the cluster if the certificate is generated by the CA authority certificate passed in the argument.

This way, we can secure our cluster is using TLS encryption. Now let's look over the port binding method to secure our web administrative screen.

Binding the web administrative port

This method will prevent the web administration port from being directly accessed from any remote machine. We will bind our port to, say, 3000 or the localhost for that matter, and generate a reverse proxy to access it from a remote location.

First open up the configuration file in your favorite editor as follows:

```
sudo vi /etc/rethinkdb/instances.d/default.conf
```

Now add the following key:

```
bind-http=localhost
```

This way, it is blocked from remote connection, but we want to access it for admin purposes; to do that, we will add a reverse proxy for the same.

Assuming you are using the Nginx package, which is quite common for the lightweight reverse proxy server, you need to add the following code in the default configuration file of Nginx. In Ubuntu, it is located at /etc/nginx/nginx.conf as follows:

```
location /rethinkdb/admin/
{
 proxy_pass http://127.0.0.1:8080;
}
```

Now you can access the web administrative portal by pointing your browser to http://hostname/rethinkdb/admin.

This way, no outside machine can connect to http://hostname:8080. We can add username and password in the admin authentication to have an extra security layer. We will look over user accounts and permissions in detail in Chapter 5, *Administration and Troubleshooting Tasks in RethinkDB*.

We have our production cluster ready and running; it's time to run some queries in our cluster.

Executing ReQL queries in a cluster

We have our cluster in place running smoothly; let's perform a ReQL query and observe the response. First we will create a new table in the `test` database. As we have learned in `Chapter 2`, *RethinkDB Query Language,* we need to use the `tableCreate()` method to create a new table.

Let's execute a query from the web administrative screen:

```
r.db("test").tableCreate('clusterTest2')
```

Here is our response object:

```
Data Explorer                                    History    ⚙    ⠿

1 | r.db("test").tableCreate('clusterTest')



                                                        Clear      Run

1 row returned in 922ms.          Tree view   Table view   Raw view   Query profile

{
    "config_changes": [
        {
            "new_val": {
                "db": "test" ,
                "durability": "hard" ,
                "id": "678446aa-4223-4c73-9d3c-2c07920cfc73" ,
                "indexes": [ ],
                "name": "clusterTest" ,
                "primary key": "id" ,
                "shards": [
                    {
                        "nonvoting_replicas": [ ],
                        "primary_replica": "Shahids_MacBook_Air_local_y7b" ,
                        "replicas": [
                            "Shahids_MacBook_Air_local_y7b"
                        ]
                    }
                ],
                "write_acks": "majority"
            } ,
            "old_val": null
        }
    ] ,
    "tables_created": 1
}
```

As you may have noticed the highlighted section, `primary_replica` is showing that this table is stored at a machine ending with _y7b, which is my second machine in the cluster. This proves that RethinkDB automatically utilizes the instances in the cluster.

Let's perform an `insert` operation on the same table and observe the response. Here is the `insert` ReQL query:

```
r.db("test").table("clusterTest").insert({name : "Shahid", age : 24})
```

Upon running it, we see that the document has been inserted in the `clusterTest` table and RethinkDB returns exactly the same response as we get when we do not use clustering. Hence, this again proves that all query routing is being done by RethinkDB automatically. See the response shown here:

Similarly, responses for other ReQL queries are also same as before. Hence we do not require any code change and we do not need to worry about utilization of our machine in the cluster; RethinkDB takes care of it automatically. This is a big feature of RethinkDB. It makes this complex management of clusters a piece of cake.

We have covered clustering in detail; Now let's move ahead to one more interesting topic from RethinkDB, that is, the replication of tables.

Performing replication of tables in RethinkDB

We have a fully working cluster with us running two instances of RethinkDB. We can perform replication in our cluster to maintain high availability of data in case of failover. Replication, as the name suggests, means keeping the copy of a table in another instance to mainly handle failover scenarios. However, replication can also help you in scaling your system to improve performance and response time.

RethinkDB provides two ways to perform replication:

- By using a web console
- By using ReQL queries

You can use the `tableCreate` ReQL method and provide values for `shards` and `replicaspershard` keys to create your replication; we have covered ReQL queries in detail in `Chapter 2`, *RethinkDB Query Language*. So, for this chapter, we will be covering replication using a web console, which is indeed a promising feature of RethinkDB (that is, easy administration).

To perform replication of tables, open your administrative screen and go to the tables screen. If you don't have any tables or database, you can create one or just select on any table to provide. When you scroll down to the shards and replication widget and click on the Reconfigure button, you will get the following screen:

As you can observe, we can create multiple shards (max to number of cluster instances, including primary) and replications. Choose the number of replications and click on **Apply configuration**. I chose three replicas in one shard.

Since we don't have enough records in our table, it will apply the settings in seconds; however, in production, this takes up to a minute depending on the size of the table. During that time, your data will not be available to the application.

Once the settings are applied, RethinkDB lists down the servers our table is using. Since I chose three replicas, RethinkDB puts the replica of the table in each instance of the cluster. As shown in the following figure, it puts the primary replica in the SEED server, that is, the server we used to create our cluster:

Servers used by this table

Shard 1   ~900 documents

Shahids_MacBook_Air_local_pnj	Primary replica	ready
Shahids_MacBook_Air_local_872	Secondary replica	ready
Shahids_MacBook_Air_local_y7b	Secondary replica	ready

As you can see in the preceding image, I already have documents in the table. RethinkDB will copy all of these documents in the replicas as well. You can perform your read, write, update, and delete operations using ReQL without worrying about the replicas.

To prove our point about failover handling, let's bring down one of the instances of the cluster and then perform the read operation. For fun, let's bring down the SEED Server itself. After stopping the SEED Server, here is what I got in the web administrative screen:

You have been disconnected from the server

The connection to the server has been lost. The server may be under heavy load.

Trying to reconnect

This implies that our primary server is down; we switch to another cluster machine and log in to its web console (if the primary is running on `port 8080`, then the first cluster machine will be running on `8081`).

Run the following query from the data explorer:

```
r.db("company").table("employees")
```

As you can see in the following image, we are still getting the document stored in the employee's table without changing any piece of query. It won't require any code change at the client end either:

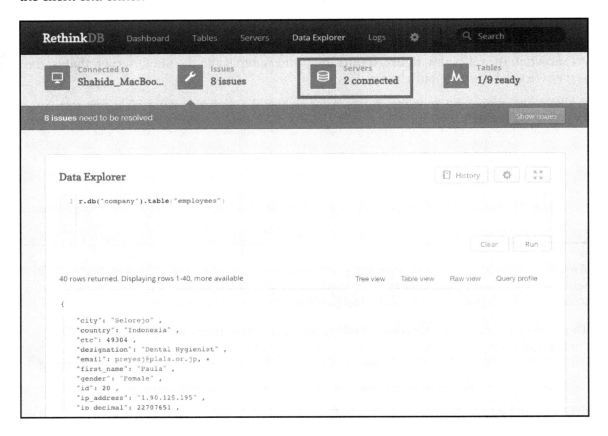

This provides us confidence in our data availability. Now let's look over the scalability; RethinkDB, by default, will read from the primary replica if the connection from the client driver is made to the SEED Server. In order to divert traffic forcefully, we can perform changes in the connection and connect it to one of the cluster machines to ensure that any request coming to the client is directed to this replica. Hence we can improve the response time plus shred down the load of the SEED Server.

We have learned how easy it is to perform replication in RethinkDB. Let's learn how to perform sharding (splitting data across the cluster) in RethinkDB.

Sharding the table to scale the database

Replication puts the same copy of the table in different RethinkDB instances in the cluster, while sharding splits the data and puts it in a different cluster. As we have studied in Chapter 1, *RethinkDB Architecture and Data Model*, RethinkDB uses the range sharding algorithm to perform the splitting of records.

You can refer to that chapter for more details on the algorithm; in this section, we will be doing sharding in our cluster.

So let's take our cluster again and perform sharding of a table. To do so, again we have two options; either do it via a web console or ReQL. I am going to use a web console for the same.

So, as you can see in the following image, we have about 900 documents in the table with random IDs (remember the mock data we generated in Chapter 3, *Data Exploration Using RethinkDB*?). The reason I am mentioning ID here is that the range sharding algorithm is going to partition our data on the basis of IDs.

For ease of understanding, let's create two shards in our cluster. Click on the reconfigure button and increment the value of the shard by 1 as shown here:

Click on **Apply configuration**. Once the partitioning has been done by RethinkDB, you can view the number of shards in the data distribution graph and how many documents each shard contains.

Here is what I have at my end:

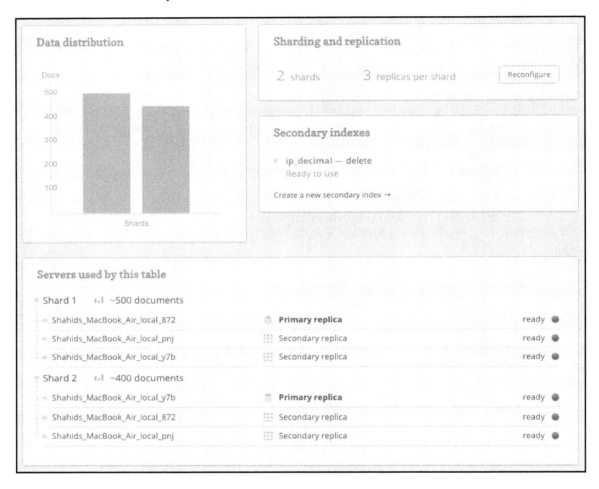

Here we've got two shards containing 500 and 400 documents; that's a total of 900 documents. The splitting of data was based on the ID column, and according to my observation, all the even number IDs goes to shard 1, while the odd ones go to shard 2. This is purely an assumption as RethinkDB does not provide any insights into how their algorithm works.

RethinkDB uses the range sharding algorithm for now but may switch to the hash sharding algorithm in future. For information on why RethinkDB is going to switch to hash sharding, follow this github pull request:
`https://github.com/rethinkdb/rethinkdb/issues/364`

As we can see, sharding results in a split of data. But does it affect ReQL queries? Mainly the read operation? No. You can perform all ReQL queries as you were doing before sharding. All of the internal logic and pointing the query to the correct shard is done by RethinkDB automatically.

In case of shard failure, as long as more than half of the voting replicas are available, RethinkDB will choose one of them as the primary replica and process the request. However, if less replicas are available, you will not be able to process the queries. For example, if we shut down two instances in our cluster, we will receive the following error upon running the query:

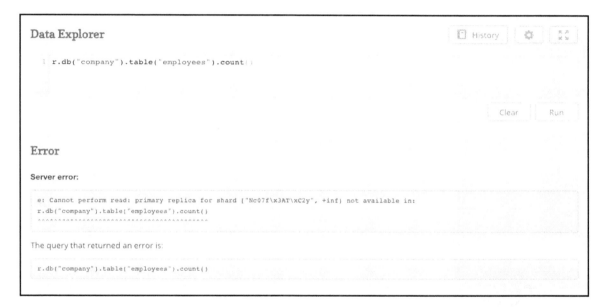

Data Explorer

History

```
1   r.db("company").table("employees").count()
```

Clear   Run

Error

Server error:

```
e: Cannot perform read: primary replica for shard ["Nc07f\x3AT\xC2y", +inf) not available in:
r.db("company").table("employees").count()
```

The query that returned an error is:

```
r.db("company").table("employees").count()
```

 Replicas which can be used during the failover process are called **voting replicas**, one which can't is called a **non-voting replicas**.

This implies that RethinkDB is not able to select the primary replica as a part of automatic failover handling. This is because we have one instance running in the cluster out of three. The minute we restart another instance, RethinkDB will vote and select the master replica, and we will receive the result of the query, as shown here:

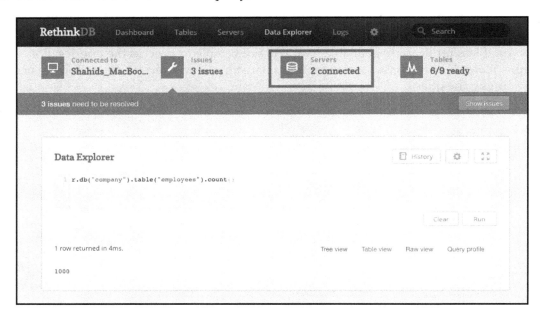

As shown in the preceding section, we have two servers out of three running; hence RethinkDB can process the queries. This sums up sharding in RethinkDB. We have looked over clustering, replication, and sharding in detail to improve the performance of the system. Let's cover the proxy node in our cluster for improving intra-cluster turnaround time and reducing CPU load.

Running a RethinkDB proxy node

We have our cluster consisting of one SEED Server and a RethinkDB instance to support the cluster. The SEED server is acting as master server (however, there is no such master/child concept in RethinkDB; we are phrasing this for understanding) to perform routing of queries and run various kinds of business logic to determine where the data is stored and where to point the request. This in turn increases the load and dependency on one RethinkDB instance. Refer to the following figure; the proxy node acts as the node to distribute the query across instances in the cluster:

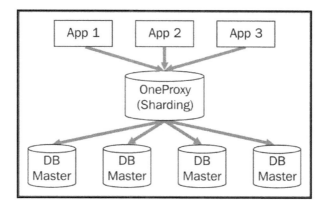

RethinkDB allows us to create a proxy node to solve such problems. The proxy node will act like a query redirector and will not store any data. We can create a proxy node in our cluster and join our other instances to it to form the cluster. The RethinkDB proxy node will:

- Reduce CPU load by doing some query processing itself
- Reduce intra-cluster traffic because it knows exactly where to point the query and sends traffic directly to it
- Act as the instance to expose to the outside world (outside of the firewall)

Let's form a proxy node in our cluster and see how it works. To create the node as a proxy, add the `proxy` parameter while starting the RethinkDB server.

Here is a command to start RethinkDB on the default port (`29015`) as a proxy node:

```
rethinkdb proxy --join localhost:29015
```

On the terminal, it shows that the proxy is ready:

```
Shahids-MacBook-Air:Desktop UnixRoot$ rethinkdb proxy --join localhost:29015
Listening for intracluster connections on port 29015
warn: Attempted to join self, peer ignored
Listening for client driver connections on port 28015
Listening for administrative HTTP connections on port 8080
Listening on cluster addresses: 127.0.0.1, ::1
Listening on driver addresses: 127.0.0.1, ::1
Listening on http addresses: 127.0.0.1, ::1
To fully expose RethinkDB on the network, bind to all addresses by running rethinkdb
  with the --bind all command line option
Proxy ready, proxy-42db4bac-f1fb-428a-90ea-f44926b5db1d
```

Open up the web admin console, as shown in the following figure; you should see that RethinkDB is connected to the proxy node instead of the name of the machine. Also, there is no RethinkDB instance connected to it and you cannot execute the query at all. Why? Simply because it's a proxy and its job is to direct the query, not to execute. Since there is no RethinkDB instance with data connected, we can't execute our queries:

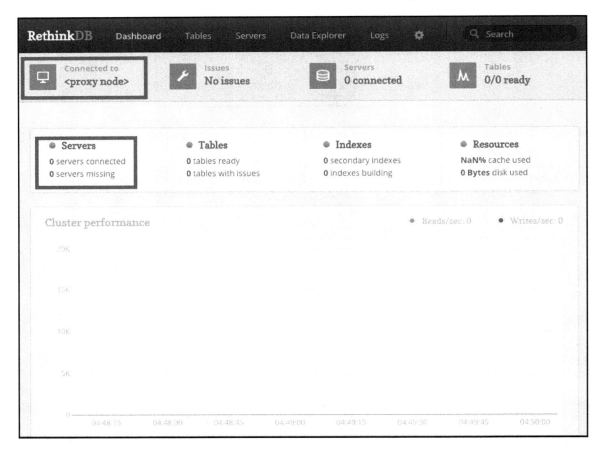

In order to form the cluster and run queries, we will add a RethinkDB instance to it. After adding four RethinkDB instances, here is our cluster, with four servers and 10 tables replicated and sharded across the cluster, as shown here:

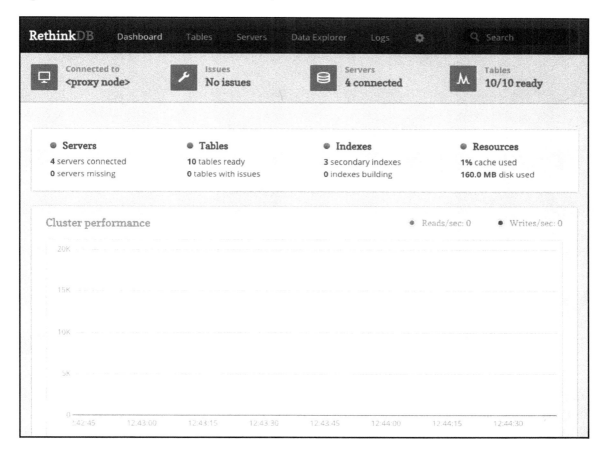

Awesome! We have our cluster ready with a proxy node. Time to run some queries! Open up **Data Explorer** and run any test query to check whether it's working okay. Here I am fetching documents from our **login** table:

```
Data Explorer                                              History    ⚙    ⤢

1  r.db("users").table("login")


                                                           Clear       Run


2 rows returned. Displaying rows 1-2        Tree view   Table view   Raw view   Query profile

{

    "email": shahid@codeforgeek.com, »
    "id": "136707e9-78d3-488e-912d-fe9247d0d180" ,
    "password": "nothingtohidehere"

}

{

    "email": shahid@codeforgeek.com, »
    "id": "cde4e290-5ee4-45cf-a1c8-c69119e8da07" ,
    "password": "nothingtohidehere"

}
```

We have our cluster with a replicated table and shards running with the proxy node. This can be easily scalable and can be deployed to production. One of the other advantages that you can avail using proxy is the de-duplication of query results coming in changefeed while running in the cluster to improve your performance.

Once we have the cluster infrastructure ready, it's our job to keep monitoring it in order to make sure we are getting the full benefits. In the next section, we are going to analyze how to monitor and evaluate our queries to keep the performance up as much as possible.

Optimizing query performance

The way recommended by RethinkDB to get great performance from the database is to use sharding, replication, and proxy nodes, which we've already learned in previous sections. However, poorly written queries can still affect your system even if you are using these techniques.

In order to refactor and find out those queries, RethinkDB provides a tool called database profiler that shows various performance parameters of queries executed on the database. You can enable this tool from the web admin console, under the **Data Explorer** section.

Once you run the query, it provides you with the following information:

- **Round trip time**: Total time taken from firing the query till the return of the result
- **Server time**: Total time taken by the database to execute the query
- **Shared access**: How many shards were used to form the result

Here is a screenshot of the query I ran to fetch all employees from the company table:

```
2 rows returned. Displaying rows 1-2          Tree view    Table view    Raw view    Query profile

  ⟳ 80ms round-trip time          ⊙ 55ms server time                ⤓ 8 shard accesses

  [                                                                      ⤷ Copy to clipboard
      {
          "description": "Evaluating table." ,
          "duration(ms)": 19.399668 ,
          "sub_tasks": [
              {
                  "description": "Evaluating db." ,
                  "duration(ms)": 0.016246 ,
                  "sub_tasks": [
                      {
                          "description": "Evaluating datum." ,
                          "duration(ms)": 0.001115 ,
                          "sub_tasks": [ ]
                      }
                  ]
              } ,
              {
                  "description": "Evaluating datum." ,
                  "duration(ms)": 0.000295 ,
                  "sub_tasks": [ ]
              }
          ]
      } ,
```

As you can see, **Query profile** provides us important information to understand and evaluate the performance of our query. This cluster is running on my local system; hence, **server time** is **55 ms**, which is also more than ideal query execution time (10-15 ms). But since the query requires a full table scan, we can expect this to be the average time.

However, let's look at improving reading time for the field-based search. Say we want to fetch the names of all employees. We can write a simple query like this in RethinkDB:

```
r.db("company").table("employees")("first_name")
```

This takes in my system around **19ms** to execute, as shown here:

We have studied indexing in Chapter 2, *RethinkDB Query Language* . It helps us to improve the reading time of a database. Let's check that by creating an index on the first_name field. Here is the query to create an index on this field:

```
r.db("company").table("employees").indexCreate("first_name")
```

RethinkDB provides the getAll() command to query an index. This command accepts two parameters as input: the value to search and the name of the index to query.

Let's try repeating the original query using this index:

```
r.db('company').table('employees').getAll("John", {index: "first_name"})
```

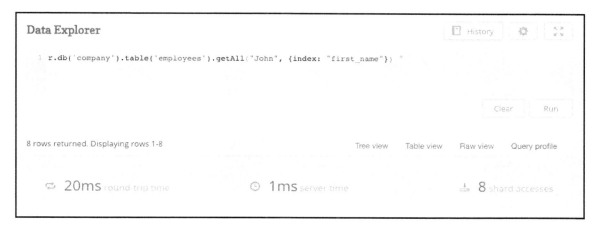

That's an improvement of 18 ms. Impressive! So this again proves that indexing does work to improve query performance.

However, for the majority of times, we as developers come across a situation where we need to run the query on more than one field or combinations of fields. In such a scenario, a single index won't work the way we expect it to. Hence, RethinkDB provides us with compound indexes as well. You can create more than one index using the `indexCreate()` ReQL command to improve the performance of your query.

Here are a few tips to keep in mind while using ReQL:

- Always use `orderBy` with indexes
- Use `getAll`, `between`, and `filter` to select the data
- Use MapReduce operations to perform aggregation
- Always try to put the commands that can execute in parallel before commands that combine the result to use query parallelization

However, query execution time is only going to work on the server time parameter. What about the network round trip time? We need to make sure that our network is of a high quality in order to keep the round trip time as low as possible.

Here is one of the best ways to ensure that the network round trip time is not too much we should be looking at an infrastructure that is already built and proven and deploy our code there instead of reinventing the wheel (unless, of course, if you come up with better solutions than them).

This sums up query optimization in RethinkDB.

Summary

In this chapter, we learned all about performance and how to achieve it in RethinkDB. We went deeper into clustering with use cases and learned how to perform replication, achieving the highest level of scalability and availability. We also learnt about sharding and how to achieve it in RethinkDB. Above all, we saw how the RethinkDB team has managed to provide us the tools and web console to perform such tedious operations easily.

We also learned about query optimization, how we can use a query profiler to monitor the time our database is taking to execute the query, and how we can use indexing to improve that time. We looked at some useful tips to help us write better queries for RethinkDB.

In the following chapter, we are going to learn about the administration of RethinkDB, how we can allow user access control, and how to perform various kinds of troubleshooting and failovers.

5
Administration and Troubleshooting Tasks in RethinkDB

In the previous chapters, we learned about how RethinkDB works and how to scale it in order to achieve high availability and a fast response time. We also learned about running ReQL queries in RethinkDB and, before moving ahead to deploy our RethinkDB database, it's important to understand how to manage and administrate the RethinkDB database.

In this chapter, we are going to learn about RethinkDB administration, mainly user accounts, roles, and failover management, and also how to perform a crash recovery in the case of failure. We will also learn about data migration and backing up the RethinkDB database. In addition to this, we will also look over some of the third-party tools that we can use to perform the monitoring of RethinkDB.

In this chapter, we will also learn the following:

- Understanding access controls and permissions in RethinkDB
- Failover handling in RethinkDB
- Performing manual and automatic backup in RethinkDB
- Data import and export in RethinkDB
- Crash recovery in RethinkDB
- Using third-party tools

At the end of the chapter, we will also look over the third-party tools available for free to perform the monitoring of RethinkDB.

Understanding access controls and permission in RethinkDB

In RethinkDB, user access control is divided into permissions and scope. Each RethinkDB user has some permissions, and these permissions in turn have scope; that is, where they can perform their respective operation with each permission.

For example, say a user named John has a read permission, and his scope is tables. He can perform read (permission) operations on tables (scope), but not on databases.

In this section, we will learn about the kinds of permission and scope RethinkDB provides for administration purposes.

Let us look over the permissions and scope of RethinkDB in detail.

There are four permissions in RethinkDB; refer to the following table to understand their effect:

Permissions	Effect
read	Allows reading the data.
write	Allows modification of data.
connect	Allows users to perform an http() command.
config	Allows user to perform configuration tasks on tables/databases, depending upon the scope.

As you can see in the preceding table, the read permission is self-explanatory, while the write permission consists of inserting records, replacing/updating, and deleting records.

We learned in Chapter 2, *RethinkDB Query Language*, that RethinkDB can perform the HTTP operation directly from the database, which can harm your database if it's open to hackers. They could dump millions of rows from the Large Hadron Collider into your database, which may bring down the whole system.

 CERN released 300 TB of data from the Large Hadron Collider. If you're interested, follow this link: http://www.theverge.com /2016/4/25/11501078/cern-300-tb-lhc-data-open-access

You can prevent this by only providing this access to trusted users. Moving on to the `config` permission, this is a kind of administrative permission where, if it's provided to the user, they can add/remove indexes, add/remove databases, reconfigure databases, and so on, depending upon the scope. We will look over the scopes in a moment.

Every permission is stored in a permissions table in the RethinkDB database. You can change the permission by using ReQL queries such as `update` or `grant`. RethinkDB encourages you to use grant for such operations.

Let's look over scopes now. RethinkDB scopes go from table, then to database, and then to global. Refer to the following table for better understanding:

Scopes	Impact
Table	Permission to work on a particular table.
Database	Permission to work on a particular database.
Global	Permission to work on all tables and databases.

As you can see, RethinkDB scopes allow you to provide permissions at the table, database, or global level.

Any permissions given to lower entities will override the higher entity permissions. What we mean is if you have write permission to the database but read permission to the table in that database, then the final access control is read for that table even though you have write permission for the database.

We have learned how permissions and roles work. Let's look over how to use them.

RethinkDB user management

Before moving ahead to creating a new user and playing with the permissions and scope, let's learn a little bit about the `admin` user of RethinkDB.

As you may have noticed, we run most of our queries from the RethinkDB data explorer and that connects to the admin user who is the default user.

The default `admin` user is a global scope user with all the permissions. Initially, it is not associated with a password, but you can do so by running a simple query such as the following:

```
r.db('rethinkdb').table('users').get('admin').update({password:
'test@2016'});
```

or

```
Start RethinkDB using --initial-password parameter.
```

If you have set the password for the admin user, you need to provide the password in the RethinkDB client to connect to the RethinkDB instance. However, in the case of the RethinkDB web console, it will bypass the password and directly show the administrative screen.

We can secure that by using proxies. We have covered that in Chapter 4, *Performance Tuning in RethinkDB*, in the *Securing clusters* section.

Let's create a new user with no password. Run the following query from Data explorer as follows:

```
r.db("rethinkdb").table("users").insert({id: 'shahid',password: false})
```

You should be seeing the response shown here:

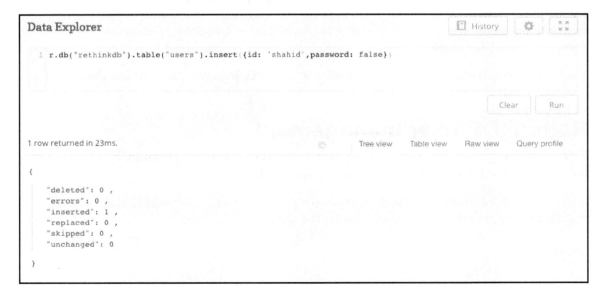

Now in order to check whether our user exists in system, let's select all users using the following query:

```
r.db("rethinkdb").table("users")
```

You should be seeing one more user document in the response of the query as shown here:

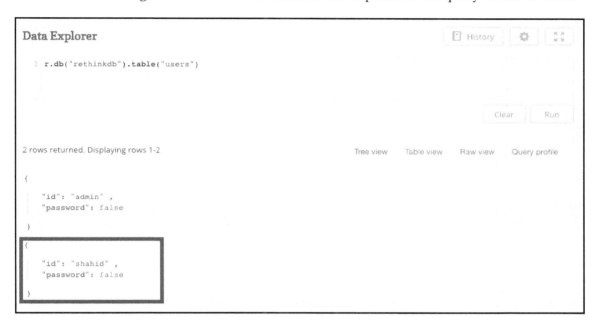

Congratulations! We have created new user using a simple insert query. However, this user can't do anything as we have not set any permissions during the creation of the user.

 In order to find out the permissions of the user, query the **permissions** table in the rethinkdb database.

Since global scope is not specific to any database or table, let's look over it first. To give our user a global scope with all permissions, we need to run the following query:

```
r.grant("shahid",{read:true,write:true,config:true});
```

Notice in the query that we have not selected any databases or tables; we are providing our user access to every database with three permissions, that is, read, write and config. You should be getting the following response:

In order to provide permissions in the database scope, we need to run the following query:

```
r.db("company").grant("shahid",{read:true,write:true,config:false});
```

We are only providing read and write permissions to our user for the database named company.

You can chain the table here to limit the permission and scope to the table using the following query:

```
r.db("company").table("user").grant("shahid",{read:true,write:false,config:
false});
```

Here, we have given read permission to our user for the user table, which resides in the company database.

This covers providing access control to the user. Let's look at how to revoke particular permissions of a user or delete a user.

To revoke the permissions of a user, you can run the `grant` query again and specify `null` or `false` to the permission you need to revoke.

For example, let's revoke the write permission of the user named `shahid`.

Here is the query:

```
r.db("company").grant("shahid",{read:true,write:false,config:false});
```

You can revoke the permission of the table scope by chaining the table name to the preceding query:

Now, in order to delete the user, you need to hard delete it from the RethinkDB user's table. So if we want to remove the user named `shahid`, here is the query:

```
r.db("rethinkdb").table("users").get("shahid").delete()
```

This will remove the user and automatically flush the permissions table. You don't need to do that manually.

Can we suspend the user for a certain length of time? Yes and no.

RethinkDB does not provide any status field for the user to suspend them, but you can do it by revoking all the permissions of the user, that is, `read`, `write`, `connect`, and `config`, and that user won't be able to do anything.

You can do it again using `grant` command, as shown here:

```
r.db("company").grant("shahid",{read:null,write:null,connect:
null,config:null});
```

After running this query, a user will be suspended. This is the workaround I found when I realized RethinkDB doesn't provide a **suspend user** feature.

This covers the user management in RethinkDB along with the access controls. Let's look at how RethinkDB handles and maintains automatic failover.

Failover handling in RethinkDB

RethinkDB provides two ways to handle the failover:

- Automatic failover handling
- Emergency repair

RethinkDB performs automatic failover handling if, and only if, the cluster has three or more RethinkDB instances running, and if a table has three or more voting replicas available. If these conditions do not match, then automatic failover handling will not occur.

We have done a quite nice demonstration of this in the *Performing replication and performing sharding* section in `Chapter 4`, *Performance Tuning in RethinkDB*, where we had three live servers running along with three replicas for each table and we shut down instances, including primary, to validate the automatic failover handling.

But what if the ideal situation happens, that is, there are only one or two RethinkDB instances alive and failover happens. Of course, RethinkDB will not perform the automatic failover; we now need to manually perform the emergency repair.

In this section, we are going to perform the emergency repair for the same cluster configuration we used throughout `Chapter 4`, *Performance Tuning in RethinkDB*.

For demonstration purposes, I purposely brought down the three RethinkDB instances running on ports `8081`, `8082`, and `8083`. Upon running the Seed Server on port `8080`, this error is shown on the web console:

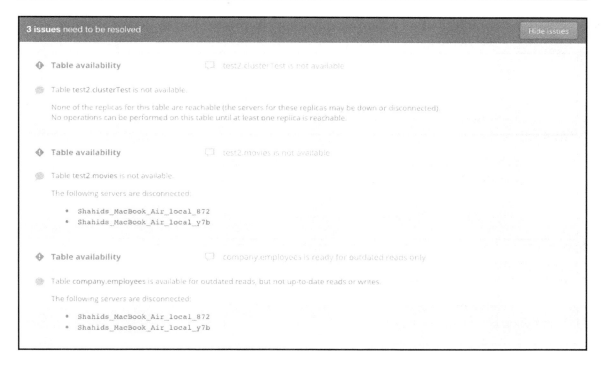

It provides us with details about the unavailability of the server and the respective tables. In order to fix this, RethinkDB provides us with the command called reconfigure.

This command accepts various parameters:

- shards: The number of shards to reconfigure
- replicas: The number of replicas to reconfigure
- primaryReplicaTag: If the replicas key is an object, then provide the primary replica tag here
- dryRun: To perform the reconfigure operation without effect, just to check the response
- nonvotingReplicaTags: Add non-voting replica tags here
- emergencyRepair: Used for emergency repair mode

What we are looking for here is the emergency repair option because we want to fix it immediately, considering we have no prior information about the setup and configuration of the cluster.

For information regarding other options please visit the documentation here: `https://www.rethinkdb.com/api/javascript/reconfigure/`

In order to use emergency repair, let's first understand how it works. Upon execution of this command, RethinkDB performs the analysis of the table and classifies it into three categories:

- **Healthy**: Replica count is more than half in the shard
- **Repairable**: The shard is not healthy, but it contains one replica of the table regardless of voting or nonvoting
- **Beyond repair**: No replica exists for the table

In our scenario, we have one database that is beyond repair because it resides on the RethinkDB instance, which is down. Plus, all of its replicas were in the same instance, so there is no way we can fix that.

However, we have one repairable replica for the employees table in the company database. Here is the error message:

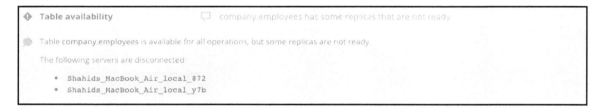

Let's run the reconfigure command using the emergencyRepair option to see if RethinkDB can fix that.

Here is the query:

```
r.db("company").table("employees").reconfigure({emergencyRepair:
"unsafe_rollback"})
```

Always use `unsafe_rollback` as the parameter to prevent destruction of unrepairable shards and replicas.

Here is the response of the query:

Data Explorer

```
1  r.db("company").table("employees").reconfigure({emergencyRepair: "unsafe_rollback"})
```

1 row returned in 116ms.

Tree view   Table view   Raw view   Query profile

```
    config_changes                    repaired    status_changes
      [                               1            [ ... ]
          {
              "new_val": { ... } ,
              "old_val": { ... }
          }
      ]
```

As you can see in the **repaired** field, it returns 1, that is, true, which tells us that RethinkDB performed the repair successfully. Let's run the query to validate this:

```
r.db("company").table("employees").limit(5)
```

The query returns the result successfully. Here is a screenshot of this:

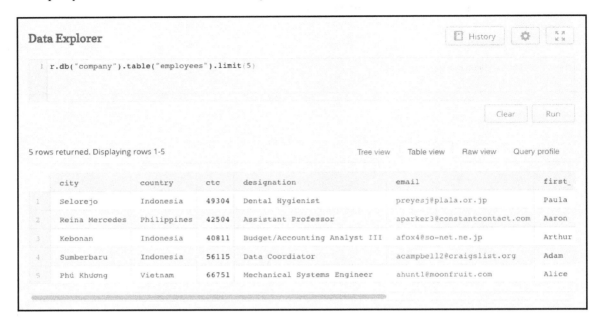

That's great. Let's check if we lost some data during the repair. This table has 1,000 records which we generated in Chapter 2, *RethinkDB Query Language,* for the data import demonstration. Here is the query I ran to check the count of the documents:

```
r.db("company").table("employees").count()
```

Here is the query response:

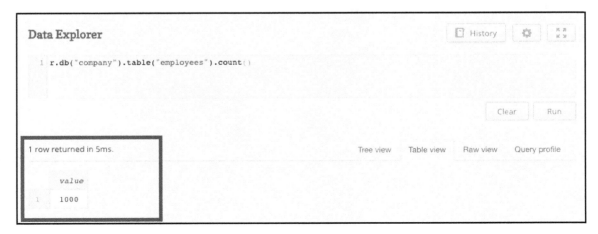

This proves there was no data loss during our repair operation. Awesome! However, emergency repair is marked as a dangerous operation by the RethinkDB team because it does not maintain any consistency and bypasses every measure RethinkDB takes to prevent data loss.

But what if data is lost during the operation? We can't blame RethinkDB for our infrastructure failure, but we can prevent this by backing up our database on a timely basis.

In next section, we are going to learn how to perform a backup of the RethinkDB databases and tables manually and how to set up an automatic job in the server to perform a backup every once in a while.

Performing a manual and automatic backup in RethinkDB

RethinkDB allows you to take a backup of the data while the system is running without affecting any other operations. Generally, in traditional databases you need to provide a locking mechanism to perform the backup, which eventually affects the working system. RethinkDB lets you back up or restore the database with no such constraints.

RethinkDB uses a client driver to perform the backup, which provides the concurrency facility, so it doesn't lock any clients while the backup process is running.

RethinkDB provides two utilities to perform the backup and restore:

- `dump` performs the backup of the cluster, database, or table
- `restore` performs the restore operation after backup

Along with learning how to take a backup of the system, it is equally and crucially important to learn how to use that backup to restore the system. We will cover restoration in the next section.

To back up the entire cluster of various RethinkDB instances, run the following command under the admin user privilege:

```
rethinkdb dump
```

This will perform the backup of the entire cluster assuming that the RethinkDB instance is running on the default port. You should receive the following response in the terminal:

```
Shahids-MacBook-Air:Desktop UnixRoot$ rethinkdb dump
NOTE: 'rethinkdb-dump' saves data and secondary indexes, but does "not" save
  cluster metadata.  You will need to recreate your cluster setup yourself after
  you run 'rethinkdb-restore'.
Exporting to directory...
[========================================] 100%
2013 rows exported from 8 tables, with 4 secondary indexes
  Done (1 seconds)
Zipping export directory...
  Done (0 seconds)
Shahids-MacBook-Air:Desktop UnixRoot$
```

This should generate a `.tar.gz` at the location where the command is executed. In my case, it's the desktop; extract the zip, and you should see a directory named after every database that, in turn, contains JSON files and metadata files. Have a look at the following screenshot for the backup file hierarchy:

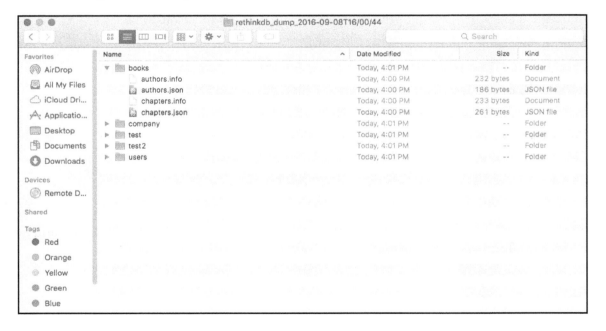

There are several arguments associated with the dump command. By default, running it with no parameter will back up the database or cluster running on port 28015. Here is a list of the supported parameters for this command:

- -c or -connect: This takes the port as the input to connect to a different port than the default.
- -f or -file: This allows you to change the default file naming convention of the backup file.
- -e or -export: This allows you to specify the database or table name to limit the databases to back up.
- -p or -password: If the admin user password is set, this specifies to perform authentication after this parameter.
- -password-file: This reads the admin password from a plain text file.
- -tls-cert: If the server is protected by TLS certification, this provides the path to the certificate to allow encrypted connections to the server.
- .-clients: This takes a number as input and performs the backup of the table simultaneously.
- -temp-dir: During the backup operation, RethinkDB uses the temporary directory to store the intermediate files. This specifies the path to change the directory.

> About -temp-dir, I personally got into the situation where the temp cache in Linux (/root/tmp) got full and the restoration process threw an error. This command rescued us from the situation.

If you like to back up a database running on port 28016 or anything else with a file named backup.zip, try this command out:

```
rethinkdb dump -c localhost:28016 -f /Users/UnixRoot/Desktop/backup.zip
```

Upon running the command, a new file named `backup.zip` will be stored on the Desktop. You should be receiving a response similar to the following screenshot:

```
Shahids-MacBook-Air:Desktop UnixRoot$ rethinkdb dump -c localhost:28016 -f /Users/UnixRoot
/Desktop/backup.zip
NOTE: 'rethinkdb-dump' saves data and secondary indexes, but does *not* save
  cluster metadata.  You will need to recreate your cluster setup yourself after
  you run 'rethinkdb-restore'.
Exporting to directory...
[========================================] 100%
2013 rows exported from 8 tables, with 4 secondary indexes
  Done (1 seconds)
Zipping export directory...
  Done (0 seconds)
Shahids-MacBook-Air:Desktop UnixRoot$
```

You can also back up a single table instead of a complete database. To do so, specify the database and table name in the `dump` command with `-e` parameter. Here is the command:

```
rethinkdb dump -c localhost:28016 -e company.employees -f
/Users/UnixRoot/Desktop/backup.zip
```

This will only back up the employees table present in the company database. You can also specify a single database in the same command.

Making backups in RethinkDB is really easy!

So far we have made backups manually, which is not suitable for a production system at all. Let's learn how to set up automatic backups for RethinkDB.

Performing automatic backups

To keep the backup process regular and to avoid any human dependencies, DevOps generally performs automation. The majority of servers run on Linux-based operating systems, and Linux provides an awesome utility called `crontab` to perform automation. For Windows users, there are utilities such as Task Scheduler and `schtash`.

 DevOps is a new term coined for infrastructure developers who perform continuous deployment tasks.

In this section, we are going to automate our backup process using the crontab utility. To perform this, we need to do it in two steps:

1. Create a script to execute at regular intervals, which in turn contains the backup commands.
2. Set up crontab to execute the script at midnight every day.

So let's do this.

The script that we are going to create is a shell script. Don't worry, it won't be very fancy; it will just have commands that we have executed in previous sections. So without any further ado, here is the shell code:

```
#!/bin/bash
echo "($(date -u)) Starting RethinkDB daily backup"
/usr/local/bin/rethinkdb-dump -f /etc/rethinkdbbackup/backup_."$(date)".zip
echo "($(date -u)) Finished creating backup"
```

The first line is for the Linux shell interpreter to identify the shell file. In the next line, we are just printing the date and text to make the log readable.

The second line is very important, and that line is actually our command to create a new backup. In order to avoid the same filename error we encountered previously, I am just appending the date to each filename.

Okay, so we have our script ready; it's time to make it executable. Run the following command to make the shell script code self-executable:

```
sudo chmod +x shellfile.sh
```

 This step is optional but required; the reason is to avoid needing one extra command to execute the shell script. Generally, you need to run it using sh <shellfile.sh>. After the preceding command, it will be ./shellcode.sh.

It's time to create a new cron job. Open the crontab utility using the following command:

```
crontab -e
```

Now we will add our cron code; here it is:

```
00 00 * * * /Users/UnixRoot/Desktop/backup.sh >>
/Users/UnixRoot/Desktop/backup.log
```

Save and quit the `crontab` utility. You should see a message indicating that a new crontab has been installed, similar to the screenshot shown here:

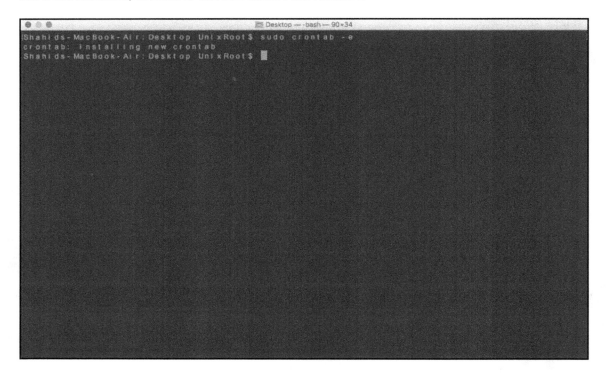

This simple utility will execute your script every midnight, which will in turn save the daily backup. You can tweak the backup script according to your needs; for example, we needed to limit the backup file to 5 MB due to some disk issue. We added a filter using the shell directory listing command, and it works.

Let us understand the syntax for cron before wrapping up this section. Here is a simple diagram to explain it:

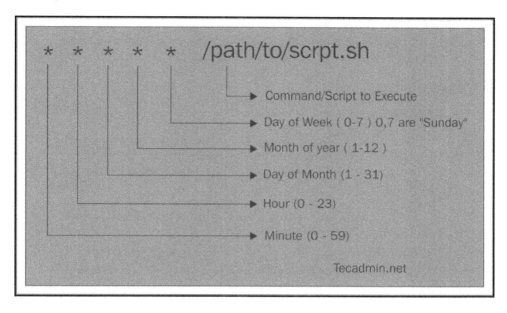

As you can see, this is quite easy. You need to specify at which time a particular task should be executed using minutes, hours, days of the month, months of the year, and days of the week. We want something to be executed every midnight, so we write 00 minutes and 00 hours, which is midnight, followed by *, which means every day and month of the year.

Coming to back to backups, you can enhance the backup process more by adding third-party APIs such as Dropbox or Google Drive to upload your backup file from the disk to the online store for better availability; however, that will incur some bandwidth expenses, but you will have data surety.

There is an amazing tool written by *Rob Conery* called *rethinkdb_nightly*, which uses crontab internally and performs a backup to the Amazon S3 server. Please refer to the following link: `https://github.com/robconery/rethinkdb_nightly`

We have done the backup process manually and automatically; it's time to perform the restoration process.

Restoring a RethinkDB database

As I have mentioned in an earlier section, RethinkDB provides a utility called `restore` to perform the backup restoration. This command takes the file path as the mandatory parameter along with the other optional parameter, which we are going to learn about in this section, in order to perform the restoration.

Here is the syntax of the command:

```
rethinkdb dump <file_name or Path>
```

This command will load the file from the path and restore it to your database cluster. This, by default, assumes that the RethinkDB instance is running on the default port, that is, `28015`. Again, like the `dump` utility, this command also provides various parameters, as follows:

- `-c` or `-connect`: This takes the port as the input in order to connect to a different port than the default.
- `-p` or `-password`: If an admin user password is set, this specifies to perform the authentication after this parameter.
- `-password-file`: This reads the admin password from a plain text file.
- `-i` or `--import`: This allows you to restore specific databases or tables.
- `-tls-cert`: If the server is protected by TLS certification, this provides the path to the certificate for signature handling.
- `-clients`: This takes a number as an input and performs the restoration of the table simultaneously.
- `-temp-dir`: During the backup operation, RethinkDB uses the temporary directory to store the intermediate files. This specifies the path required to change the directory.
- `--force`: When used, it will import data that exists in a table.
- `--no-secondary-indexes`: It prevents the creation of a secondary index during restoration.

If your RethinkDB instance is running on a port other than the default, specify it using the `-c` parameter. You can also limit which database or table performs the restoration on by using the `-i` parameter.

The RethinkDB team has worked really hard to make admin operations like these really easy. Backing up and restoring databases is a nightmare task in database development. RethinkDB pushes the limit of it to make it as easy as it can be.

In the next section, we will learn how to perform the migration of data using the backup and restore method in RethinkDB.

Data import and export in RethinkDB

RethinkDB provides the facility to dump existing data either coming from traditional databases such as MySQL and MSSQL in a suitable format, that is, CSV or JSON, or freshly generated JSON documents.

In Chapter 3, *Data Exploration Using RethinkDB*, we used the import utility to dump a JSON file consisting of 1,000 documents directly into a table. In this section, we are going to refresh the import utility.

Here is the command:

```
rethinkdb import -f <file path> --table <Database name>.<table name>
```

You can also specify the port options and other configuration; for more information, please visit Chapter 3, *Data Exploration Using RethinkDB*.

Let's look at a few use cases where we can really make use of the import utility.

Importing data from MySQL to RethinkDB

MySQL is no doubt one of the most popular and widely used SQL database engines, and is used by giants such as Facebook and Google. If you want to switch your stack from MySQL to RethinkDB, you need to do some of the tweaks and migration.

There are two ways, as far as I know:

- Using a third-party migration tool
- Performing the migration manually

If you would like to do the migration using a ready-made tool, then **methink** is the one!

Calder Coalson of Google made an awesome CLI-based tool called methink, which performs the migration from MySQL to RethinkDB.

It's a node module, so you need to first install it globally. Here is the command:

```
npm i --g methink
```

Once it is installed, execute the command to begin the migration. Here is the syntax:

```
mysql2rethink -h <host> -u <user name> -p <password> -d <mysql database> -t
<mysql table name> -D <rethinkdb database> -T <rethinkdb table name>
```

Replace the values with the actual configuration and it will perform the migration from MySQL to RethinkDB.

Another way to do it, if you don't want to use the migration tool, you can export the table from the database into CSV format, then using the RethinkDB `import` utility to enter the data into the RethinkDB table.

That's for MySQL; similarly, you can perform the migration from any conventional database if it supports CSV or JSON export formats. If not, there are ways to convert the existing data in formats such as XML to JSON or CSV. In the next section, we will learn how to perform the migration from MongoDB to RethinkDB, which is most likely the case with the majority of users.

Importing data from MongoDB to RethinkDB

To import data from MongoDB to RethinkDB, we need to export our collections from MongoDB first. Before moving ahead, let's clarify the terminologies used here. Refer to the following table:

Terms	MongoDB	RethinkDB
Database	Database	Database
Table	Collection	Table
Rows	Document	Document
Columns	Fields	Fields

All the terms are the same, except tables in RethinkDB are called collections in MongoDB. So let's do the data migration.

For demonstration purposes, I created a collection in a MongoDB test database and added some documents to it. Refer to the following screenshot:

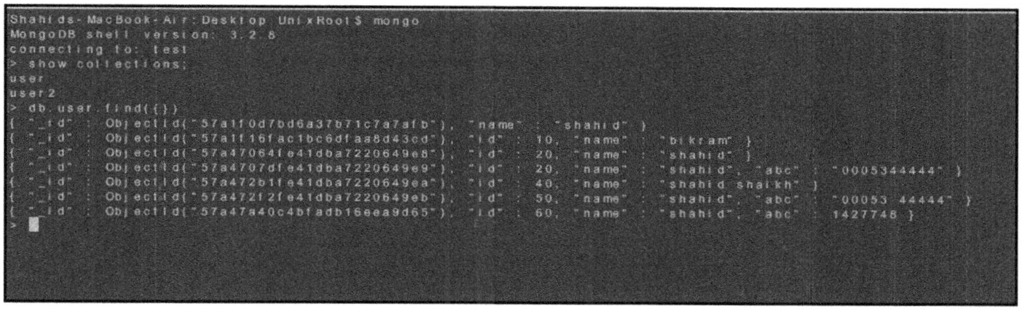

To export this collection, we need to run the export utility of MongoDB. Here is the syntax:

```
mongoexport --db <database name> --collection <collection name> --out <file path>
```

So to export our collection, I executed this command:

```
mongoexport --db test --collection user --out user.json
```

Since the collection contains fewer records, it exported them in nanoseconds. Refer to the following screenshot:

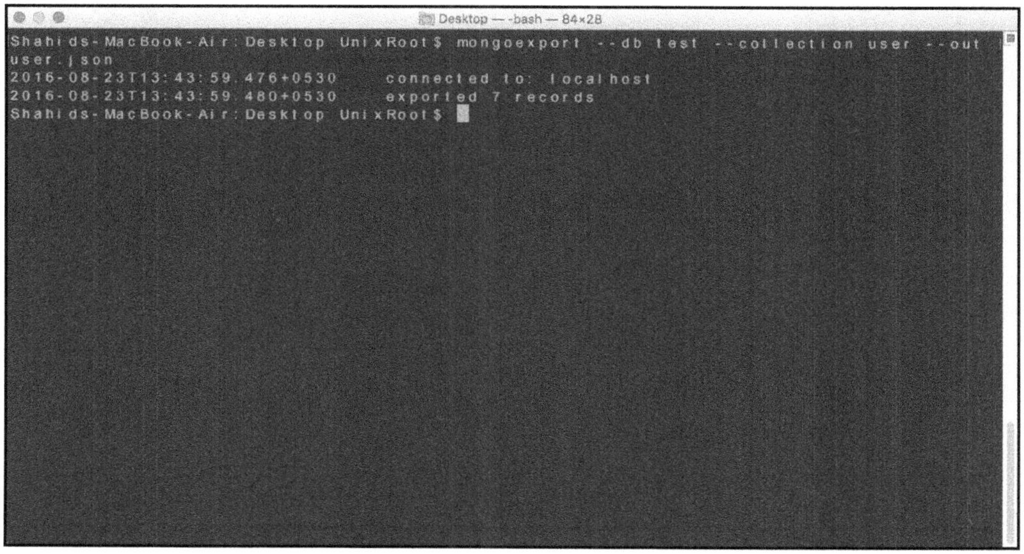

Alright, it's time to import this data into our RethinkDB database. Here is the command to do so:

```
rethinkdb import -f <file path> --table <db>.<table>
```

In the case of this migration, we need to specify which primary key RethinkDB should use. Here is the command that we executed to import our data from Mongo to RethinkDB:

```
rethinkdb import -f user.json --table test.users --pkey id
```

This will import the documents present in the `user.json` file to our users table in the test database. Refer to the following screenshot: 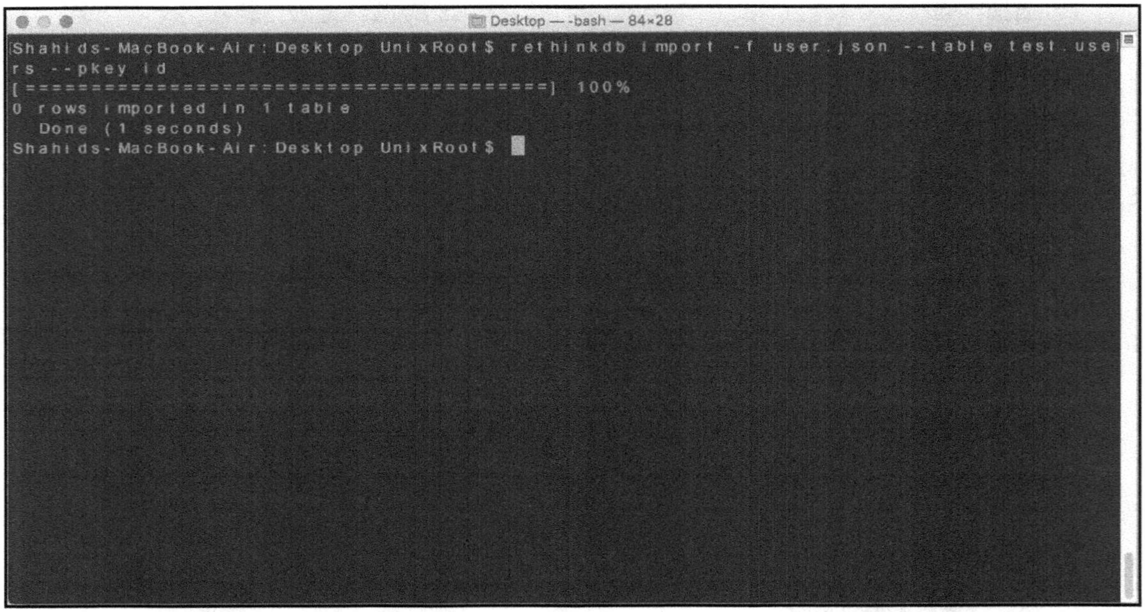

Let's validate whether our data has been successfully imported into our database by running the ReQL query to fetch all the documents from the table. Here is the query:

```
r.db("test").table("users")
```

And here is the result, as shown in the following screenshot:

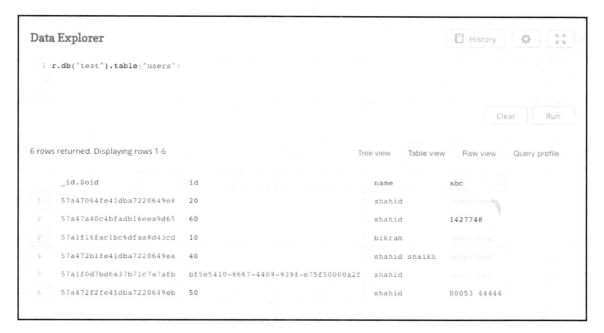

Congratulations! We have successfully migrated the collection from MongoDB to RethinkDB.

At the time of writing, there were no migration tools available to do this. Maybe one of you can take inspiration from this and write one for the community.

We have done SQL and NoSQL database migration to RethinkDB. Pretty much every NoSQL database comes with an export utility, so the steps to perform the migration are pretty much going to be the same.

RethinkDB is often updated, and some updates contain important fixes. In this scenario, you need to upgrade your RethinkDB instance and perform the migration of old data to the newer version of RethinkDB.

In the next section, we are going to learn how to perform the data migration from an older version of RethinkDB to a newer version.

Data migration to an updated version

In order to switch to a new version of RethinkDB, the data migration should happen in three steps:

1. Export all of your cluster data.
2. Upgrade RethinkDB.
3. Import all clusters into RethinkDB.

To perform the export operation, you can use the RethinkDB `dump` utility. Once a backup has been successfully created, you can download the latest version of RethinkDB and run the installer.

Once the installation is complete, use the RethinkDB `import` utility to bring all the data back from the cluster in the database.

Please make a note of this: the backup process stores the data and table metadata, but not the cluster configuration. Once the restore operation is over, you need to re-create your cluster.

During this operation you may need to perform some additional steps depending upon your RethinkDB version.

After the completion of the restore operation, you need to manually rebuild the secondary indexes. You can do this by using the following command:

```
rethinkdb index-rebuild
```

If your RethinkDB version is 1.6 or less, then you are trying to upgrade and migrate your data to newer version, you need to use the import script written by the RethinkDB team. This script has not been tested by the RethinkDB team for newer versions.

You can download the script from
`https://github.com/rethinkdb/rethinkdb/tree/02b4f29e1e7f15b3edffcb68bf015578ec5783ab/scripts/migration`, and to run this you need to install the Ruby runtime.

First, export all of the data using the command shown here:

```
import_export.rb --export --host HOST --port PORT
```

Then install RethinkDB and delete the `rethinkdb_data` folder. To import it into a newer version of RethinkDB, use the following command:

```
import_export.rb --import <DIR PATH> --host HOST --port PORT
```

That's it. RethinkDB will import all of the old data into the newer version.

Crash recovery in RethinkDB

If RethinkDB crashes, you, as an administrator, can perform troubleshooting by looking at the logs. RethinkDB, by default, writes logs in the most descriptive way possible.

The logs are classified into INFO, WARN, and ERROR. If there's a crash, you can look for the ERROR logs by doing a simple GREP operation. GREP is the Unix/Linux utility to perform the basic and advanced search in the system. It accepts a string, a regex, and so on as a parameter and searches for the query across the system or in a specified folder. In the following screenshot, we searched for the term in our log file:

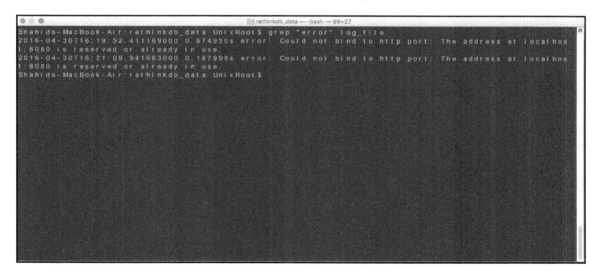

If the error relates to a cache size, say it's too low or out of size, the quick way to fix it is of course increasing the cache size. You can increase it by passing `--cache-size` followed by memory unit in MBs or putting it in a RethinkDB configuration file.

If the error is not trackable, you can directly ask the RethinkDB team by creating issues in GitHub at `https://github.com/rethinkdb/rethinkdb/issues` or asking a question on the official IRCInternet relay chat at `http://webchat.freenode.net/?channels=#rethinkdb`.

We have seen various administration operations so far in this chapter. Let's look at some third-party tools provided by the active members of the RethinkDB community to use and get more from RethinkDB.

Using third-party tools

The RethinkDB community contributes free tutorials, docs, books, and third-party tools. In this section, we are going to cover some of the best third-party tools that you can use with RethinkDB.

ReQLPro

ReQLPro is a clean, modern graphical software that helps you to browse your data in an easy and simple manner. ReQLPro is in beta. You can download it from `http://utils.codehangar.io/rethink#downloads`.

Once the download is complete, run the installer and enter your e-mail address to begin. You should see a similar screen to this:

Click on the + button and add the new RethinkDB connection. By default, RethinkDB runs on port 28015. Add the details in the form as shown here:

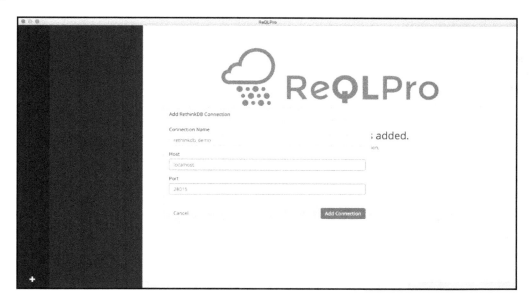

Once ReQLPro connects to RethinkDB, it will show you a successfully connected message like this:

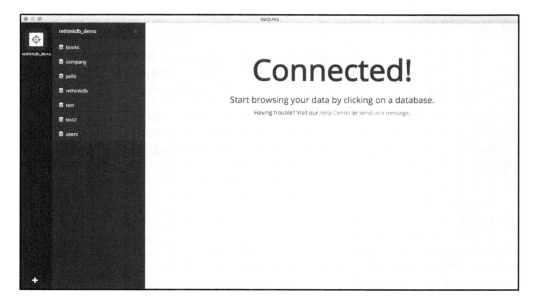

As you can see in preceding screenshot, all of the databases are listed on the side pane. You can click on them and it will expand and list down the tables that resides within that database. Refer to the following screenshot for reference:

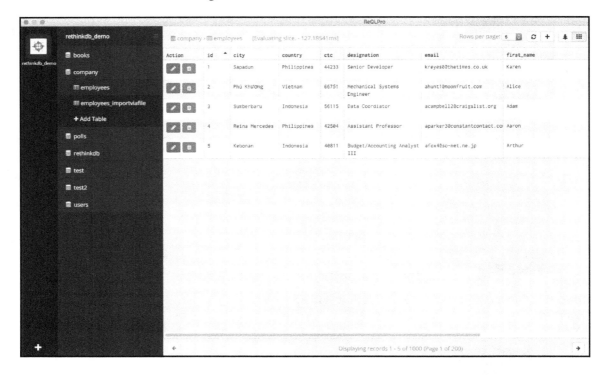

Apart from browsing the data, you can also add new databases, add new tables in databases, and modify the existing data. This tool is really good and I have personally used it to avoid running queries again and again to fetch the documents.

There is only one limitation of this software, which is that it is a desktop-based application that won't work when we have teams working together on a RethinkDB cluster. But there is another awesome implementation, which is a web-based RethinkDB data browser, just like phpmyadmin for MySQL.

Chateau

Chateau is web-based data browser for RethinkDB. It is available for free and requires Node.js to run. Before moving ahead, make sure you have Node.js installed and running.

Install Chateau as the global accessible package using **Node Package Manager** (**NPM**) as follows:

```
npm i --g chateau
```

Depending upon your network connection, it will take a moment to install all required dependencies.

After installation, if your RethinkDB running on default port and port 3000 is free to accept connection, then you can immediately start Chateau using the following command:

```
Chateau
```

It will start the server and listen on port 3000. Point your browser to <domain>: <3000> to view the Chateau screen. Refer to the following screenshot:

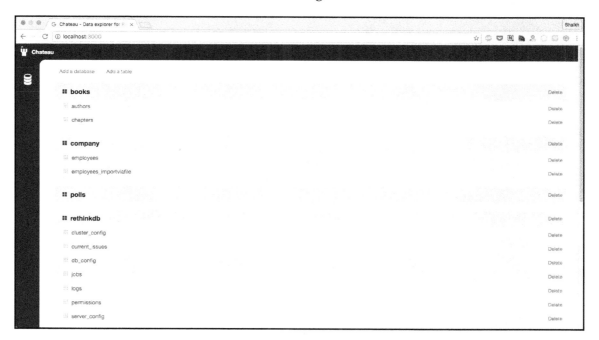

You can browse your data by clicking on any database and tables. Since this is a web platform, anyone from your team can access it during the development.

If you want to change the configuration of the port or RethinkDB instance, you can change the configuration file to achieve that.

In Mac- or Linux-based systems, global node modules get installed in the following location:

```
/usr/local/lib/node_modules/
```

You need to browse to that location and switch to the `chateau` directory. Inside, there is a file called `config.template.js`; open that file and make changes accordingly:

```
// RethinkDB settings
exports.host = 'localhost';      // RethinkDB host
exports.port = 28015;            // RethinkDB driver port
exports.authKey = '';            // Authentication key
// Express settings
exports.expressPort = 3000;      // Port used by express
exports.debug = true;            // Debug mode
exports.network = '127.0.0.1'    // Network the node app will run on
```

This software made a few assumptions, such as that RethinkDB should run with an admin user, and this software does not have an authentication mechanism, so putting it live on the Internet isn't recommended. However, running it on an intranet with your team will work like a charm!

Summary

We have covered administrating RethinkDB along with user management and access controls. We have also learned how RethinkDB performs failover handling automatically and how to manually perform failover handling. At the end, we covered some amazing third-party tools that can help us during development with RethinkDB.

In the next chapter, we are going to learn about RethinkDB deployment using PaaS services such as Amazon and compose.io. We will also learn about Docker and deploying RethinkDB with Docker.

6
RethinkDB Deployment

In previous chapters, we learnt about how RethinkDB works, how to perform complex queries, and how to manage the RethinkDB instance, along with troubleshooting RethinkDB and crash recovery. So we are now ready to deploy our RethinkDB cluster to the development environment.

In this chapter, we are going to learn various ways in which we can successfully deploy our RethinkDB instance.

In this chapter, we will learn about **Platform as a Service (PaaS)** applications such as Amazon which allow us to deploy RethinkDB in one click and pay as you go.

We will also look at a very important aspect of deployment which is quite popular nowadays: Docker. Docker is a container-based solution to perform deployment without worrying about the existing infrastructure of various servers.

At the end of the chapter, we will also learn about deploying RethinkDB to a standalone server.

We are going to cover the following topics:

- Deploying RethinkDB using PaaS services
- Deploying RethinkDB using Docker
- Deploying RethinkDB to a standalone server

Deploying RethinkDB using PaaS services

PaaS applications allow one-click installation of RethinkDB. There are mainly three PaaS services that are widely recognized and we are going to see all of them. They are as follows:

- Amazon Web Services
- Compose.io
- DigitalOcean

All three services are paid but you can get free access for a limited time. If you choose the Amazon EC2 server, then it's free for 750 hours. While Compose.io provides 30 days' free access, DigitalOcean allows free access only if there is an offer running or you were referred by someone.

Let's begin with **Amazon Web Services** (**AWS**).

Deploying RethinkDB on AWS

AWS is very powerful and popular cloud hosting service for enterprise. AWS provides very flexible pricing and a wide range of products ready to be installed. To begin with, you need to create an account at AWS and provide your billing information.

In this section, we will go through setting up the Amazon web instance for our RethinkDB. To begin with, first log in to your account and visit the Amazon marketplace. The Amazon marketplace is a store that contains free and premium products to buy and install in either an existing or a new Amazon instance.

Search for RethinkDB in the search box and you should be viewing a similar screen to the one shown here:

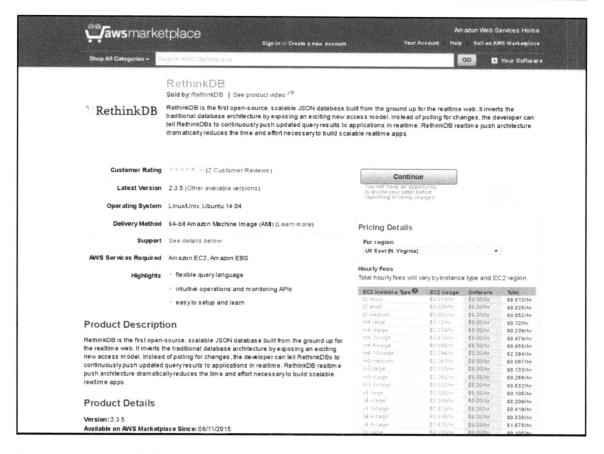

As you can see, RethinkDB provides free installation at AWS. You can choose the server as per your budget; the recommended one is **t2.small**. However, **t2.micro** will work if you just want to test it out.

Click on **Continue** and it will lead you to the review page, as shown below in the screenshot. Make sure you have chosen the correct **Instance Type**:

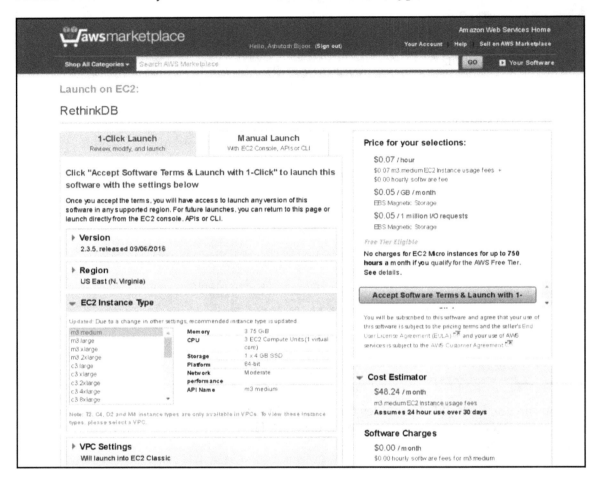

As you can see in the preceding screenshot, I have selected **m3.medium** as the instance type because I need it for other purposes (some office work) too. You can choose the Region, database version, and so on as, given in the screenshot.

The recommended instance for RethinkDB in AWS is **t2.micro** for simple testing. However, it is totally dependent upon your needs and requirements.

Once you are done reviewing, click on the **Accept Software Terms & Launch** button, which will lead you to the following screen that will confirm the creation of an Amazon instance:

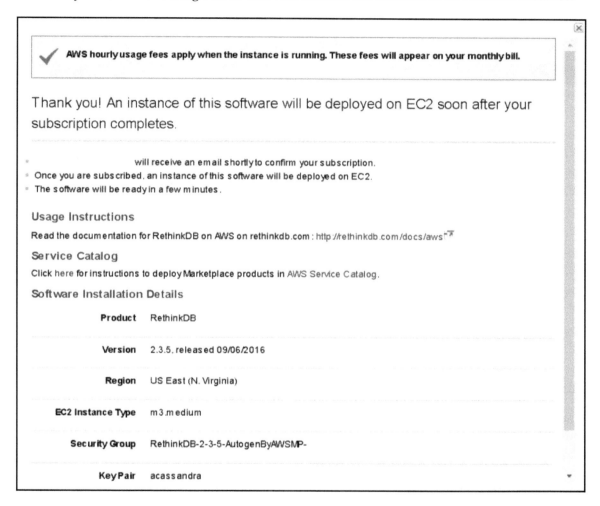

Amazon will send you an e-mail about the subscription and its charges. Close the screen and Amazon will prepare the instance; you can see the progress in the Amazon marketplace itself, as shown in the following screenshot:

Once you see it in **running** stage, click on the **Manage in AWS Console** link and it will redirect you to the AWS console. On the console, you can see various details, such as **Public IP**, **Public DNS**, **Name**, **Instance ID**, and so on, as shown in the following screenshot:

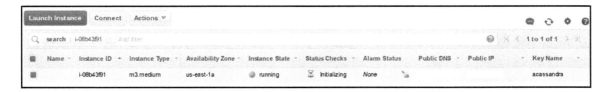

Now, we need to set up our RethinkDB instance, copy public DNS or IP from the instance screen, and hit that using the browser, and it will lead to you the setup screen of RethinkDB, as shown here:

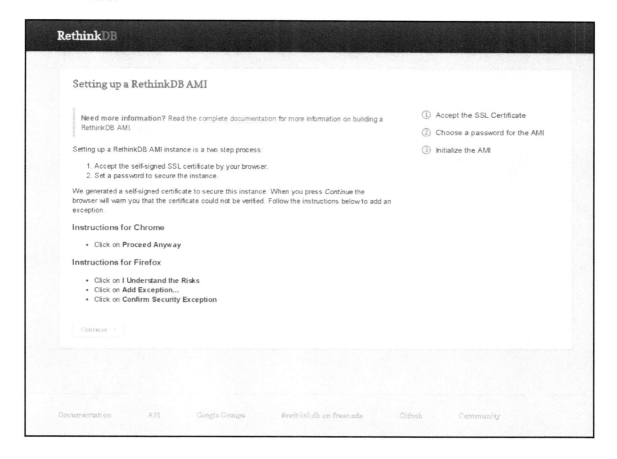

Amazon uses self-signed SSL certificates; since the browser takes that as a security breach, you need to manually approve the SSL request. The following description is given in the preceding screenshot, click on **Continue** and it will lead you to the password setup screen as shown here:

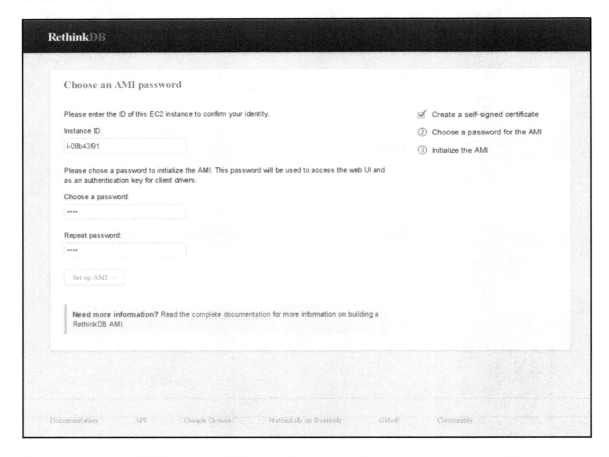

Copy the **Instance ID** from the AWS console screen and use a strong password to set up RethinkDB. Click on **Set up AMI** once you have filled in the password and **Instance ID**.

Amazon will set up RethinkDB on your AWS instance; you can check the progress as shown in the following screenshot:

Once the setup is done, you can visit your IP or DNS and provide your credentials (username is admin) and you can login to the web console of RethinkDB.

Now, in order to perform the existing data import in a fresh RethinkDB instance on AWS, you need to perform the shell login. Go to the management console of AWS and click on the **Connect Instance** button. A popup window similar to the following screenshot will display various ways to connect to your instance and perform admin operations:

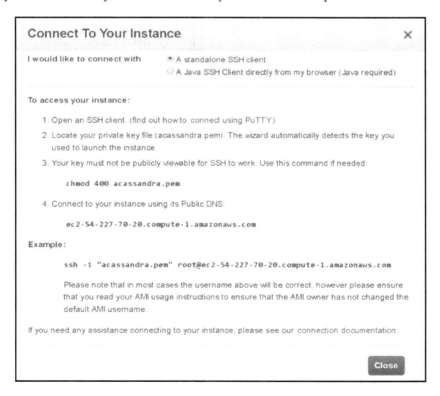

Once you log in, you can use the import/export feature of RethinkDB to put your data in the fresh RethinkDB instance.

This sums up the deployment on AWS; let's see how to deploy RethinkDB on Compose.io.

Deploying RethinkDB on Compose.io

Compose.io is an IBM-owned database deployment company. It provides one-click deployment for production-ready databases. With Compose, you get the great pricing which is more or less equivalent to Amazon AWS but also you get a secured, scalable database server.

Compose provides production-ready deployment for databases such as Redis, Mongo, ElasticSearch, and of course RethinkDB. In this section, we are going to learn how to deploy RethinkDB on Compose.

First thing, you need to sign up for a Compose account. They provide a 30-day free trial but they take payment details first, so keep your credit card ready with you.

Visit `https://app.compose.io/signup/svelte/` to sign up for a new account.

As shown in the following screenshot, fill in your details and from the right-hand pane, choose **RethinkDB**:

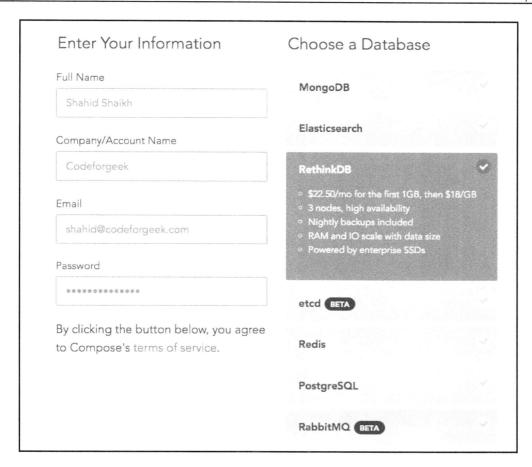

In the next step, add your payment details and you should be good to go.

It will take a few moments to create your account; Compose will send you a verification e-mail.

Once it completes the signup, it will take you to the Dashboard and you should be viewing a similar screen to the one shown here:

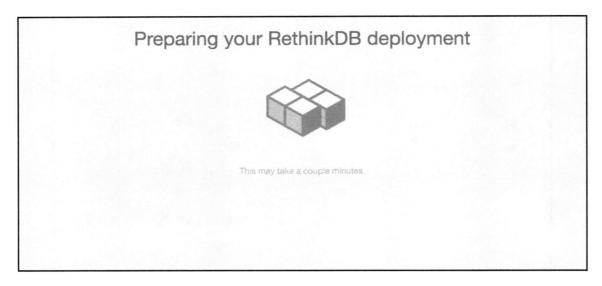

It will take a few minutes to set up and configure RethinkDB in the Compose server.

Once **Compose** sets up RethinkDB, you should be viewing a similar screen to this:

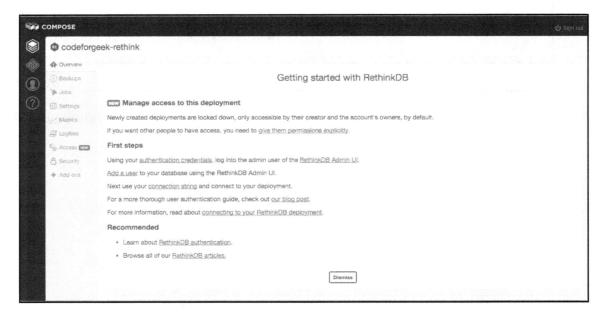

As you can see in the preceding screenshot, Compose provides you with everything you need: a protected web admin console, a connection string for your middle layer, and instructions to get you out of trouble.

In the **Overview** tab, scroll down to see the web admin console link. Click on that and it will ask for the username and password. The username is admin and you can get the password on the same screen.

Here is my web admin console after a successful login:

Congratulations! You have just deployed your working RethinkDB instance on Compose.

Compose uses self-signed encryption to protect data transmission across the network. However, you can change the certificate if you wish. To do so, go to the SSL Certificate tab, as shown in the following screenshot:

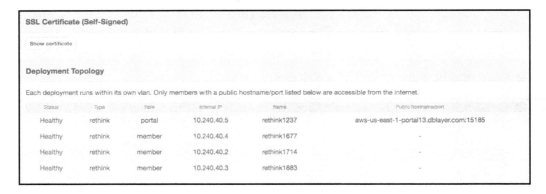

In case you want to deploy your existing cluster to Compose, you need to have SSH access to perform the import operation. By default, Compose disables SSH access; you can enable it from the **Security** tab, as shown here:

Activate the SSH and it will provide you with further details. You can also add a specific IP address from where you want to access the Server, just to add extra security.

Compose provides log details as well; it gets updated every week and will provide you with quick access to the log.

You can also add new team members in Compose and let them be part of the deployment. You can do this by visiting the **Access** tab, as shown in the following screenshot:

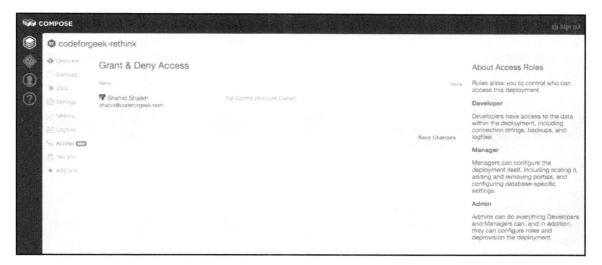

Compose does have other options, such as **Backup**, **Jobs**, and so on, which is quite useful. You, as deployment manager, can at any time scale your **Compose** account according to your needs. For instance, if traffic increases to your database and you need to increase the memory size, all you need to do is to go to the **Scaling** section and change the size of the memory, as shown in the following screenshot:

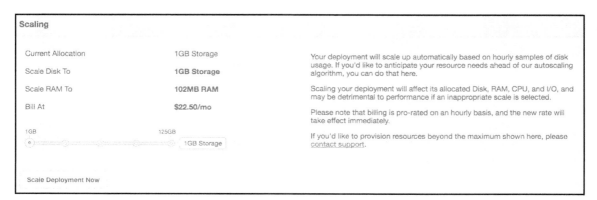

This sums up Compose. Let's move on to learning about deploying RethinkDB on the DigitalOcean Server.

Deploying RethinkDB on DigitalOcean

DigitalOcean has been a key player in cloud hosting for affordable prices. It says *it's built for developers*, and after using it for a year, I can justify same. It includes a range of products ready to install in one click (including RethinkDB), plus the price range starts from $5 a month, which is really cheap if you consider other PaaS providers.

You can expand the size of the Droplet in terms of memory or disk size in future, according to your needs. DigitalOcean also has variable pricing options, where it will charge you based on resources used.

To begin with, visit DigitalOcean's official site at `https://digitalocean.com` and create your account; it will not ask for payment details now because you haven't created your Droplet yet. **Droplet** is the term DigitalOcean coined for **Virtual Private Server** (**VPS**) instances.

Once you have created an account, log in to DigitalOcean and you should be viewing a similar screen to this:

This screen will list the droplets you have created. Now let's create one fresh droplet for our deployment. Click on the **Create Droplet** button and it will take you to the Droplet creation screen.

Here, instead of selecting the distribution, click on the **One-click apps** tab and choose the **Horizion w/ RethinkDB on 14.04** option, as shown in the following screenshot:

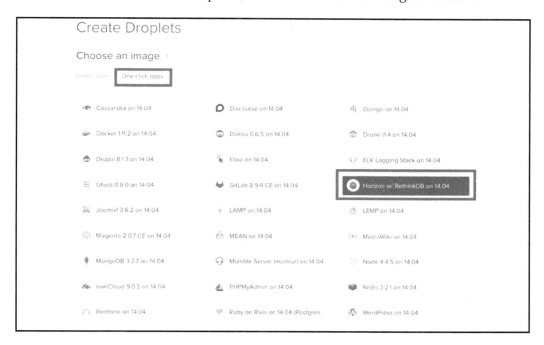

Scroll down and select the pricing model; a $10 Droplet will suffice for deployment. It will give us 1 GB RAM and 30 GB SSD drive; refer to the screenshot for the same:

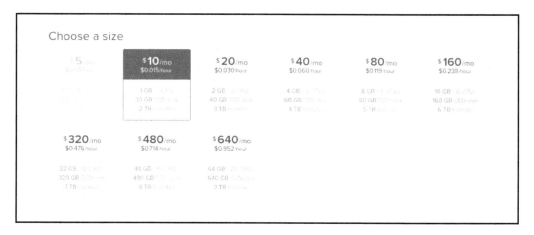

Next choose the data center; choose the location which is your targeted audience to trim down the network round-trip times. I am choosing **Bangalore.** Please check the following screenshot:

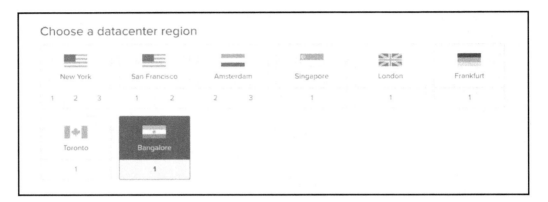

You can choose additional services according to your requirements; for a testing deployment server, I am not selecting any additional services but for production I would certainly like to have **Backups** for sure:

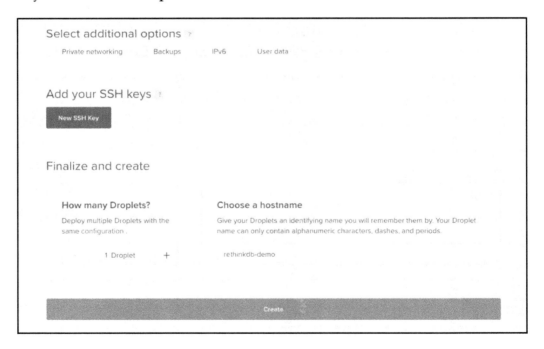

Name your droplet and click on the **Create** button.

It will take a few moments to set up your **Droplets**; you can see the progress from the **Dashboard** page:

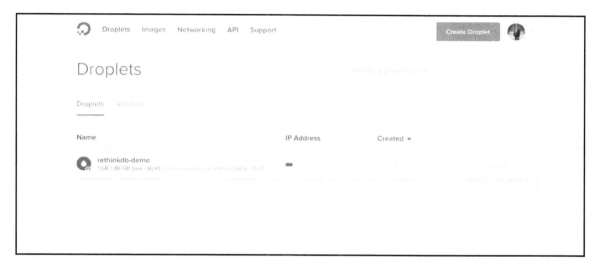

Once the droplet is created, you will get an email from DigitalOcean with the access details, as shown in the following screenshot:

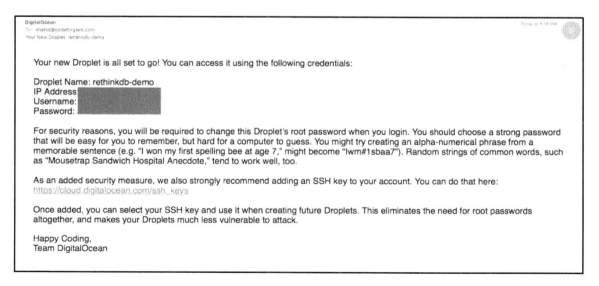

Now perform the SSH to your server using the following command:

```
ssh username@droplet-ip
```

Use the password sent in the email to log in when the terminal prompts for a password; immediately after the first login to the Droplet, DigitalOcean will ask you to change your password. Use a secure password and once you have done that, it will let you log in to the Droplet.

Refer to the following screenshot:

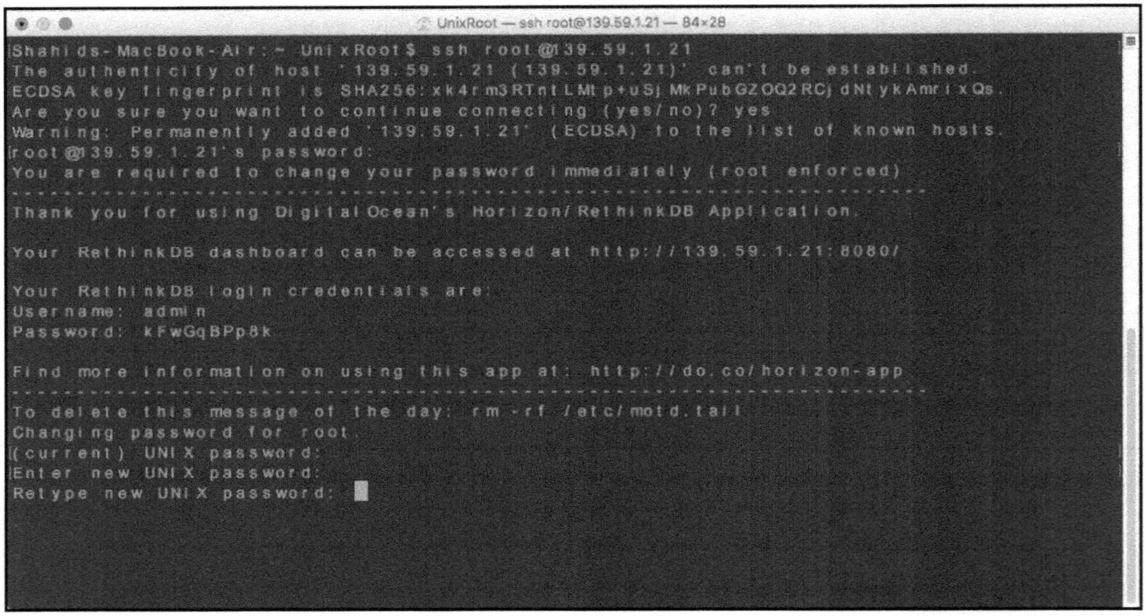

As you can see inpreceding screenshot, it also shows you the RethinkDB web console link, username, and password; copy the link and hit the URL from the browser.

Enter your username and password; once validated, you should be able to view the web console screen as shown here:

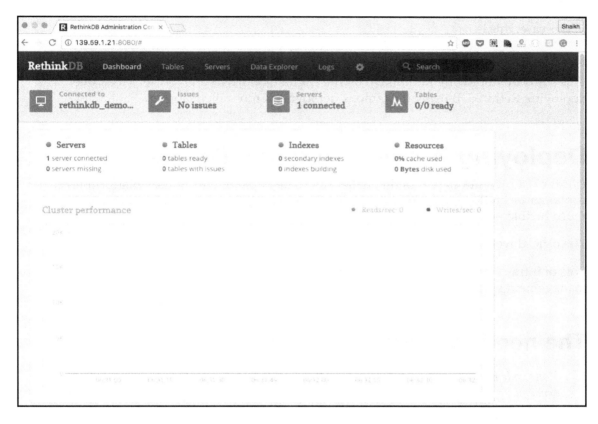

Congratulations! You have successfully deployed RethinkDB on DigitalOcean.

Now, in order to put your cluster online, you need to perform the import/export operation we discussed in `Chapter 5`, *Administration and Troubleshooting Tasks in RethinkDB*.

 In case you are having trouble putting the Rethinkdb imported file to the Server, you can do this by `FTP` or using the `SCP` command. I would recommend the `SCP` command as it will not require any extra installation of FTP software.

The syntax is as follows:

```
scp your_username@remotehost.edu:foobar.txt /some/local/directory
```

In our case, this is:

```
scp root@droplet-ip: import.zip /home/
```

This sums up deploying RethinkDB on the DigitalOcean Server. Now let's look over deploying RethinkDB using the famous deployment tool called Docker.

Deploying RethinkDB using Docker

Docker is a revolutionary tool that helps automate deployments. It uses platform-level container technology to make it easy to compose isolated software components in a reproducible way.

The official website of Docker is as follows: https://www.docker.com/

Lots of infrastructure-related tools, ranging from self-hosted PaaS applications to cluster management systems, are built around the Docker ecosystem.

The need for Docker

> *Your code is not working in Production? But it's working on the QA (quality analysis server)!*

I am sure you have heard statements like these in your team during the deployment phase. Well no more of that, Docker everything and forget about the infrastructure of different environments, say, QA, Staging and Production, because your code is going to run Docker container not in those machines, hence write once, run everywhere.

In this section, we will learn how to use Docker to deploy a RethinkDB Server or PaaS services. I am going to cover a few docker basics too; if you are already aware of them, please skip to the next section.

Installing Docker

Docker is available for all major platforms, such as, Linux-based distributions, Mac, and Windows. Visit the official website at `https://www.docker.com/` and download the package suitable for your platform.

We are installing Docker in our machine to create a new Docker image. Docker images are independent of platform and should not be confused with Docker for Mac or Docker for Windows. It's referred to as a Docker client too.

Once you have installed the Docker, you need to start the Daemon process first; I am using a Mac so I can view this in the launchpad, as shown here:

Upon clicking that, it will open up a nice console showing the Docker official logo and an indication that Docker is successfully booted, as shown in the following screenshot:

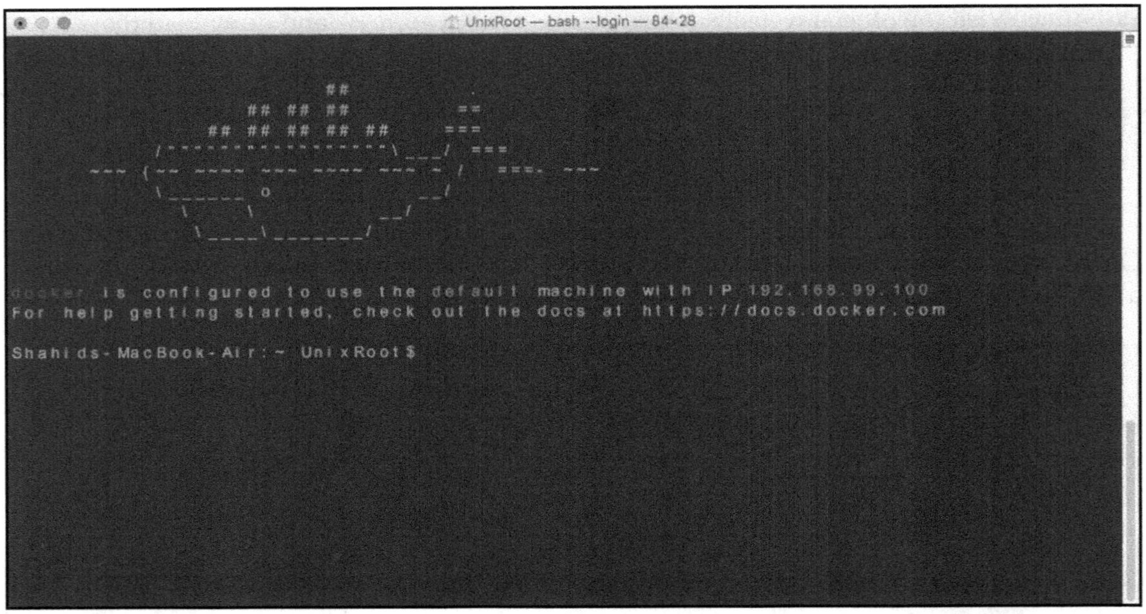

Now we can begin creating our Docker image that in turn will run RethinkDB.

Creating a Docker image

For installing our RethinkDB on Ubuntu inside the Docker, we need to install the Ubuntu operating system. Run the following command to install a Ubuntu image from the official Docker hub repository:

```
docker pull ubuntu
```

This will download and install the Ubuntu image in our system. We will later use this Ubuntu image and install our RethinkDB instance; you can choose different operating systems as well.

Before going to the Docker configuration code, I would like to point out the steps we require to install RethinkDB on a fresh Ubuntu installation:

- Update the system
- Add the RethinkDB repository to the known repository list
- Install RethinkDB
- Set the data folder
- Expose the port

We are going to do this using Docker. To create a Docker image, we require `Dockerfile`.

Create a file called `Dockerfile` with no extension and apply the code shown here:

```
FROM ubuntu:latest
# Install RethinkDB.
RUN \
  apt-get update && \
  echo "deb http://download.rethinkdb.com/apt `lsb_release -cs` main" >
/etc/apt/sources.list.d/rethinkdb.list && \
  apt-get install -y wget && \
  wget -O- http://download.rethinkdb.com/apt/pubkey.gpg | apt-key add - &&
\
  apt-get update && \
  apt-get install -y rethinkdb python-pip && \
  rm -rf /var/lib/apt/lists/*
# Install python driver for rethinkdb
RUN pip install rethinkdb
# Define mountable directories.
VOLUME ["/data"]
# Define working directory.
WORKDIR /data
# Define default command.
CMD ["rethinkdb", "--bind", "all"]
# Expose ports.
#   - 8080: web UI
#   - 28015: process
#   - 29015: cluster
EXPOSE 8080
EXPOSE 28015
EXPOSE 29015
```

The first line is our entry point to the Ubuntu operating system, then we are performing an update of the system and using the installation commands recommended by RethinkDB here: https://www.rethinkdb.com/docs/install/ubuntu/.

Once the installation is complete, we install the rethinkdb python driver to perform the import/export operation.

The next two commands mount a new volume in Ubuntu and telling RethinkDB to use that volume.

The next command runs rethinkdb by binding all the ports and exposing the ports to be used by the client driver and web console.

In order to make this a docker image, save the file and run the following command within the project directory:

```
docker build -t docker-rethinkdb.
```

Here, we are building our docker image and giving it a name docker-rethinkdb; upon running this command, Docker will execute the Dockerfile and you're on.

The representation of the previous steps is shown here:

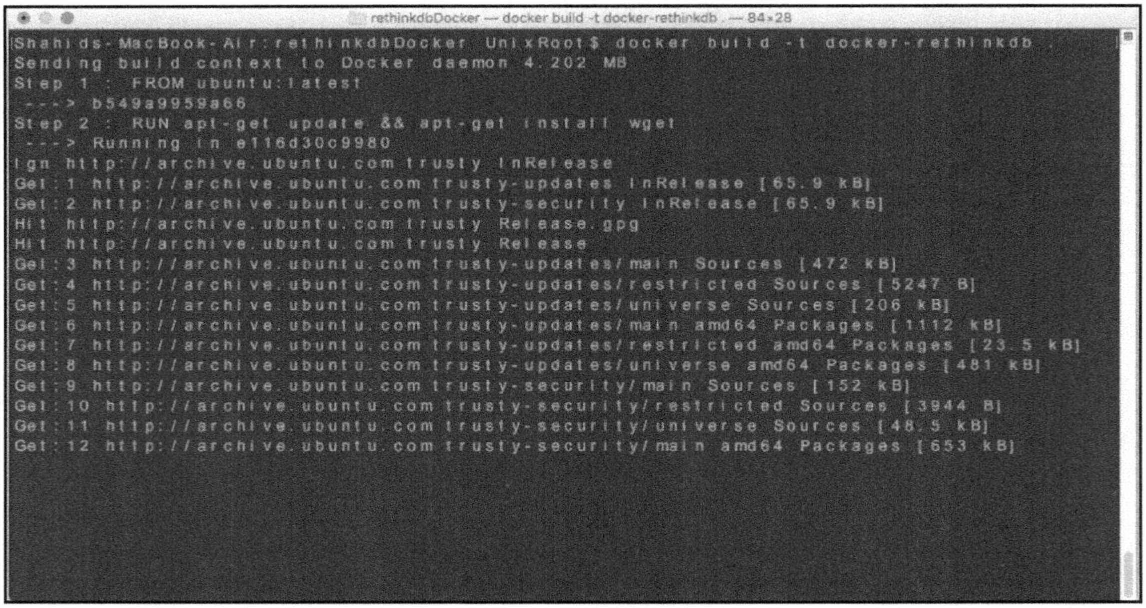

Once everything works, and I am sure it will, you will see a success message in the console, as shown here:

```
---> 63b3d1dd1a36
Removing intermediate container 90a47ac672c2
Step 4 : VOLUME /data
 ---> Running in ce8c48366f4b
 ---> 984a7c10db7d
Removing intermediate container ce8c48366f4b
Step 5 : WORKDIR /data
 ---> Running in 9e229381f14c
 ---> 5d9a8ae62e50
Removing intermediate container 9e229381f14c
Step 6 : CMD rethinkdb --bind all
 ---> Running in f81a7f0910ff
 ---> 49b4e272b0c3
Removing intermediate container f81a7f0910ff
Step 7 : EXPOSE 8080
 ---> Running in e005ace9b807
 ---> 7ed460292ebf
Removing intermediate container e005ace9b807
Step 8 : EXPOSE 28015
 ---> Running in d9ded08e64da
 ---> 40dfa7016f18
Removing intermediate container d9ded08e64da
Step 9 : EXPOSE 29015
 ---> Running in 6a01c8bafde1
 ---> f1a13e1b3b8f
Removing intermediate container 6a01c8bafde1
Successfully built f1a13e1b3b8f
Shahids-MacBook-Air:rethinkdbDocker UnixRoot $
```

Congratulations! You have successfully created a docker image for RethinkDB. If you want to see your image and its properties, run the following command:

```
docker images
```

And this will list all the images of Docker, as shown in the following screenshot:

```
Shahids-MacBook-Air:rethinkdbDocker UnixRoot $ docker images
REPOSITORY                    TAG            IMAGE ID         CREATED            SIZE
docker-rethinkdb              latest         f1a13e1b3b8f     30 seconds ago     396.6 MB
rethinkdb                     latest         e30940c8232c     9 days ago         183.9 MB
google-captcha                latest         1bb51d6f9158     6 weeks ago        507.2 MB
<none>                        <none>         ee66c61db93b     6 weeks ago        507.2 MB
shahid/ubuntu-node-hello      latest         506e6a57925b     5 months ago       507.2 MB
<none>                        <none>         8c5896accd32     5 months ago       360.2 MB
<none>                        <none>         bad9c147f800     5 months ago       507.2 MB
ubuntu                        latest         b549a9959a66     5 months ago       188 MB
node                          latest         1de2e178998e     5 months ago       644.2 MB
centos                        centos6        fc73b108c5ae     5 months ago       228.9 MB
Shahids-MacBook-Air:rethinkdbDocker UnixRoot $
```

Awesome! Now let's run it.

To access the web portal, we need to run our docker image and bind port 8080 of the docker image to some port of our machine; here is the command to do so:

```
docker run -p 3000:8080 -d docker-rethinkdb
```

As per the command above, -p is used to specify port binding, the first is the target and second port is source, that is, Docker port and -d is used to run it in the background or daemon.

This will run the docker image in the background; to extract more information about this process, we need to run the following command:

```
docker ps
```

This will list all the running images called as a container, along with the information, as shown in the following screenshot:

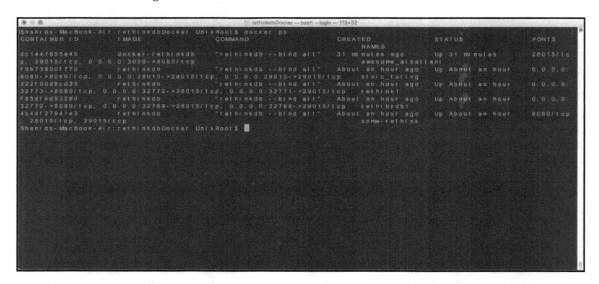

You can also check the logs of specific containers using the following command:

```
docker logs <container id>
```

Now, in order to access the RethinkDB web console from our machine, we need to find out the IP address on which the Docker machine is running. To get that, we need to run the following command:

```
docker-machine ip default
```

This will print out the IP. Copy the IP and hit IP:3000 from the browser to view the RethinkDB web console, as shown here:

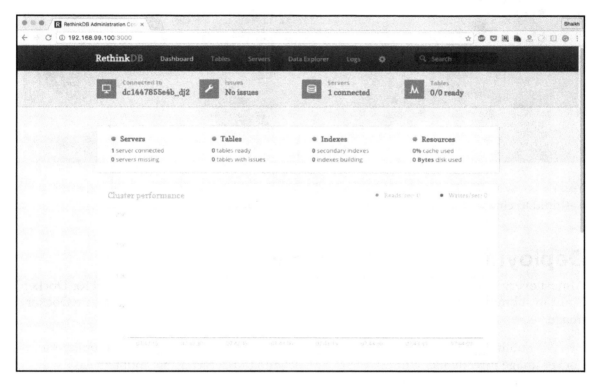

So we have docker running and accessible from the browser. In order to import and export the data, we need to log in to our Docker image. To do that, run the following command:

```
docker exec -i -t <container-id>  /bin/bash
```

This will log in to the docker image running Ubuntu; refer to the following screenshot:

You can now run the `rethinkdb` command to perform the data import to the existing RethinkDB cluster.

Deploying the Docker image

Almost every PaaS service we have covered in earlier sections provides support for Docker. You can submit your Dockerfile to `git` and clone it anywhere if you want to create Docker image.

You can submit the whole docker image (not `Dockerfile`) to **Dockerhub** and pull your docker image directly using the `docker pull` command, which is no doubt an easy way because you will be directly working on the image running on the server.

Till now, we have learned about RethinkDB deployment on PaaS services such as Amazon, DigitalOcean, and Compose.io, as well as using Docker. In the next section, we are going to learn about deploying RethinkDB on a standalone server.

Deploying RethinkDB on a standalone server

If you want to deploy RethinkDB other than on PaaS services then you need to perform a custom installation, which is going to be different per operating system.

To give an example, let's consider the server is running Ubuntu 15.04 and we want to install RethinkDB on it.

To do that, we need to execute the following commands:

1. First, update Ubuntu:

   ```
   sudo apt-get update
   ```

2. Install the RethinkDB repository in the repository list of Ubuntu using the following command:

   ```
   echo "deb http://download.rethinkdb.com/apt `lsb_release -cs`
   main" >/etc/apt/sources.list.d/rethinkdb.list
   ```

3. Install WGET to download the executable files of RethinkDB using the following command:

   ```
   sudo apt-get install --y wget
   ```

4. Download the RethinkDB repository to the system using the following command:

   ```
   wget -O- http://download.rethinkdb.com/apt/pubkey.gpg | apt-key
   add -
   ```

5. Update the repository to effect the changes:

   ```
   sudo apt-get update
   ```

6. Install RethinkDB using the following command:

   ```
   apt-get install -y rethinkdb
   ```

It will take some time to install RethinkDB on your system and, once completed, you can run RethinkDB using the command line.

These steps are going to be similar for any other flavor of Linux distribution, with little change in the commands.

Summary

In this chapter, we have covered RethinkDB deployment. We started with PaaS services and covered each PaaS service, such as Amazon, DigitalOcean, and Compose.io in detail. Then we moved on to RethinkDB using Docker and learned how to create our own RethinkDB image. We also covered how to deploy RethinkDB in a custom standalone server.

In the next chapter, we are going to learn about extending RethinkDB with other popular services such as Elasticsearch, RabbitMQ, and so on. So stay tuned!

7
Extending RethinkDB

In the last chapter, we learned various ways to deploy RethinkDB. We studied PaaS applications, Docker, and custom installation and deployment of RethinkDB.

So far, we have studied solely RethinkDB and its various features. It's time to take one step forward and extend RethinkDB to meet the real-world challenges of databases.

In this chapter, we are going to learn how to extend RethinkDB to perform facet searches using very a famous database, **ElasticSearch**, and how to extend the RethinkDB changefeed feature with a message queue such as **RabbitMQ** to have a full-fledged automated change notifier.

In this chapter, we will cover the following topics:

- Integrating RethinkDB with ElasticSearch
- Integrating RethinkDB with RabbitMQ
- Understanding the RethinkDB protocol
- Third-party libraries and tools

We will also learn about the basics of ElasticSearch and the essentials you need to know before moving ahead with integration. This chapter is all about integrating RethinkDB with other amazing tools to architect an advanced, highly capable system.

So without any further ado, let's begin!

Integrating RethinkDB with ElasticSearch

To perform real-time full text search, it is recommended to use ElasticSearch-a database made for searches. ElasticSearch is a very advanced search database based on Apache Lucene, which allows you to perform full text searches efficiently.

Before we go ahead with integration, let's look over some basics of ElasticSearch.

Introducing ElasticSearch

ElasticSearch is real-time, distributed, document-oriented, and full-text-based search database. It provides you with immediate search availability with very easy-to-use RESTful APIs.

ElasticSearch is based upon Apache Lucene but with more advanced features, such as geo-location, did-you-mean search suggestion, autocomplete, and much more. It also provides schemaless architecture so that you can start very quickly; just dump your existing data in ElasticSearch as documents and it will make it searchable in no time, just like that!

In order to begin with ElasticSearch, let me explain you some terms and what they mean. ElasticSearch indeed uses a database layer but the terminology is different. In ElasticSearch, a database is called an index and a table is called a type:

```
ElasticSearch Index ==> database
ElasticSearch table ==> type
```

Keep this mind because most of the time, people tend to mix them up.

As I have mentioned earlier, ElasticSearch provides easy-to-use RESTful APIs for developers to easily integrate it with almost any programming language. We will look over that in upcoming section.

Let's learn about installing ElasticSearch.

Installing ElasticSearch

The ElasticSearch team has worked really hard to make things as easy as possible. So is the installation; all you have to do here is go to the downloads page of ElasticSearch (https://www.elastic.co/downloads/elasticsearch) and download the latest version.

At the time of writing this book, the latest and stable version of ElasticSearch is 2.4.1.

Alternatively, you can also download a docker image of elasticsearch (`https://hub.docker.com/_/elasticsearch/`) and run it using docker.

Extract the downloaded file and go to the `bin` folder. This folder contains various files related to ElasticSearch for different operating systems, as you can see in the following screenshot:

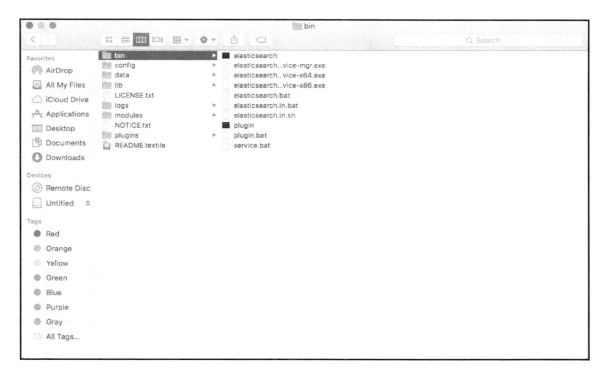

ElasticSearch contains various executable files which you can use, depending upon your operating system. For Windows, use the executable (`.exe`) file and for Mac and Linux based systems, use the `elasticsearch` file.

Since I am using Mac, I need to run the `elasticsearch` file to start ElasticSearch.

 Make sure you have the latest Java runtime installed on your system. Preferred is Java 7 or 8. You can run the `java -v` command to check the version. If it's lower than Java 7, then visit the Java download page at http://www.oracle.com/technetwork/java/javase/downloads/index.ht ml and update.

Start ElasticSearch using the following command in the `bin` folder:

```
./elasticsearch
```

This will boot up ElasticSearch, and to check whether it has started successfully or not, just send a `GET HTTP` request to `localhost:9200` or point your browser to the same URL. In this screenshot, I am making a CURL request to `localhost:9200`:

```
Shahids-MacBook-Air:~ UnixRoot$ curl localhost:9200
{
  "name" : "Kyle Gibney",
  "cluster_name" : "elasticsearch",
  "version" : {
    "number" : "2.3.5",
    "build_hash" : "90f439ff60a3c0f497f91663701e64ccd01edbb4",
    "build_timestamp" : "2016-07-27T10:36:52Z",
    "build_snapshot" : false,
    "lucene_version" : "5.5.0"
  },
  "tagline" : "You Know, for Search"
}
Shahids-MacBook-Air:~ UnixRoot$
```

As you can, it returns a nice document in response saying: `You know, for Search`. This is an indication of a successful startup of ElasticSearch.

Let's look over some RESTful actions that can come handy while performing integration with RethinkDB.

Performing operations in ElasticSearch

As I have mentioned in an earlier section, ElasticSearch provides RESTful APIs to perform indexing and searching operations. In this section, we will use a few of them to get started with ElasticSearch. Mainly, we will create new documents in index and perform a search over it. So let's get started.

To create a new document in the type resides in Index, ElasticSearch provides the following API:

```
POST ==> /{index-name}/{type-name}
With
JSON {} data.
```

So, for example purposes, let's assume that the index name is `twitter`, the type name is `tweets`, and ElasticSearch is running on a local machine, on the default port. This is how the request will look:

```
POST ==> http://localhost:9002/twitter/tweets
{
    "tweet" : "Hello World!",
    "user": "John",
    "userId": 1024
}
```

This will create a new document inside the `tweets` type residing in the `twitter` API.

 If an index does not exist, ElasticSearch will create it automatically instead of throwing an error. The same is true for type. This is because ElasticSearch promotes schemaless architecture. But you can manually create an index and a type using the `createIndex` and `Mapping` API.

One of the ways to test ElasticSearch is by using an API simulator, and POSTMAN is one of the best. As you can see in the next screenshot, I am sending a POST request to the URL I mentioned previously:

Let's do a search.

Suppose we would like to get all the tweets regardless of who tweeted them. We can do this by hitting the same API that we used to create an Index with the POST HTTP request but with different post data:

```
POST ==> http://localhost:9200/twitter/tweets/_search
{
    "query" : {
        "match_all" : {}
    }
}
```

This should return the following response:

```
{
  "took": 75,
```

```
"timed_out": false,
"_shards": {
  "total": 5,
  "successful": 5,
  "failed": 0
},
"hits": {
  "total": 2,
  "max_score": 1,
  "hits": [
    {
      "_index": "twitter",
      "_type": "tweets",
      "_id": "AVdl9CYpQvF9124G826H",
      "_score": 1,
      "_source": {
        "tweet": "Hello World!",
        "user": "John",
        "userId": 1024
      }
    },
    {
      "_index": "twitter",
      "_type": "tweets",
      "_id": "AVdmAO8mQvF9124G826N",
      "_score": 1,
      "_source": {
        "tweet": "ElasticSearch is great",
        "user": "Mary",
        "userId": 1025
      }
    }
  ]
}
}
```

Let's run more queries where we would like to search for tweets having ElasticSearch in them:

```
POST ==> http://localhost:9200/twitter/tweets/_search

{
    "query" : {
        "match" : {
            "tweet": "elasticsearch"
        }
    }
}
```

In the POST data, we are sending the query to return all the results that contain the word `elasticsearch` in them. Here is the response:

```
{
  "took": 141,
  "timed_out": false,
  "_shards": {
    "total": 5,
    "successful": 5,
    "failed": 0
  },
  "hits": {
    "total": 1,
    "max_score": 0.15342641,
    "hits": [
      {
        "_index": "twitter",
        "_type": "tweets",
        "_id": "AVdmAO8mQvF9124G826N",
        "_score": 0.15342641,
        "_source": {
          "tweet": "ElasticSearch is great",
          "user": "Mary",
          "userId": 1025
        }
      }
    ]
  }
}
```

You can learn more about searching with ElasticSearch at the ElasticSearch official docs (`https://www.elastic.co/guide/en/elasticsearch/reference/current/search-search.html`). Now let's look over the real problem of integrating RethinkDB with ElasticSearch.

The problem statement

So far we know the basics of ElasticSearch and how to index and search a document. The real problem is how to integrate RethinkDB with ElasticSearch. There are two proposed solutions:

- **Solution #1**: Write a program to perform polyglot persistence across RethinkDB and ElasticSearch
- **Solution #2**: Hook the RethinkDB changefeed to ElasticSearch to perform the synchronization automatically on the go

In both the solutions, we need to use the changefeed to find out any changes in the table so that we can do the syncing in ElasticSearch. However, if we can find something which is already built and can be used with some configuration then that will be prevent lot of development and testing time of custom program.

Luckily, RethinkDB team has been working on such ElasticSearch plugin which can be used along with `Logstash` – Another product by ElasticSearch team to generate events and log to perform the synchronization.

Hence, we will be solving our problem using the solution #2.

This is how its, going to work:

- RethinkDB pushes changes to logstash using the logstash plugin
- Logstash will take the changes and sync them with ElasticSearch

`Logstash` will be acting as a glue between RethinkDB and ElasticSearch. To begin with, we need to first download the logstash software.

It is available for free and it's platform independent. Visit the download page of `Logstash` (`https://www.elastic.co/downloads/logstash`) and download the appropriate file format.

Once the download is complete, you can run `logstash` by executing the `logstash` file from the `bin` folder.

Now let's perform the synchronization; first things first, let's download the plugin written by the RethinkDB team for `logstash`.

Go to the bin folder in the download copy of logstash and execute the following command:

```
./plugin install logstash-input-rethinkdb
```

It will download and install the plugin, which we will need later. After completion of the plugin installation, it will show a success message in the console as shown in this screenshot:

We have everything in place; let's understand the basic commands of `logstash` before performing the actual thing for better understanding:

```
logstash input {--source such as RethinkDB-- } output { --destination such
as ElasticSearch-- }
```

By default, `logstash` already contains the plugin for ElasticSearch and we have installed the plugin for RethinkDB.

Let's perform the synchronization.

Start RethinkDB and ElasticSearch in a different terminal and then run the following command in the terminal. Make sure you are in the `bin` folder of `logstash`:

```
./logstash -e '
 input {rethinkdb
    {host => "localhost"
     port => 28015
     auth_key => ""
     watch_dbs => ["company"]
     watch_tables => ["company.employees"]
     backfill => true
     }}
 output { elasticsearch {}}'
```

Let's understand what we did previously.

We have followed the syntax of `Logstash` and, in the input object, provided the `rethinkdb` credentials. There are three more keys:

- `watch_dbs`: The array of the database list to look for changes
- `watch_tables`: The array of the table list to look for changes
- `backfill`: Whether or not to synchronize existing data in source, boolean

We added the company database and employees table that we have used throughout the book. This table consists of more than 1,000 documents.

In the output object, we added ElasticSearch details with a blank object. The blank object will instantiate it with default credentials and will automatically create Index and type.

However, you can provide custom information as well, such as host details, SSL, proxy, document type, and so on. You can see the list of supported options here: https://www.elastic.co/guide/en/logstash/2.1/plugins-outputs-elasticsearch.html

Once the command is executed successfully, you can see the following message:

```
Shahids-MacBook-Air:bin UnixRoot$ ./logstash -e '
> input {rethinkdb
>     {host => "localhost"
>      port => 28015
>      auth_key => ""
>      watch_dbs => ["company"]
>      watch_tables => ["company.employees"]
>      backfill => true
>     }}
> output { elasticsearch {}}'
Settings: Default pipeline workers: 4
Eventmachine loop started
Creating db feed for company
Feed for db 'company' registered
Watching table company.employees []
Pipeline main started
```

This means `logstash` has created a successful connection between RethinkDB and ElasticSearch.

Since we haven't provided the Index and type name, Logstash will create one with the name `logstash-current-timestamp`, as shown in the following screenshot:

```
health status index             pri rep docs.count docs.deleted store.size pri.store.size
yellow open   randomindex         5   1          8            0     35.6kb         35.6kb
yellow open   testindex           5   1          1            0      4.1kb          4.1kb
yellow open   twitter             5   1          2            0      7.7kb          7.7kb
yellow open   usa-cigarettes      5   1        444            0      1.4mb          1.4mb
yellow open   employee            5   1          0            0       795b           795b
yellow open   logstash-2016.09.27 5   1       1001            0    718.9kb        718.9kb
```

Since we have asked Logstash to synchronize the existing data in RethinkDB, let's check whether it exists or not.

Open your API simulator and hit the following request:

```
POST ==> http://localhost:9200/logstash-2016.09.27/logs/_count
```

This will return the number of documents present in the ElasticSearch; for me, it is showing 1,001 documents. Here is my response:

```
{
  "count": 1001,
  "_shards": {
    "total": 5,
    "successful": 5,
    "failed": 0
  }
}
```

If you want to see all the documents, just replace `_count` with `_search` in the URL.

 By default, Logstash creates a type named `logs`.

Ok! So we have the existing document in the ElasticSearch index. Let's check what happens if we create a new document in RethinkDB. Ideally, it should index it in ElasticSearch too.

Open the RethinkDB web console by visiting `localhost:8080` and execute the following query from the Data Explorer section:

```
r.db("company").table("employees").insert({
  "city": "Selorejo" ,
  "country": "Indonesia" ,
  "ctc": 49304 ,
  "designation": "Dental Hygienist" ,
  "email": "john@abc.or.jp",
  "first_name": "John" ,
  "gender": "Male" ,
  "ip_address": "1.90.125.195" ,
  "ip_decimal": 22707651 ,
  "last_name": "Reyes",
  "id": 1024
})
```

This will create a new document in the employees table and `logstash` will be notified about this change.

Upon the new event of document addition, Logstash will index it automatically in ElasticSearch. The same will happen for deletion, update and so on. ElasticSearch maintains versions of records; so if you update any document, then instead of updating that directly to the ElasticSearch document, ElasticSearch will create a new copy and call it version 2.

This sums up integrating ElasticSearch with a RethinkDB changefeed. Let's see some use cases where this method will save a lot of your time.

Integration use cases

Listed below are some of the use cases I think ElasticSearch can be used.

Search engine

This method can be useful if you are building a crawler and want a full-fledged search engine. You can use any crawler program, such as **Apache Nutch**, to perform the crawling of the website and index it in RethinkDB for detailed storage and index link, description, body, and so on in ElasticSearch so that it can be easy to search.

Static website search

Static websites are becoming a new trend but with search challenges. This approach can be helpful where the backend of the site is dynamic but the frontend is static. You can use this to build an automated search engine by putting new links in RethinkDB and search items in ElasticSearch.

In the next section, we are going to integrate RabbitMQ with RethinkDB.

Integrating RethinkDB with RabbitMQ

RabbitMQ is a message broker. If you think of how a broker of any kind works, then it would be easy for you to understand the working of RabbitMQ too. Say you are consulting a property broker, so you become the person who is initiating a request to purchase property. Let's name you Producer–a guy who is producing a request.

Broker is a guy who has a list of properties that have been listed by other people. Let's name one of those people Consumer of your producer's request. Eventually, Producer is going to buy the property of Consumer.

Broker has lists of properties; let's name the listing Property queue. So, Producer wants some property; it adds the request to Broker. Broker looks over his listing and tries to match the correct consumer.

That's exactly how RabbitMQ works. Except that there is no commission charge and there is no property!

RabbitMQ exchanges messages between a producer and a consumer using the message queue. There can be multiple producers putting their message in the queue and multiple consumers listening to it. There is no size limit to the queue; as long as your system supports it, you can keep exchanging messages.

So, to summarize the working, refer to the diagram shown here:

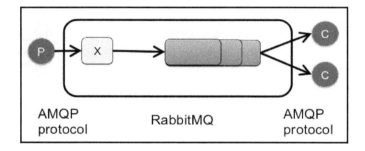

As you can see in the preceding diagram, the producer exchanges the message and that gets added to the queue, and there are multiple consumers who are listening to the queue to obtain some message from one or more producers.

But should every consumer have to deal with every message the producer sends? If so, then is there a lack of security and any performance issues?

Well, there isn't. To answer this technically, allow me to introduce topics in the RabbitMQ queue. You can create a topic, send and receive messages on that topic, and ignore the rest.

So far, we know how RabbitMQ works, but you might be wondering, *Why do I need to integrate it with RethinkDB?* Valid question.

If you observe, the producer (that is, the one who is sending the event) is actually the program itself. This will create a possibility of a bottleneck; what if the producer is down or there is a lag in sending the message?

RethinkDB has the changefeeds feature, which allows you to subscribe to changes of any table. If we can somehow integrate the RabbitMQ with the changefeed, then there is no need to write code to generate messages every time; plus the performance is going to be awesome.

In this section, we are going to do exactly the same, but before we do so, I would like to run you through some basics of RabbitMQ, such as quick installation, plus writing a sample code to observe the working. If you have already worked with RabbitMQ and know the implementation part, please skip the next section and jump right to the integration section.

So let's move ahead and learn about installation of RabbitMQ.

Installing RabbitMQ

The RabbitMQ installer is available for all major operating systems. RabbitMQ is also available as source code, which you can build on your own, and it is also listed on various package managers such as Ubuntu, Homebrew, and so on.

To download RabbitMQ for your operating system, visit the official download page: `https://www.rabbitmq.com/download.html`

Since I am using Mac and RabbitMQ is available on the Homebrew package manager, I am going to use that to install it on my system.

First, update `Homebrew`:

```
brew update
```

Then install RabbitMQ using the following command:

```
brew install rabbitmq
```

This will download, extract, and build RabbitMQ in your system. Once the installation is complete, we need to add the installation path in our system profile to start RabbitMQ using the terminal.

To do so, run this command:

```
cd ~ && nano .bash_profile
```

Add the following line in the file:

```
PATH=$PATH:/usr/local/sbin
```

Save and close the nano editor. Restart the terminal and run the following command:

```
rabbitmq-server
```

This will start the server and you will get a message at terminal as shown in the following screenshot:

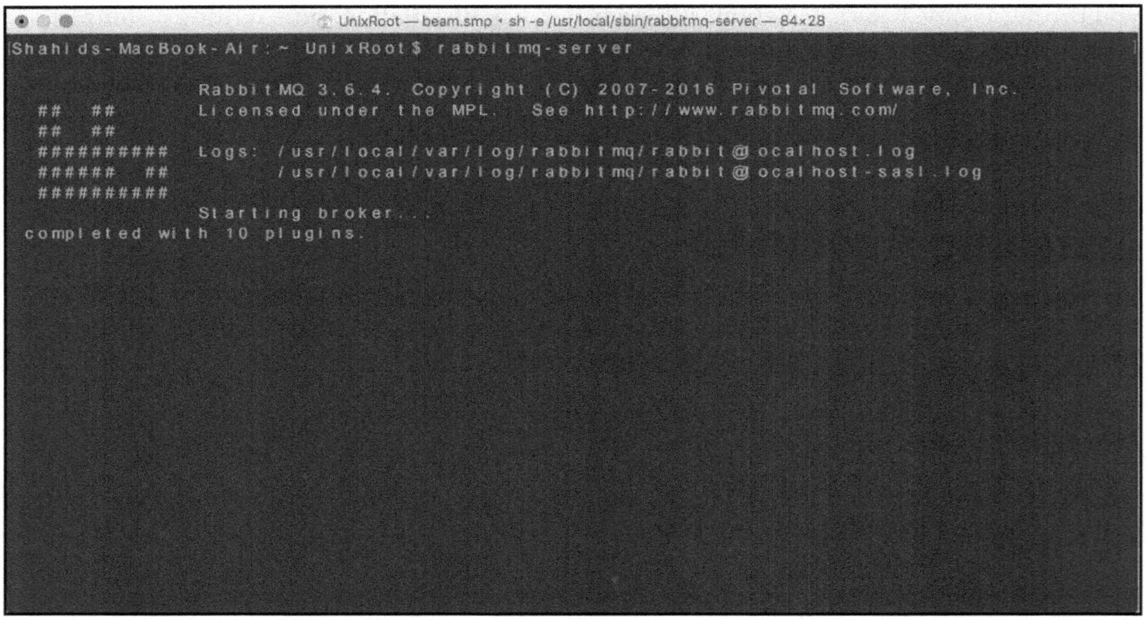

Ok! We have installed RabbitMQ successfully, let's develop a simple use case to warm up ourselves up before moving ahead to integration.

The use case we are going to develop is a simple message exchange where the producer will emit the message and the consumer will receive it from the channel in RabbitMQ.

I am going to develop it in Node.js. There are going be two files in the project, producer.js and consumer.js, with node modules.

First, let's install the client module of RabbitMQ called amqplib from NPM.

Here is the command:

```
npm i -S amqplib
```

This will install the module and make the entry in `package.json`.

Now let's move ahead and write some code for `Producer.js`.

First, we need to require our module, as shown here:

```
var amqp = require('amqplib/callback_api');
```

The next step is to connect to RabbitMQ instance. Here is the code to do that:

```
amqp.connect('amqp://localhost:5672', function(err, conn) {
});
```

This will return two callback variables. We will use a connection variable returned by the function to create a new channel.

Here is the code to create a new channel:

```
amqp.connect('amqp://localhost:5672', function(err, conn) {
  conn.createChannel(function(err, ch) {
    // Create queue
  });
});
```

So we have connected to a RabbitMQ instance and created a channel. Now we can create as many queues as we want and send and receive messages. To create a new queue, we will use the `assertQueue()` function. Here is the code to create a new queue in the channel:

```
amqp.connect('amqp://localhost:5672', function(err, conn) {
  conn.createChannel(function(err, ch) {
    // Create queue
    var q = 'hello';
    ch.assertQueue(q, {durable: false});
  });
});
```

This will create a new queue inside the channel, named `hello`. We will listen to this queue, that is, the `hello` queue, at the consumer end.

Now all we need is sending a message. Here is the code to do so:

```
amqp.connect('amqp://localhost:5672', function(err, conn) {
  conn.createChannel(function(err, ch) {
    // Create queue
    var q = 'hello';
    ch.assertQueue(q, {durable: false});
    ch.sendToQueue(q, new Buffer('Hello World!'));
    console.log(" [x] Sent 'Hello World!'");
  });
});
```

So we have the producer code ready to connect to RabbitMQ, create a new channel, create a new queue, and send the message. Now we require a consumer to listen to the queue and receive messages.

In consumer.js, we will again require the amqp module and connect to our RabbitMQ instance. We will create a channel at the consumer as well and create a new queue with the same name, that is, hello. Creating a queue with the same name is critical and important to combine the producer and consumer.

Instead of sending the message, in consumer.js, we will use the consume function. Here is the complete code:

```
var amqp = require('amqplib/callback_api');
amqp.connect('amqp://localhost:5672', function(err, conn) {
  conn.createChannel(function(err, ch) {
    var q = 'hello';
    ch.assertQueue(q, {durable: false});
    console.log(" [*] Waiting for messages in %s. To exit press CTRL+C",
q);
    ch.consume(q, function(msg) {
      console.log(" [x] Received %s", msg.content.toString());
    }, {noAck: true});
  });
});
```

The only difference between the producer.js code and consumer.js code is the consume() function.

Let's run the code.

Open up two terminals and run the code using the following command:

```
node producer.js
node consumer.js
```

You should be seeing the messages being exchanged between producer and consumer:

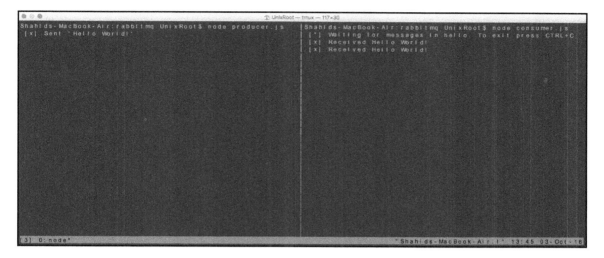

Congratulations! You have successfully created a RabbitMQ-based message exchange system. Since we now know the basics and did our warm-up, let's move ahead to a real working set, that is, integrating RethinkDB changefeeds with the RabbitMQ messaging system.

Here is what we are going to do in steps at the producer end:

1. Connect to RethinkDB instance.
2. Create a database and table if they do not exist.
3. Connect to RabbitMQ.
4. Create a channel and queue.
5. Attach a changefeed to the table, and on each change, add a message to the queue.

Here is what we are going to do in steps at the Consumer end:

1. Connect to RabbitMQ.
2. Create a channel and bind queue.
3. Listen for the messages.

So let's code it. Again, we are going to use Node.js for the same. Let's make the code in the same way as we devised the steps.

Developing producer code

As we studied in the preceding section, we are going to develop producer code; it will push messages in RabbitMQ as soon as our data in the RethinkDB table changes.

Connecting to the RethinkDB instance

Here we are importing the `rethinkdb` and `rabbitmq` node modules in our code and connecting to the default instance of RethinkDB:

```
var r = require('rethinkdb');
var amqp = require('amqplib');
var rethinkConn;
r.connect({host: 'localhost', port: 28015}).then(function(conn) {
    // Setup RethinkDB connection
    rethinkConn = conn;
}).catch(r.Error.RqlDriverError, function(err){
    console.log(err.message);
    process.exit(1);
});
```

In the preceding code, we are using the official node module of RethinkDB to perform the database-related operations. Here we are using connect function to perform the connection to our instance and this function returns a promise, that is, success and error functions. Here, `then()` is the success scenario and `catch()` is the error scenario function. You can also use callback, but promise seems more readable in code.

https://medium.com/@ilyothehorrid/writing-code-for-humans-5b80a8
9f439c#.gh377yy9u

The next step is to create a database and table. Here is the code to do so.

Creating a database and table if they do not exist

In this step, we will create a database and table in our RethinkDB instance if it doesn't exist. RethinkDB returns an error if the database or table already exists; we are ignoring that error and only catching the driver-level error in our code:

```
var r = require('rethinkdb');
var amqp = require('amqplib');
var rethinkConn;
```

```
r.connect({host: 'localhost', port: 28015}).then(function(conn) {
    // Setup RethinkDB connection
    rethinkConn = conn;
}).catch(r.Error.RqlDriverError, function(err){
    console.log(err.message);
    process.exit(1);
}).then(function createDB(){
    return r.dbCreate('change_example').run(rethinkConn);
}).finally(function createTable(){
    return r.db('change_example').tableCreate('mytable').run(rethinkConn);
}).catch(r.Error.RqlRuntimeError, function(){
})
```

This code will execute in order and create a database and table if they don't exist.

Please note that if the database or table already exists in RethinkDB, then it throws an error, but that is a kind of positive use case for us, so we are ignoring that error.

Ok! RethinkDB is ready with the database and table. Let's connect to the RabbitMQ instance, which is our step 3.

Connecting to RabbitMQ

We just need to append the then() function in the trail and connect to the RabbitMQ instance. Here is the code to do so:

```
var r = require('rethinkdb');
var amqp = require('amqplib');
var rethinkConn;
var rabbitConn;
r.connect({host: 'localhost', port: 28015}).then(function(conn) {
    // Setup RethinkDB connection
    rethinkConn = conn;
}).catch(r.Error.RqlDriverError, function(err){
    console.log(err.message);
    process.exit(1);
}).then(function createDB(){
    return r.dbCreate('change_example').run(rethinkConn);
}).finally(function createTable(){
    return r.db('change_example').tableCreate('mytable').run(rethinkConn);
}).catch(r.Error.RqlRuntimeError, function(){
}).then(function(){
    // Setup rabbit connection
    return amqp.connect('amqp://localhost:5672');
});
```

Next, we need to create a new channel in RabbitMQ.

Creating a channel and queue

Here we will use the `createChannel()` to create a new channel, and to create a new queue, we will use the `assertExchange()` function:

```
var r = require('rethinkdb');
var amqp = require('amqplib');
var rethinkConn;
var rabbitConn;
var channel;
var exchange = 'rethinkdb';
r.connect({host: 'localhost', port: 28015}).then(function(conn) {
    // Setup RethinkDB connection
    rethinkConn = conn;
}).catch(r.Error.RqlDriverError, function(err){
    console.log(err.message);
    process.exit(1);
}).then(function createDB(){
    return r.dbCreate('change_example').run(rethinkConn);
}).finally(function createTable(){
    return r.db('change_example').tableCreate('mytable').run(rethinkConn);
}).catch(r.Error.RqlRuntimeError, function(){
}).then(function(){
    // Setup rabbit connection
    return amqp.connect('amqp://localhost:5672');
}).then(function(conn){
    rabbitConn = conn;
    return rabbitConn.createChannel();
}).then(function(ch){
    channel = ch;
    return channel.assertExchange(exchange, 'topic', {durable: false});
});
```

Till now, we have completed four steps, and now comes the main part, that is, creating a changefeed and pushing the message in the RabbitMQ queue for any change.

Attaching a changefeed and integrating the RabbitMQ queue

Here, we are going to first attach the changefeed to the table once, and for each change, it will return us a cursor. We will then loop over the cursor and find out what kind of change it is, that is, update, delete, or create, and then add the message in the queue. Here is the complete code to perform this action:

```
var r = require('rethinkdb');
var amqp = require('amqplib');
var rethinkConn;
var rabbitConn;
var channel;
var exchange = 'rethinkdb';
r.connect({host: 'localhost', port: 28015}).then(function(conn) {
    // Setup RethinkDB connection
    rethinkConn = conn;
}).catch(r.Error.RqlDriverError, function(err){
    console.log(err.message);
    process.exit(1);
}).then(function createDB(){
    return r.dbCreate('change_example').run(rethinkConn);
}).finally(function createTable(){
    return r.db('change_example').tableCreate('mytable').run(rethinkConn);
}).catch(r.Error.RqlRuntimeError, function(){
}).then(function(){
    // Setup rabbit connection
    return amqp.connect('amqp://localhost:5672');
}).then(function(conn){
    rabbitConn = conn;
    return rabbitConn.createChannel();
}).then(function(ch){
    channel = ch;
    return channel.assertExchange(exchange, 'topic', {durable: false});
}).then(function(){
    // Listen for changes on our table
    return
r.db('change_example').table('mytable').changes().run(rethinkConn);
}).then(function(changeCursor){
// to be continued on next page
// Feed changes into rabbitmq
    changeCursor.each(function(err, change){
        if(err){
            console.log(err.msg);
            process.exit(1);
        }
        var routingKey = 'mytable.' + typeOfChange(change);
```

```
              console.log('RethinkDB -(', routingKey, ')-> RabbitMQ')
              channel.publish(
                  exchange, routingKey, new Buffer(JSON.stringify(change)));
          });
  }).catch(function(err){
      console.log(err.message);
      process.exit(1);
  });
  function typeOfChange(change) {
      // Determines whether the change is a create, delete or update
      if(change.old_val === null){
          return 'create';
      } else if(change.new_val === null){
          return 'delete';
      } else {
          return 'update';
      }
      return 'something'
  }
```

As you can see in the code, we are first attaching the changefeed to our table using the code shown here:

```
  return r.db('change_example').table('mytable').changes().run(rethinkConn);
```

Then in the next function, we are looping over the cursor and determining what kind of change this is using our custom function. RethinkDB provides changefeed data in two objects:

```
  new_val : {},
  old_val: {}
```

As the name implies, they contain old and new values in case of deletion or updation, and there will be no old value if the record is just created. We are using this assumption in our typeOfChange() function to determine the operation type.

After that we are adding new message to our RabbitMQ queue using the publish function. Hence, for each change, we are going to get a new message in the queue automatically.

This completes the Producer part. Let's code the Consumer now.

Developing the consumer code

We have completed our producer; it is ready to listen for changes in the RethinkDB instance and put messages in the RabbitMQ queue. In this section, we are going to develop consumer code to listen for messages in our RabbitMQ queue.

Here we do not require to connect to RethinkDB because we don't have database interaction here. Let's connect to RabbitMQ directly.

Connecting to RabbitMQ

```
var amqp = require('amqplib');
var rabbitConn;
var channel;
var exchange = 'rethinkdb';
var queue;
// Create the rabbit connection
amqp.connect('amqp://localhost:5672').then(function(conn){
    rabbitConn = conn;
    return rabbitConn.createChannel();
});
```

Now we need to create a channel and bind the queue.

Creating a channel and binding the queue

Here, we will again create a channel, but for listening purposes, the name of the channel must be the same as the Producer one. After that, we will bind a queue, which will receive new messages from the Producer:

```
var amqp = require('amqplib');
var rabbitConn;
var channel;
var exchange = 'rethinkdb';
var queue;
amqp.connect('amqp://localhost:5672').then(function(conn){
    rabbitConn = conn;
    return rabbitConn.createChannel();
}).then(function(ch){
    channel = ch;
    return channel.assertExchange(exchange, 'topic', {durable: false});
}).then(function(){
    return channel.assertQueue('', {exclusive: true});
}).then(function(q){
    queue = q.queue;
```

```
    // Bind the queue to all topics about 'mytable'
    return channel.bindQueue(queue, exchange, 'mytable.*');
});
```

Here we are creating a new channel and queue, and in the last function, we are binding our queue to listen for all messages containing `mytable` topics, which is the table in our RethinkDB. At last we need to now consume all the messages.

To do so, we are going to use the `consume()` function to receive all messages. Here is the code:

```
var amqp = require('amqplib');
var rabbitConn;
var channel;
var exchange = 'rethinkdb';
var queue;
amqp.connect('amqp://localhost:5672').then(function(conn){
    rabbitConn = conn;
    return rabbitConn.createChannel();
}).then(function(ch){
    channel = ch;
    return channel.assertExchange(exchange, 'topic', {durable: false});
}).then(function(){
    return channel.assertQueue('', {exclusive: true});
}).then(function(q){
    queue = q.queue;
    // Bind the queue to all topics about 'mytable'
    return channel.bindQueue(queue, exchange, 'mytable.*');
}).then(function(){
    console.log('Started listening...');
    channel.consume(queue, function(msg){
        // Handle each message as it comes in from RabbitMQ
        var change = JSON.parse(msg.content);
        var tablename = msg.fields.routingKey.split('.');
        console.log(tablename, '-> RabbitMQ -(',
                msg.fields.routingKey, ')-> Listener');
        console.log(JSON.stringify(change, undefined, 2));
        console.log(new Array(81).join('=') + '\n')
    })
});
```

In the `consume` function, we are parsing the JSON and displaying it in the terminal. Let's run them and see whether it's working.

Thanks to the RethinkDB team for providing this amazing piece of code!

To run the code, we need to first start the RethinkDB and RabbitMQ servers. After starting them, execute the code using following command:

```
node producer.js
node listener.js
```

Now, to see them working, we need to perform some operation in the RethinkDB table. For example, we add a new record.

Open up the RethinkDB web console and execute the following query:

```
r.db("change_example").table("mytable").insert({name: "Shahid"})
```

Once you've executed it, observe the console. RethinkDB will notify about the change to our Producer and it will add it in the message queue, which our consumer program will listen.

Refer to the following screenshot:

As you can see in the terminal, we are getting details of the operation type along with the data. That means our changefeed is successfully integrated with the RabbitMQ message queue. Congratulations!

This completes the integration of RethinkDB with RabbitMQ. In the next section, we are going to learn about RethinkDB protocols to understand the internal working of RethinkDB needed to write drivers and plugins for RethinkDB.

Understanding the RethinkDB protocol

RethinkDB provides steps for developers who are willing to write client drivers for it in any programming language. These steps are combined to form a small protocol. In this section, we are going to learn this protocol.

The protocol consists of following steps:

1. Open a connection to RethinkDB.
2. Perform a handshake.
3. Query serialization.
4. Send a message.
5. Get a response.

Like every other protocol, RethinkDB also uses **Transmission control protocol** (**TCP**) to perform the steps mentioned previously.

In order to connect to a RethinkDB instance, open a TCP connection to the RethinkDB Server; by default, the port is 28015.

Before the client driver can perform the query, it needs to perform authentication with the Server in three specific calls one after another; this process is also called handshake. Once this handshake operation is completed, the client driver can execute a query on the RethinkDB Server.

The handshake operation, in a nutshell, works as shown in the following diagram:

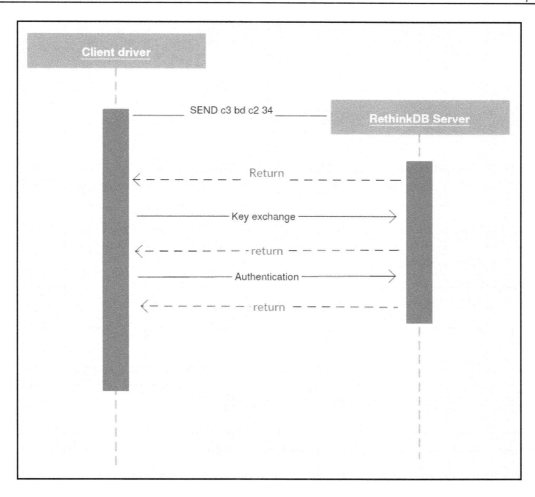

As you can see, the first step is to send the 32-bit integer number to get the server details. If the number is not valid, the RethinkDB Server will return the error.

If the number is valid, RethinkDB will send the JSON response containing the protocol versions and server version, something like this:

```
{
    "success": true,
    "min_protocol_version": 0,
    "max_protocol_version": 0,
    "server_version": "2.3.0"
}
```

Now, as the second step in the handshake, the client driver needs to provide the protocol version it wishes to use, the authentication method, and the authentication key in JSON format.

Currently the supported authentication method is SCRAM-SHA-256 only. In authentication key, client driver needs to provide user name and randomly generated nonce. Example payload is shown here:

```
{
    "protocol_version": 0,
    "authentication_method": "SCRAM-SHA-256",
    "authentication": "n,,n=user,r=rOprNGfwEbeRWgbNEkqO"
}
```

Upon successful exchange, RethinkDB will send JSON response with a success key as boolean value, and if it's true, then it will contain the salt and iteration with the random nonce to generate the authentication key for next call.

In final call of handshake, the client driver needs to send authentication key with the generated key given by RethinkDB in the previous response.

If authentication is successful then the client driver can start executing queries and receive response.

This sums up the handshake part of the protocol. Let's look over some of the third-party libraries and tools available as client drivers and ORMs.

Third-party libraries and tools

There are official and community-supported libraries available for various programming languages such as Node.js and Python, and integration such as RabbitMQ and ElasticSearch.

For Express.js in Node, you can use RethinkDB as a session store too; there is a module available for that, called express-session-rethinkdb.

All of these tools are listed at the official page of libraries here:
`https://www.rethinkdb.com/docs/frameworks-and-libraries/`.

Summary

This was one of the very informative and experimental chapters. We learned how to take the functionality of RethinkDB and expand its working with other awesome tools such as ElasticSearch and RabbitMQ.

We integrated ElasticSearch with RethinkDB to perform the facet search in such a way that any data update is automatically reflected in ElasticSearch.

We also learned how to integrate RabbitMQ with RethinkDB to have an automatic message exchange system.

In the next chapter, we are going to do some practical coding and develop a real-time system using Node.js and RethinkDB.

8
Full Stack Development with RethinkDB

In previous chapters, we learnt about how RethinkDB works, and how to deploy it, manage it, and extend it. Till now, we haven't discussed much about developing applications using RethinkDB and how it can help you to solve real-time application problems such as notifications and so on.

In this chapter, we will study how to develop an application using Full Stack technology, that is, all layers of applications using the same programming language. I, being a Full Stack programmer myself and an expert in Node.js, will be choosing JavaScript for developing our application.

In this chapter, we will cover the following topics:

- Data modeling for our application
- Creating a Node.js server and routes
- Integrating RethinkDB with Node.js
- Integrating AngularJS in the frontend
- Socket.io integration for message broadcasting

At the end, we will learn how to run and deploy our app in the cloud. The application we are going to develop is a **polling** application where the user can create new poll and anonymous people can come and vote. We will be using a RethinkDB changefeed to broadcast the poll count across every client so that polling will be in real time and always up to date.

Just to give you a glimpse, here is how the application will look like at the end of the development.

This is the screen where the user will create a new poll:

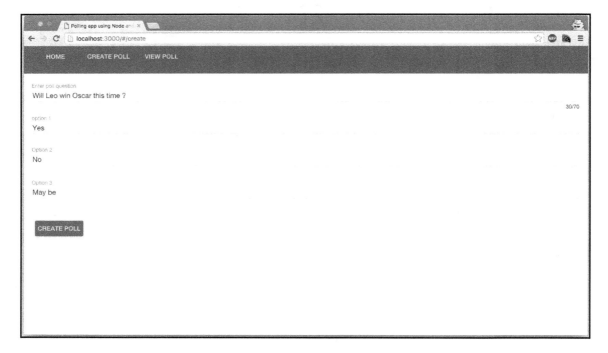

This is the screen where the user views the live updates of the voting:

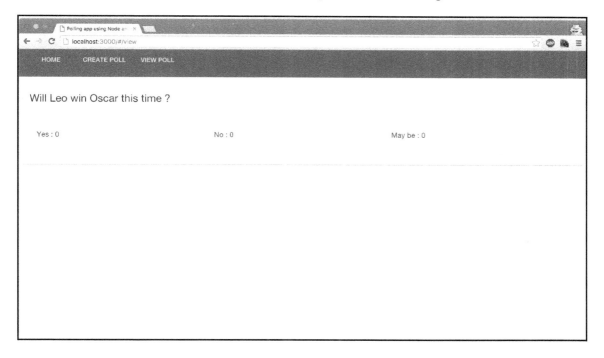

Before moving ahead with project creation and installation, let's understand what we will be building throughout this chapter.

We will be creating polling application where users can:

- Create a poll with three options
- Vote on any poll
- View the stats of polls in real time

The reason why we have three options for polls is to design a concrete database design to store and process the polls and votes.

Here is the technology stack that we are going to use to build our application:

- **Frontend**: HTML, CSS, AngularJS
- **Middle-layer**: Node.js
- **Backend**: RethinkDB (of course)

At the time of writing, Angular 2 is released, but I am not used to it due to the introduction of TypeScript, hence I am going to use Angular 1.5.0, which is still used widely in production.

One more thing: there is a suitable reason as to why we used to develop this (that is, polling) application with RethinkDB, and that is the real-time monitoring. The whole point to prove via this application is how easy it is with RethinkDB to build such a complex application. It will be complex if you use traditional databases such as MySQL (no offense to MySQL though, we still love you).

Before stepping toward development, make sure you have the latest version of Node.js installed in your application. We are going to use some ES6 (Ecma script 6) features to build our app, which requires Node.js 6.0.0 or higher.

Project structure

We are using Node.js in the middle-layer. Node.js code needs to be properly structured to maintain and reuse it in future. In this section, we are going to divide our application in a way to achieve high cohesion and less code coupling.

Here is our project structure:

- Controllers
- Models
- Node_modules
- View
- `app.js` file
- Package.json

The code base is separated in models (code dealing with database), controllers (code dealing with models and view), and view (frontend of the application). This kind of code division is proven to be more robust and highly cohesive.

Controllers generally take care of routes and communication between models and views. They accept the request from the view, transfers it to the model, and then updates the view when it receives the data from the the models.

Models contain code dealing with database operation. Models are not exposed to the outside world, that is, the frontend cannot call model code directly. Every request must go through controllers to models and vice versa.

The view contains all frontend related codes including JS, CSS, and so on.

The main application code resides in the `app.js` file. Package.json will provide the project level details and dependencies required to run the project.

So, let's begin the development.

Data modeling for our application

Since our data is unified and should be visible in an accurate manner to every administrator across the world, we are going to store our polls in the following manner:

```
{
  "Question" : "Which is best phone?",
  "polls" : [
    {
      "option" : "iPhone", vote : 0
    },
    {
      "option" : "Android", vote : 0
    }
  ]
}
```

As you are aware, in RethinkDB we store documents (JSON for geeks) and for our application we are going to store data in the former manner.

Each poll created by admin will be stored in RethinkDB and on each vote, we will update the `vote` field of our specific document, which in turn will be broadcast to every connected client to reflect the change.

Although there is no restriction on us to perform mandatory data modeling, NoSQL databases provide us the power to have schema less design. This data modeling is just for representation and explanation purposes.

Let's move ahead and begin our development with Node.js server creation.

Creating a Node.js server and routes

We need an HTTP server to expose API's and serve static files to the browser. To create a server in Node.js, Express.js is the node module that is very stable, popular, and widely used.

So let's begin. The first thing we require is a `package.json` file. The recommended way to do it is by using the `npm init` command.

 Use `npm init --y` to avoid answering the prompt questions.

Here is the sample `package.json` for reference:

```
{
  "name": "polling-app-node-rethinkdb",
  "version": "1.0.0",
  "description": "",
  "main": "app.js"
}
```

Once the `package.json` is created, we can install dependencies that are required to run the project. They are:

- **Express**: Web framework.
- **RethinkDB**: RethinkDB official client driver
- **Socket.io**: Socket module for message exchange to the client

Along with this, we also need the following dependencies for development purposes:

- **Async**: Asynchronous handling utility
- **Body-parser**: Middleware for parsing the incoming data

Install all these node modules using the following command:

```
npm install --save express rethinkdb socket.io async body-parser
```

This will install and write the entries for dependencies in the package.json file.

 Did you check out Yarn (https://yarnpkg.com/)? It is a new package manager for JavaScript based on NPM.

All right! We have what we need. Let's write our Node.js server.

Here is a basic skeleton code for the simple server, which says Hello World to the user:

```
var express = require('express');
var bodyParser = require('body-parser');
var app = express();
var http = require('http').Server(app);
var router = express.Router();
router.get('/', function(req, res){
  res.send('<h1>Hello world</h1>');
});
app.use(bodyParser.json());
app.use('/',router);

http.listen(3000, function(){
  console.log('listening on port 3000');
});
```

Ok, let's learn what we have done in the preceding code base.

Lines 1 and 2 are importing dependencies. In line 3, we are creating a new instance of Express.

Line 4 is where we are attaching the Express instance to HTTP server. We need to do this for Socket integration; otherwise Express already has a wrapper for most of the HTTP function.

In line 5, we are calling the Router function to create Express routes.

Line 7 to 9 is where the new route is registered to Express. You can't use it unless you explicitly assign it to Express using the .use() method, which we are doing in line 11.

In line 10 we add body-parser middleware for parsing HTTP data and then at the end we listen to port 3000 for incoming requests.

Let's run the app to check whether we've got this right.

Save the code and run it using the `node app.js` command. You should then see a similar screen to the following:

Open up the browser and hit `localhost:3000` on the URL. You should then be viewing a screen similar to the following:

We have our Node.js server running; let's add the routes required for our application. We are going to use the REST principle to develop our web service. The endpoint for the API would be:

```
{ HTTP methods } -> /polls
```

So, to create a new poll, we will hit the following request:

```
POST /polls { poll data }
```

And to retrieve a poll, we will use the following:

```
GET /polls/{:id}
```

We will define these routes in our `controller` folder. To do that, we need to a file that takes care of the `indexing` of all the routes. Here is the `index.js` code, which in turns additional new routes and expose them for further processing:

```
var express = require('express');
var router  = express.Router();
/**
  * @description
  * First route will handle the static html file delivery.
  * Second route will handle the API calls.
*/
router.use('/',require('./home'));
router.use('/polls',require('./polls'));
module.exports = router;
```

As you can see in the preceding code, we are adding new routes in our router instance and passing the files that contain the code for that route. This way, our code is cleaner, highly cohesive, and less coupled.

Let's work on actual routes now. The first route needs to deliver the static files; since we don't have it right now, we are going to just send simple HTML messages instead when the user requests our server.

Here, is the code for `home.js`, placed in the `controllers` folder:

```
var express = require('express');
var router = express.Router();
router.get('/',function(req,res) {
  res.send('<h1>Hello World</h2>');
});
module.exports = router;
```

Here we are adding a new route and exposing it using the `module.exports` function. It's very important to expose the routes in order to access the code outside of the scope.

Let's write our `polls.js` code for polling related routes. Here is the code structure:

```
var express = require('express');
var router  = express.Router();
router.route('/')
  .get(function(req,res) {
    // Code to fetch the polls.
  })
  .post(function(req,res) {
    // Code to add new polls.
  })
  .put(function(req,res) {
    // Code to update votes of poll.
  });
module.exports = router;
```

From each of the routes, we will call specific models that will in turn deal with RethinkDB. Since we don't have these functions ready, we are going to leave the controller code as it is and write the model functions.

Before moving to models, we need to tell Express to use this controller. Here is the updated `app.js` code (changes are highlighted):

```
var express = require('express');
var bodyParser = require('body-parser');
var app = express();
var http = require('http').Server(app);
/**
  Adding the controllers.
*/
app.use(bodyParser.json());
app.use(require('./controllers'));
http.listen(3000, function(){
  console.log('listening on port 3000');
});
```

Notice that we are not adding the filename in the middleware because Node.js will automatically require the file named as `index.js`.

Learn more about how `require` actually works at the following: `http://r equirejs.org/docs/node.html`.

Let's integrate RethinkDB with Node.js and write some model functions.

Integrating RethinkDB with Node.js

We have a basic skeleton of controllers in place and now we need to write some model functions to deal with the RethinkDB database.

One of the basic functions we need is to perform the connectivity to the database and RethinkDB instance.

The reason why we need two functions is because we are going to create the database from the application code. To do that, we need a database instance connection instead of a database connection.

Here is the function to do both of the operations:

```
"use strict";
var rethinkdb = require('rethinkdb');
connectToRethinkDbServer(callback) {
   rethinkdb.connect({
      host : 'localhost',
      port : 28015
   }, function(err,connection) {
      callback(err,connection);
   });
}
connectToDb(callback) {
   rethinkdb.connect({
      host : 'localhost',
      port : 28015,
      db : 'polls'
   }, function(err,connection) {
      callback(err,connection);
   });
}
```

As the name implies, these functions will connect to a RethinkDB instance or database and return back the connection.

Now we need to write the function that will set up our database, that is, perform the following operations in order:

1. Connect to RethinkDB.
2. Create a database if one does not exist.
3. Create a table in the database if one does not exist.

Here is the code to do this; we are using the `async` node module for asynchronous handling:

```
"use strict";
var rethinkdb = require('rethinkdb');
var async = require('async');
class db {
  setupDb() {
    var self = this;
    async.waterfall([
      function(callback) {
        self.connectToRethinkDbServer(function(err,connection) {
          if(err) {
            return callback(true,"Error in connecting RethinkDB");
          }
          callback(null,connection);
        });
      },
      function(connection,callback) {
        rethinkdb.dbCreate('polls').run(connection,function(err, result) {
          if(err) {
            console.log("Database already created");
          } else {
            console.log("Created new database");
          }
          callback(null,connection);
        });
      },
      function(connection,callback) {
rethinkdb.db('polls').tableCreate('poll').run(connection,function(err,resul
t) {
          connection.close();
          if(err) {
            console.log("table already created");
          } else {
            console.log("Created new table");
          }
          callback(null,"Database is setup successfully");
        });
      }
    ],function(err,data) {
      console.log(data);
    });
  }
  connectToRethinkDbServer(callback) {
    //code shown in previous paragraph
  }
  connectToDb(callback) {
```

```
    //code shown in previous paragraph
  }
}
module.exports = db;
```

So what we have done here is create a new function named `setupDb()` in the class called `db`. Inside that function, we performed the following tasks.

The first function in `async.waterfall` is creating a connection to RethinkDB server using our function.

In the next function, we create a new database; if a database already exists, RethinkDB will throw an error, which is a good case for us.

In the next function, we create a new table inside the database; if a table already exists, RethinkDB will throw an error, which is again a good case for us.

 `async.waterfall` is a function that executes your code in waterfall manner, that is, passing the result of each data to the next function. For more information about async and its functions, visit the GitHub page (ht tps://github.com/caolan/async).

We will call this function as the first thing when our application starts, to ensure that we have RethinkDB set up and in place. To do that, we need to change our `app.js`. Here is the updated `app.js` with changes highlighted:

```
var express = require('express');
var bodyParser = require('body-parser');
var app = express();
var http = require('http').Server(app);
var db = require('./models/db');
/**
  Adding the controllers.
*/
var dbModel = new db();
/**
  Setting up the database and creating table.
*/
dbModel.setupDb();
app.use(bodyParser.json());
app.use(require('./controllers'));
http.listen(3000, function(){
  console.log('listening on port 3000');
});
```

Now if you run the app.js file, you should view a similar console to this:

All right then, we can connect to RethinkDB and create our database and tables. Let's write some RethinkDB related functions that we are going to need for our polling application.

We need functions to perform the following operations:

- Creating new polls
- Updating votes
- Getting all polls

Let's write them one by one. First we are going to create a new file, polls.js, in our models folder, which is going to contain the code for the previously mentioned operations.

This is how polls.js looks with basic structure:

```
"use strict";
var rethinkdb = require('rethinkdb');
var db = require('./db');
var async = require('async');
class polls {
}
module.exports = polls;
```

Ok! Moving on, the first function is to create a new poll in our RethinkDB database. Here is the code:

```
"use strict";
var rethinkdb = require('rethinkdb');
var db = require('./db');
var async = require('async');
```

```
class polls {
  addNewPolls(pollData,callback) {
    async.waterfall([
      function(callback) {
        db.connectToDb(function(err,connection) {
          if(err) {
            return callback(true,"Error connecting to database");
          }
          callback(null,connection);
        });
      },
      function(connection,callback) {
        rethinkdb.table('poll').insert({
            "question" : pollData.question,
            "polls" : pollData.polls
        }).run(connection,function(err,result) {
          connection.close();
          if(err) {
            return callback(true,"Error happens while adding new polls");
          }
          callback(null,result);
        });
      }
    ],function(err,data) {
      callback(err === null ? false : true,data);
    });
  }
}
module.exports = polls;
```

We have created a new function called `addNewPolls()`, which accepts the data we need to create a new poll in the system (the data will come from controllers, remember MVC) and returns the callback function.

This function performs two things in waterfall manner:

- Connects to a RethinkDB database
- Adds new entries in the table

In the first function inside the `async.waterfall`, we are calling our `connectToDb()` function that we wrote in a previous section.

In the next function, we are using the `insert()` function of ReQL to add new documents in the database. Pretty simple!

Ok! Moving to the next function, in order to let the user vote, we need a function to update the count of the votes for the particular choice.

Here is the function for updating the vote:

```
votePollOption(pollData,callback) {
  async.waterfall([
    function(callback) {
      db.connectToDb(function(err,connection) {
        if(err) {
          return callback(true,"Error connecting to database");
        }
        callback(null,connection);
      });
    },
    function(connection,callback) {
rethinkdb.table('poll').get(pollData.id).run(connection,function(err,result
) {
        if(err) {
          return callback(true,"Error fetching polls to database");
        }
        for(var pollCounter = 0; pollCounter < result.polls.length;
pollCounter++) {
          if(result.polls[pollCounter].option === pollData.option) {
            result.polls[pollCounter].vote += 1;
            break;
          }
        }
rethinkdb.table('polls').get(pollData.id).update(result).run(connection,fun
ction(err,result) {
          connection.close();
          if(err) {
            return callback(true,"Error updating the vote");
          }
          callback(null,result);
        });
      });
    }
  ],function(err,data) {
    callback(err === null ? false : true,data);
  });
}
```

Again, the first function is performing the connection to the database. The next function is important and it needs to be discussed in detail.

In the second function, we will be doing the following:

1. Fetching the poll based on ID (we will get the ID from the UI).
2. Checking whether the option the user opted to vote is in our poll.
3. If it exists, we will update the vote count by 1 and then update the field in the table.

This step makes sure that the vote is properly maintained. We will use the get() function to retrieve the document and then loop over the options to find and update the vote count.

Once the vote option is found, we will again run RethinkDB get() and update() to update the vote count in our table. This step is important, too.

So we have the vote function as well; the only model function remaining is the retrieval of the polls.

We know we can use the get() method of ReQL to retrieve documents. Here is the code to do so:

```
getAllPolls(callback) {
  async.waterfall([
    function(callback) {
      db.connectToDb(function(err,connection) {
        if(err) {
          return callback(true,"Error connecting to database");
        }
        callback(null,connection);
      });
    },
    function(connection,callback) {
      rethinkdb.table('poll').run(connection,function(err,cursor) {
        connection.close();
        if(err) {
          return callback(true,"Error fetching polls to database");
        }
        cursor.toArray(function(err, result) {
          if(err) {
            return callback(true,"Error reading cursor");
          }
          callback(null,result);
        });
      });
    }
```

```
    ],function(err,data) {
      callback(err === null ? false : true,data);
    });
  }
```

We are connecting to the database and in the next function running the `get()` ReQL method to fetch all documents. However, RethinkDB returns us a stream instead of a complete document. To fetch the data from the stream, we use the `toArray()` function, which collects and transforms the stream into an array of objects, just what we need.

Congratulations! We have completed the models. However, they are of no use if we don't hook them with controllers.

Remember the skeleton code of `polls.js` in the `controllers` folder? We are going to call each of these functions based on the routes. Here is the updated code of the controller calling each function of models:

```
var express = require('express');
var router = express.Router();
// require model file.
var pollModel = require('../models/polls');
router.route('/')
  .get(function(req,res) {
    // Code to fetch the polls.
    var pollObject = new pollModel();
    // Calling our model function.
    pollObject.getAllPolls(function(err,pollResponse) {
      if(err) {
        return res.json({"responseCode" : 1, "responseDesc" :
pollResponse});
      }
      res.json({"responseCode" : 0, "responseDesc" : "Success", "data" :
pollResponse});
    });
  })
  .post(function(req,res) {
    // Code to add new polls.
    var pollObject = new pollModel();
    // Calling our model function.
    // We need to validate our payload here.
    pollObject.addNewPolls(req.body,function(err,pollResponse) {
      if(err) {
        return res.json({"responseCode" : 1, "responseDesc" :
pollResponse});
      }
      res.json({"responseCode" : 0, "responseDesc" : "Success","data" :
pollResponse});
```

```
      });
    })
    .put(function(req,res) {
      // Code to update votes of poll.
      var pollObject = new pollModel();
      // Calling our model function.
      // We need to validate our payload here.
      pollObject.votePollOption(req.body,function(err,pollResponse) {
        if(err) {
          return res.json({"responseCode" : 1, "responseDesc" :
pollResponse});
        }
        res.json({"responseCode" : 0, "responseDesc" : "Success", "data" :
pollResponse});
      });
    });
module.exports = router;
```

In the REST principle, the HTTP method describes an operation, that is, GET should perform the retrieval of data, POST should create, PUT should update, and so on. We have done something similar; for our GET route we are calling the getAllPolls() function.

To create a new poll, that is, POST request, we call the addNewPolls() function and pass the HTTP body data (here, body-parser comes to the rescue), which is in JSON format.

To update the vote, that is, PUT request, we call the votePollOption() function and pass the HTTP body data, which is in JSON format.

It's tough to digest all this code without seeing it in action, so let's do that. Lift the RethinkDB server and start your Node.js server then call the APIs from any API simulator.

First, we will create a new poll; hit the following URL with the sample data:

```
POST /polls
{
    "question" : "Best phone ? ",
    "polls" : [
        {
            "option" : "Android", "vote" : 0
        }
    ]
}
}
```

This will return the following response if you are using the simulator (CURL symbols will work too):

```
Pretty  Raw  Preview        JSON ⌄    ≡|
  1 ▾ {
  2        "responseCode": 0,
  3        "responseDesc": "Success",
  4 ▾      "data": {
  5           "deleted": 0,
  6           "errors": 0,
  7 ▾         "generated_keys": [
  8               "f4eba54d-644c-4c27-b8a9-846fded0cef7"
  9           ],
 10           "inserted": 1,
 11           "replaced": 0,
 12           "skipped": 0,
 13           "unchanged": 0
 14        }
 15   }
```

Let's check whether the poll is created or not. Hit the following URL:

```
GET /polls
```

It will return all the polls in the RethinkDB database in JSON format similar to the following:

```
  1 ▾ {
  2        "responseCode": 0,
  3        "responseDesc": "Success",
  4 ▾      "data": [
  5 ▾        {
  6             "id": "f4eba54d-644c-4c27-b8a9-846fded0cef7",
  7 ▾           "polls": [
  8 ▾             {
  9                  "option": "Android",
 10                  "vote": 1
 11               }
 12             ],
 13             "question": "Best phone ? "
 14          }
 15        ]
 16   }
```

Now we need to test the update vote API. Hit the following request:

```
PUT /polls
{
    "id" : "f4eba54d-644c-4c27-b8a9-846fded0cef7",
    "option" : "Android"
}
```

We need the `id` of the poll and option to do the voting; hence we are providing that in the HTTP body. Refer to the following screenshot for the response:

```
 1 ▾ {
 2       "responseCode": 0,
 3       "responseDesc": "Success",
 4 ▾    "data": {
 5         "deleted": 0,
 6         "errors": 0,
 7         "inserted": 0,
 8         "replaced": 1,
 9         "skipped": 0,
10         "unchanged": 0
11      }
12   }
```

Well it seems our API's are working. We have done the backend development, let's write some frontend code and make it work.

Integrating AngularJS in the frontend

We are using AngularJS as a frontend framework. AngularJS became a sensation right after its release. Recently, Google – the maintainer of the AngularJS project, announced Angular 2.0 with TypeScript – a static parsing language built on top of JavaScript.

In this chapter, we will use Angular v1.5, which is widely used and stable. For styling, we are going to use the Material design concept built again by Google. To use both of them, we first need to install it. There are four ways to do so:

- Install via Bower
- Install via NPM
- Install via Yarn
- Install manually

I am a big fan of Bower due to its simplicity and ease of use. However, you can use any approach to install Angular.

First we need to install Bower. Run the following command in the terminal to install Bower:

```
npm install bower -g
```

You may need to provide sudo access to it.

Once it is installed globally, let's add it as a developer dependency for consistent package installation. Run the following command to do this:

```
npm install bower --save-dev
```

Once done, we can install our Angular and material design libraries. Run the following command in the terminal and make sure you are in the view directory:

```
bower install angular-material -D &&
bower install angular-route &&
bower install angular-messages
```

-D will install dependencies needed by Angular material, which is Angular and other small libraries.

This will install all of the dependencies and you should view the bower_components directory in the view folder.

Moving forward, let's code our home page. Here is the simple HTML code:

```
<!DOCTYPE html>
<html>
  <head>
    <meta charset="utf-8">
    <title>Polling app using Node and RethinkDB</title>
    <link href="./bower_components/angular-material/angular-material.css"
rel="stylesheet" />
  </head>
```

```
    <body ng-app='starterApp' layout='column' ng-
controller='pollingController'>
        <script src="./bower_components/angular/angular.js"
type="text/javascript" ></script>
        <script src="/socket.io/socket.io.js" type="text/javascript"></script>
        <script src="./bower_components/angular-route/angular-route.js"
type="text/javascript" ></script>
        <script src="./bower_components/angular-messages/angular-messages.js"
type="text/javascript" ></script>
        <script src="./bower_components/angular-animate/angular-animate.js"
type="text/javascript" ></script>
        <script src="./bower_components/angular-aria/angular-aria.js"
type="text/javascript" ></script>
        <script src="./bower_components/angular-material/angular-material.js"
type="text/javascript" ></script>
        <script src="./js/app.js"></script>
        <md-toolbar layout="row" flex="1">
          <md-menu-bar>
            <md-menu>
              <md-button ng-href="/#/">Home</md-button>
            </md-menu>
            <md-menu>
              <md-button ng-href="/#/create">Create poll</md-button>
            </md-menu>
            <md-menu>
              <md-button ng-href="/#/view">View Poll</md-button>
            </md-menu>
          </md-menu-bar>
        </md-toolbar>
      <div flex layout="column" layout-align="left" ng-view>
      </div>
    </body>
</html>
```

In the preceding HTML code, we are including all of our dependencies at the home page because what we are going to build is a single page application, so the browser needs all of the code pieces it requires at once.

After including the libraries, we are creating a simple menu with links. The home page somehow looks like this:

In the home page, you should notice that we are using the `ng-view` directive to run our single page application. In our Angular application, we will be using the Angular built-in router to perform the single page routing.

Here is the Angular code for routing:

```
var app = angular.module('starterApp',
['ngMaterial','ngRoute','ngMessages']);
app.config(function($routeProvider){
     $routeProvider
          .when('/',{
               templateUrl: 'home.html'
          })
          .when('/create',{
               templateUrl: 'create.html'
          })
          .when('/view',{
               templateUrl: 'view.html'
          });
});
app.controller('pollingController',function($scope,$http,socket) {
 // controller code
});
```

In the preceding code, we have first initialized the Angular app and then injected each module we need. One of them is the router. We are defining the router using `app.config()` and for each endpoint specifying the path of the HTML file.

In the home page, we are going to display all polls. Here is the home page HTML code:

```
<md-content flex id="content" layout='column'>
  <md-card ng-repeat='pollInfo in pollData' ng-
hide="hiddenrows.indexOf($index) !== -1">
    <md-card-title>
    <md-card-title-text>
        <span class="md-headline">{{pollInfo.question}}</span>
      </md-card-title-text>
    </md-card-title>
    <md-card-content>
    <md-radio-group layout="column" ng-model="pollInfo.selected" ng-
change='updateVote($index)'>
      <md-radio-button ng-repeat="polls in pollInfo.polls" ng-
value="polls.option" aria-label="{{ polls.option }}">
        {{ polls.option }}
      </md-radio-button>
    </md-radio-group>
    </md-card-content>
  </md-card>
</md-content>
```

We are using `ng-repeat` to iterate over the polls and creating the simple `div` that contains the title of the post and three options.

We need to fetch the polls before we load the home page, so we need to do it as soon as the controller loads. Here is the code where we are calling our GET API to retrieve all the polls:

```
app.controller('pollingController', function($scope, $http, socket) {
  $scope.pollData = [];
  // Load polls when app initialise.
  getPollData();
  /**
    * @function
    * @description fetch the polls from RethinkDB and render it in UI.
  */
  function getPollData() {
    $http.get("/polls").success(function(response){
      $scope.pollData = response.data;
    });
  }
});
```

And in the HTML code of the homepage, we use the `pollData` scope variable to show all the polls in a nice, presentable view.

This is how it will look in the browser:

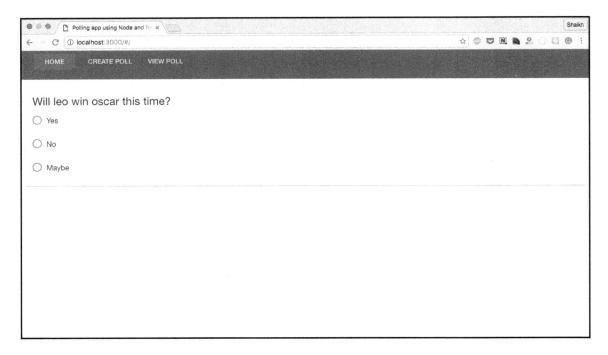

As you can see in the preceding screenshot, each poll option is a radio button and upon clicking it, we will update the count in our database. So we need to call our PUT API to update the vote count.

If you observe the preceding HTML code, we call the `updateVote()` function whenever the user selects any option. Here is the code for this:

```
app.controller('pollingController',function($scope,$http,socket) {
  $scope.pollData = [];
  $scope.hiddenrows = [];
  getPollData();
  function getPollData() {
    //code shown above
  }
  $scope.updateVote = function(index) {
    var data = {
      "id" : $scope.pollData[index].id,
      "option" : $scope.pollData[index].selected
```

```
    };
    $http.put("/polls",data).success(function(response) {
      if(response.responseCode === 0) {
        $scope.hiddenrows.push(index);
      } else {
        console.log("error");
      }
    });
  }
});
```

We also hide polls that users have already voted on in order to avoid multiple voting from the same computer. We are doing this by using the `ng-hide` directive of Angular. When a user is voting, we are simply hiding that option after registering their vote.

The next screen is the **CREATE POLL** screen; in this screen, we need to let the user create a new poll with three options. Here is the HTML code to do this:

```
<md-content layout-padding>
    <form name="projectForm">
      <md-input-container class="md-block">
        <label>Enter poll question</label>
        <input md-maxlength="70" required name="question" ng-
model="formData.pollQuestion">
        <div ng-messages="projectForm.question.$error">
          <div ng-message="required">This is required.</div>
          <div ng-message="md-maxlength">The name has to be less than 70
characters long.</div>
        </div>
      </md-input-container>
      <md-input-container class="md-block">
        <label>option 1</label>
        <input required name="option1" ng-model="formData.pollOption1">
        <div ng-messages="projectForm.option1.$error">
          <div ng-message="required">This is required.</div>
        </div>
      </md-input-container>
      <md-input-container class="md-block">
        <label>Option 2</label>
        <input required name="option2" ng-model="formData.pollOption2"/>
        <div ng-messages="projectForm.pollOption2.$error" role="alert">
          <div ng-message="required">This is required.</div>
        </div>
      </md-input-container>
      <md-input-container class="md-block">
        <label>Option 3</label>
        <input required name="option3" ng-model="formData.pollOption3"/>
        <div ng-messages="projectForm.pollOption3.$error" role="alert">
```

```
            <div ng-message="required">This is required.</div>
        </div>
    </md-input-container>
    <md-input-container class="md-block">
        <md-button class="md-raised md-primary" ng-
disabled="projectForm.$invalid" ng-click="submitPoll($event)">Create
Poll</md-button>
    </md-input-container>
    </form>
  </md-content>
```

The code is really very simple: it contains the input for adding the title of the poll and three radio buttons for options. When we click it, we are calling the submitPoll() function, which in turn is going to call our Node.js API to add a new poll in RethinkDB.

Before going to the Angular code, let's look at the output for the preceding code. Here is what it looks like:

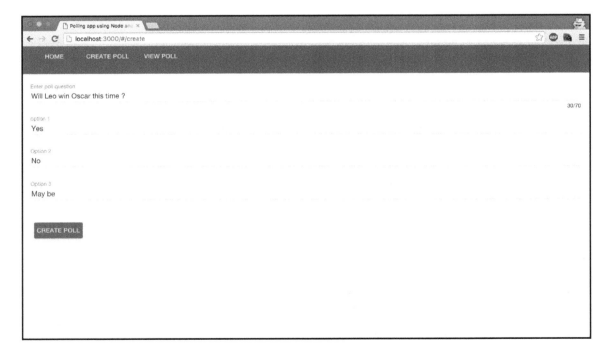

Here is the Angular code for the submitPoll() function in controllers:

```
$scope.submitPoll = function(ev) {
  var data = {
    "question" : $scope.formData.pollQuestion,
    "polls" : [{
      "option" : $scope.formData.pollOption1, "vote" : 0
    },{
      "option" : $scope.formData.pollOption2, "vote" : 0
    },{
      "option" : $scope.formData.pollOption3, "vote" : 0
    }]
  };
  var message = {"title" : "", "message" : ""};
  // Calling the API to add new poll.
  $http.post('/polls',data).success(function(response) {
    if(response.responseCode === 0) {
      message.title = "Success !";
      message.message = "Poll is successfully created";
      data["id"] = response.data.generated_keys[0];
      // Updating pollData to update the view, this will automatically
update and render the new vote at home page.
      $scope.pollData.push(data);
    } else {
      message.title = "Error !";
      message.message = "There is some error happened creating poll";
    }
    // Upon Error or success, dialogue box will appear with message.
    $mdDialog.show(
      $mdDialog.alert()
.parent(angular.element(document.querySelector('#popupContainer')))
        .clickOutsideToClose(true)
        .title(message.title)
        .textContent(message.message)
        .ok('Got it!')
        .targetEvent(ev)
    );
  });
}
```

Alright, let's try to understand this code. From line one to ten, we are constructing the JSON document, which we will pass in our API. In line 11, we are calling our API and upon success, updating the home page by inserting a new object in the `$scope.pollData` variable. Since it's bound to the frontend, we do not require the browser to refresh to see the new poll on screen.

In the next lines of code, we are displaying the nice dialog box offered by Google material design to inform the user about the poll creation.

The only screen that is left right now is the **VIEW POLL** screen. In this screen, the user will see the live update of the vote count.

Here is the HTML code for this:

```
<md-content flex id="content" layout='column'>
  <md-card ng-repeat="pollInfo in pollData">
    <md-card-title>
    <md-card-title-text>
        <span class="md-headline">{{pollInfo.question}}</span>
      </md-card-title-text>
    </md-card-title>
    <md-card-content>
      <md-list>
  <md-list-item class="md-3-line">
    <div class="md-list-item-text" layout="column" ng-repeat="polls in
pollInfo.polls">
      <h3 ng-value="polls.option" aria-label="{{ polls.option
}}">{{polls.option}} : {{polls.vote}}</h3>
      </div>
  </md-list-item>
  <md-divider ></md-divider>
</md-list>
    </md-card-content>
  </md-card>
</md-content>
```

It's quite a simple screen. We are using our `$scope.pollData` variable to iterate through the polls and instead of showing radio buttons, it's a simple label. Here is the output for it:

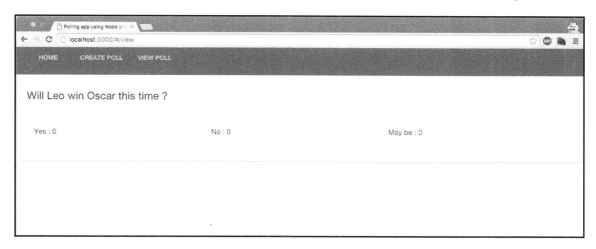

We need to make sure that this page updates as soon as someone performs the voting. In order to do that, we need to do the following:

1. Emit the change as soon as someone votes.
2. Broadcast the change across connected devices.

For task 1, RethinkDB changefeed is the answer. For task 2, the most widely used is `socket.io`, which we have already installed.

To implement task 1, that is, RethinkDB changefeed, we need to add a listener for our RethinkDB table and once the change happens, emit the event message for the connected client.

Socket.io integration for message broadcasting

Here is the code that will perform the RethinkDB changefeed operation and event broadcasting:

```
var rethinkdb = require('rethinkdb');
var db = require('./db');
var pollObject = new db();
module.exports = function(socket) {
  pollObject.connectToDb(function(err,connection) {
  if(err) {
    return callback(true,"Error connecting to database");
  }
  // Look over this line carefully.
  // we are invoking changes() function on poll table.
  // On every change it will give us data.
  rethinkdb.table('poll').changes().run(connection,function(err,cursor) {
    if(err) {
      console.log(err);
    }
    // We are scrolling over the cursor data and broadcasting the changes
using socket.
    cursor.each(function(err,row) {
      console.log(JSON.stringify(row));
      if(Object.keys(row).length > 0) {
        socket.broadcast.emit("changeFeed",{"id" : row.new_val.id,"polls" :
row.new_val.polls});
      }
    });
  });
  });
};
```

In the preceding code, we are writing a function that can be used as many times a user wishes to invoke it. Here we are first connecting to the database using our existing function, which we wrote in an earlier section, and then attaching a changefeed to it.

Once any change occurs, we are looping through the stream and if some data exists, then we broadcast it using the `socket` function. Simple, isn't it?

Let's invoke it as soon as our app starts, add this line of code in `app.js`:

```
var io = require('socket.io')(http);
var feed;
// On connection to the socket, just invoking the function.
io.on('connection',function(socket) {
  feed = require('./models/feeds')(socket);
});
```

This will invoke the new feed as soon as at least one client is connected to the server. This sums up the backend. All we need now is to listen for this event in our Angular code.

To make sure Angular listen for this change, we need to first initialize the Socket in our Angular app. Socket is available as `factory` in AngularJS. Here is the code to do so:

```
app.factory('socket',function(){
  // This is where our app running.
  var socket = io.connect('http://localhost:3000');
  return socket;
});
```

This will return the socket object after connecting to our server. Make sure the URL is correct. Once you get the socket object, all you need to do is listen for the events and if any change is happening, update the `$scope.pollData` variable.

Here is the socket listener:

```
  // This is the event we are emitting from Server.
  socket.on('changeFeed',function(data) {
    // $scope.apply will make the change in HTML screen.
    for(var pollCounter = 0 ;pollCounter < $scope.pollData.length;
pollCounter++) {
      if($scope.pollData[pollCounter].id === data.id) {
        $scope.pollData[pollCounter].polls = data.polls;
        $scope.$apply();
      }
    }
```

I believe the code is quite simple; we are looping over the data coming from the backend, and if any poll ID matches the poll already present then it updates the poll count. This will make sure that the vote count is updated as soon as people vote.

You can always download the code from the source code provided to you and run it and have fun. Try to do this using multiple browsers to see the real working scenario.

Summary

This chapter was full of code and implementations. We started with an application introduction and what we are going to build and did it by steps. We modeled the database; we developed the backend system, and then, finally, a frontend. I can say this chapter is one of the key chapters in this book because we used whatever we learned and made something useful out of it.

The next chapter is going to be more fun; we are going to implement a Polyglot Persistence engine using our RethinkDB. Polyglot Persistence is a concept where we synchronize various databases at once. Let's move on to the next chapter, where we will see this and much more in detail.

9
Polyglot Persistence Using RethinkDB

In the last chapter, we went through all the stages of development required to build an application using RethinkDB. We have done the data modeling, code structure, and finally the frontend design. Building an application where real-time data is required is one of the best-suited cases for RethinkDB; however, there is something more than just real-time data where we can hook RethinkDB. It is **Polyglot Persistence**.

In this chapter, we will cover the following topics:

- Introducing Polyglot Persistence
- Using the RethinkDB changefeed as a Polyglot agent
- Developing a proof-of-concept application with MongoDB and MySQL
- Developing the Polyglot agent
- Developing event consumers
- Running the app
- Further improvements

So let's begin.

Introducing Polyglot Persistence

In 2006, Neal Ford coined the term called **Polyglot programming**, which in short tells you to use different programming languages which are best suited to solve a specific problem instead of trying to solve all problems using a single programming language. He suggested that there are different programming languages which are best suited for particular things, such as Java for data processing, Erlang for functional programming, and so on.

As the field of databases is growing, we have lots of different databases to solve different kinds of problems.

For example, SQL is still suited for user-based applications such as Quora, NoSQL is suited for large-batch processing and analytics such as Hadoop, and real-time databases such as RethinkDB are suited for building interactive real-time applications.

For more information, read why Quora uses MySQL at:
`https://www.quora.com/Why-does-Quora-use-MySQL-as-the-data-sto`
`re-instead-of-NoSQLs-such-as-Cassandra-MongoDB-or-CouchDB`.

Having these options at hand, we should not stick to using one database for all purposes, but instead we should use a variety of databases to match our needs. However, having various sources of database requires extra caution, which is synchronization. Using different databases and maintaining the synchronization between them is called Polyglot Persistence.

To most of us, the term Polyglot Persistence looks simple, but it's really not. When you dive into architecture details, you need to figure out lots of details, some of them being:

- **Choosing the databases**: This can be complex due to performance metrics of various database
- **Choosing the entry database**: The database where data manipulation happens first
- **Choosing the transaction necessity**: Does your application require transaction or not?

There is one point I would like to mention: even if you make a mistake when choosing the database or transaction needs, you can always redo it without affecting the existing system because database engines are separate processes running probably on different machines and the consumer really has no idea that the data coming to his/her request is from which database.

Please note, I have personally developed and deployed such a system and eventually did make a mistake on choosing the entry database, although, I changed it later without any downtime. I would love to share the project details but it's confidential and I am the one who signed the non-disclosure agreement but I will share my experience and try to help you out as much as possible.

I am sure till now you have grasped the concept in one sentence *Using lots of databases and maintaining the data synchronization*.

As mentioned, the entry database, that is, a database where creation, updates, and deletion happens first, is then synchronized to other concerned databases. So we need some kind of agent which tells the other databases about the change in the entry database. I am sure you are getting what I mean to say here: RethinkDB changefeed can act as the agent.

In the next section, we are going to learn how RethinkDB can help us to implement the agent for the other databases or I should say you've already got it.

Using the RethinkDB changefeed as a Polyglot agent

I am sure changefeed does not require any introduction now. We have already used or discussed it in almost every chapter. In this section, we are going to learn why RethinkDB can act as a Polyglot agent.

As I have mentioned in the previous section, synchronizing various kinds of databases requires the following two important things:

- An event to trigger the process
- Database-specific listeners

Any time we add/update/delete the data in our entry database, an event must be triggered in order to start the process of synchronization. Then we need a database-specific listener who in turn performs the data manipulation in the respective databases.

So to trigger an event, we need to first know that there is some kind of change happening in the database. You can do this easily by writing an extra piece of code if the program which is doing the manipulation in the database is written or controlled by you. However, if the manipulation is done by the various processes which you can't control then the database is the one from where the event should be fired.

Considering this, RethinkDB is the best-suited case here. All we need is to assign a changefeed to the table or query and emit an event every time there is a change.

Listeners will then perform their database-level task to manipulate the data. You can of course hook a distributed level transaction here if needed and make sure every database is synchronized and, if any error occurs, roll back from every database.

So we have learned why RethinkDB is best suited for the Polyglot agent. In the next section, we are going to develop an application to prove what we have discussed in the previous sections.

Developing a proof-of-concept application with MongoDB and MySQL

Till now, we have learned about Polyglot Persistence and why RethinkDB is best suited for it. It's time to get to work and prove that this kind of system can be implemented with RethinkDB. In this section, we are going to develop an application that will use three databases, RethinkDB, MySQL, and MongoDB, where RethinkDB will act as an entry database.

We will develop an application where you can perform the CRUD operation in RethinkDB and all changed data will be synchronized automatically to MySQL and MongoDB.

Consider the following diagram:

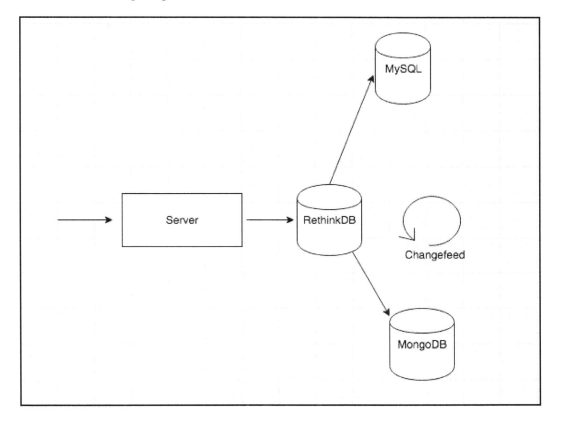

As you can see in the preceding diagram, the server will first perform the data manipulation in RethinkDB and by using the changefeed we will notify and update MongoDB and MySQL.

Before moving ahead to the code part, let's do some quick data modeling for all three databases. We are going to store personal data related to the users. Here is the simple data model schema for RethinkDB:

```
{
    "id": "string",
    "name":  "string",
    "gender": "string"
    "dob" : "Date",
    "location" : "string"
}
```

Here is the sample schema for MongoDB:

```
{
    "_id": "string",
    "rethinkId": "string"
    "name":  "string",
    "gender": "string"
    "dob" : "Date",
    "location" : "string"
}
```

As you may notice, we have added one more ID field named `rethinkId`, which will eventually store the ID of the RethinkDB document. This is good way to have distributed indexing.

Now for MongoDB; you may not need to create a database and collection beforehand because we are going to use mongoose ORM, which takes care of definition-level queries for MongoDB. However, for MySQL, we need to manually create the database and table definition before writing the code.

So let's do that.

Install MySQL or, I would say, the complete package of XAMPP to access the **phpMyAdmin** screen for data access.

Installation of XAMPP depends upon different operation systems. You can visit their official site at `https://www.apachefriends.org/index.html` to download the stable version of XAMPP.

Once done, open up **phpMyAdmin** by visiting `http://localhost/phpmyadmin` from your browser. Type in the name of the database you require and hit the Create button, as shown in the screenshot:

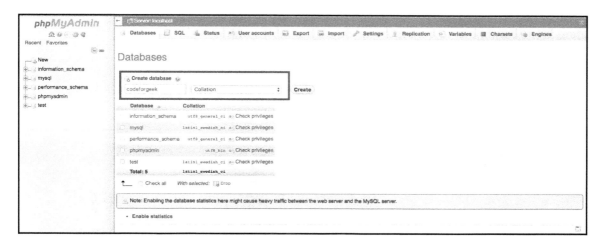

Once the database is created, create a new table named `users` inside it with the properties shown in the screenshot:

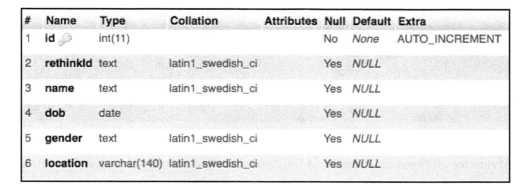

#	Name	Type	Collation	Attributes	Null	Default	Extra
1	id	int(11)			No	*None*	AUTO_INCREMENT
2	rethinkId	text	latin1_swedish_ci		Yes	*NULL*	
3	name	text	latin1_swedish_ci		Yes	*NULL*	
4	dob	date			Yes	*NULL*	
5	gender	text	latin1_swedish_ci		Yes	*NULL*	
6	location	varchar(140)	latin1_swedish_ci		Yes	*NULL*	

So we have the database and tables in place. Let's begin the implementation. The first step is to set up the project environment.

Setting up the project

I am going to use Node.js to develop this POC. The best practice to begin the Node.js project is by creating a `package.json` file using `npm` command.

Here is the command to generate a basic `package.json` file:

```
npm init --y
```

This will generate the `package.json` file with default values. Refer to the following screenshot:

The next step is to install all of our dependencies needed for the project. We are going to need drivers for all three databases and the `Express` module for web server handling.

Here is the command to install all the dependencies:

```
sudo npm i --S rethinkdb mysql mongodb mongoose async express body-parser
```

This will take a moment depending upon the Internet speed at your end. Once the installation is complete, we are good to go to the development phase. In development, the first thing we need is a server.

Developing a server using Express

To develop a server using the Express module, we need to first load the module, configure the routes, and then listen on specific ports for requests.

This is how we load the Express module:

```
const express = require('express');
```

We need to create a new instance of the class. Here is how we do it in Node.js:

```
const app = express();
```

The next step is to configure the routes. We are going to put our routes code in a separate file, say users.js. This is how to configure it in our server.

First require the router file:

```
const routes = require('./users');
```

Then configure Express to use these routes:

```
app.use(routes);
```

Once done, we can now start our server using the following code:

```
app.listen(4000,() => {
  console.log("Listening to port 4000");
});
```

So, eventually, the complete code base will look something like this:

```
const express = require('express');
const bodyParser = require('body-parser');
const app = express();
const routes = require('./users');
app.use(bodyParser.json());
app.use(routes);
app.listen(4000,() => {
  console.log("Listening to port 4000");
});
```

We did develop our server but it won't work without a route. Let's develop sample routes for CRUD operations. You can find these codes in the users.js file.

Case – reading all users' data

We are going to use our `Model` function, the `getAllUsers()` function, to retrieve all data from RethinkDB and return it to the client:

```
const express = require('express');
const router = express.Router();
const userModel = require('./userModel');
router.route('/')
  .get((req,res) => {
    let userObject = new userModel();
    userObject.getAllUsers(function(err,userResponse) {
      if(err) {
        return res.json({"responseCode" : 1, "responseDesc" :
userResponse});
      }
      res.json({"responseCode" : 0, "responseDesc" : "Success", "data" :
userResponse});
    });
  });
module.exports = router;
```

Here is the `getAllUsers()` function in the `userModel.js` file:

```
const rethinkdb = require('rethinkdb');
const db = require('./db');
const async = require('async');
class Users {
  getAllUsers(callback) {
    async.waterfall([
      function(callback) {
        var userObject = new db();
        userObject.connectToDb(function(err,connection) {
          if(err) {
            return callback(true,"Error connecting to database");
          }
          callback(null,connection);
        });
      },
      function(connection,callback) {
        rethinkdb.table('users').run(connection,function(err,cursor) {
          connection.close();
          if(err) {
            return callback(true,"Error fetching users from database");
          }
          cursor.toArray(function(err, result) {
            if(err) {
              return callback(true,"Error reading cursor");
```

```
        }
          callback(null,result)
        });
      });
    }
  ],function(err,data) {
    callback(err === null ? false : true,data);
  });
  }
}
```

In the last chapter, we used a similar `Model` function to perform CRUD operations on the RethinkDB database. Here, we have first made a connection to the database using the predefined function in our `db.js` file, which we used in the last chapter as well, and then we ran the ReQL query to retrieve all documents related to the user.

RethinkDB returns the stream so we need to iterate and collect all the documents before returning it to the user. We do this using the `toArray()` function of RethinkDB.

Since the `db.js` code is similar to the one used in the last chapter with a different database name, I don't think there is a need to explain it again here.

Case – creating a new user

We are going to use our `Model` function `addNewUser` to create a new user in a RethinkDB table and return the response to the client:

```
const express = require('express');
const router = express.Router();
const userModel = require('./userModel');
router.route('/')
  .post((req,res) => {
    let userObject = new userModel();
    userObject.addNewUser(req.body,function(err,userResponse) {
      if(err) {
        return res.json({"responseCode" : 1, "responseDesc" :
userResponse});
      }
      res.json({"responseCode" : 0, "responseDesc" : "Success","data" :
userResponse});
    });
  });
module.exports = router;
```

Here is our `Model` function to add the new user in the RethinkDB table:

```
const rethinkdb = require('rethinkdb');
const db = require('./db');
const async = require('async');
class Users {
  addNewUser(userData,callback) {
    async.waterfall([
      function(callback) {
        var userObject = new db();
        userObject.connectToDb(function(err,connection) {
          if(err) {
            return callback(true,"Error connecting to database");
          }
          callback(null,connection);
        });
      },
      function(connection,callback) {
rethinkdb.table('users').insert(userData).run(connection,function(err,resul
t) {
          connection.close();
          if(err) {
            return callback(true,"Error happens while adding new user");
          }
          callback(null,result);
        });
      }
    ],function(err,data) {
      callback(err === null ? false : true,data);
    });
  }
}
module.exports = Users;
```

In this function, we are first connecting to our database and then running the `insert()` query of ReQL to perform the creation of a new document in the RethinkDB table. The `userData` variable contains the incoming data from the client passed by the router to this function.

This is for the creation of the new user. Let's move to a use case where we need to update the existing document.

Case – updating user data

In this use case, we are going to use our `Model` function `updateUser` to update the information of the user in the RethinkDB table and return the response to the client:

```
const express = require('express');
const router = express.Router();
const userModel = require('./userModel');
router.route('/')
  .put((req,res) => {
    let userObject = new userModel();
    userObject.updateUser(req.body,function(err,userResponse) {
      if(err) {
        return res.json({"responseCode" : 1, "responseDesc" :
userResponse});
      }
      res.json({"responseCode" : 0, "responseDesc" : "Success","data" :
userResponse});
    });
  });
module.exports = router;
```

Here is our `Model` function to update the user information in the RethinkDB table:

```
const rethinkdb = require('rethinkdb');
const db = require('./db');
const async = require('async');
class Users {
  updateUser(userData,callback) {
    async.waterfall([
      function(callback) {
        var userObject = new db();
        userObject.connectToDb(function(err,connection) {
          if(err) {
            return callback(true,"Error connecting to database");
          }
          callback(null,connection);
        });
      },
      function(connection,callback) {
rethinkdb.table('users').get(userData.id).run(connection,function(err,resul
t) {
        if(err) {
          return callback(true,"Error fetching users from database");
        }
        // update users
        result = userData;
rethinkdb.table('users').get(userData.id).update(result).run(connection,fun
```

```
ction(err,result) {
              connection.close();
              if(err) {
                return callback(true,"Error updating the user");
              }
              callback(null,result);
            });
          });
        }
      ],function(err,data) {
        callback(err === null ? false : true,data);
      });
    }
}
module.exports = Users;
```

In this function, we are first making a connection to the database and then running two queries in the pipe. First, we will find whether any user exists using the ID and if it exists, we will update it with the incoming payload and run the update ReQL query to make the effect in the database.

With this, we are left with our final use case, deleting the user.

Case – deleting the user

In this use case, we are going to use our Model function deleteUser to delete the information of the user in the RethinkDB table and return the response to the client:

```
const express = require('express');
const router = express.Router();
const userModel = require('./userModel');
router.route('/')
  .delete((req,res) => {
    let userObject = new userModel();
    userObject.deleteUser(req.body,function(err,userResponse) {
      if(err) {
        return res.json({"responseCode" : 1, "responseDesc" :
userResponse});
      }
      res.json({"responseCode" : 0, "responseDesc" : "Success","data" :
userResponse});
    });
  });
module.exports = router;
```

Here is our `Model` function to delete the user information from RethinkDB:

```
const rethinkdb = require('rethinkdb');
const db = require('./db');
const async = require('async');
class Users {
  deleteUser(userData,callback) {
    async.waterfall([
      function(callback) {
        var userObject = new db();
        userObject.connectToDb(function(err,connection) {
          if(err) {
            return callback(true,"Error connecting to database");
          }
          callback(null,connection);
        });
      },
      function(connection,callback) {
        // find and delete user
rethinkdb.table('users').get(userData.id).delete().run(connection,function(
err,result) {
          connection.close();
          if(err) {
            return callback(true,"Error deleting the user");
          }
          callback(null,result);
        });
      }
    ],function(err,data) {
      callback(err === null ? false : true,data);
    });
  }
}
module.exports = Users;
```

In this function, we are first making a connection to the database and then running two queries in the pipe. First, we are finding out whether any user exists using the ID and if it exists, we are deleting the user using the `delete` ReQL command.

So now we are done with all the required CRUD use cases, let's move ahead with integrating RethinkDB in Node.js, that is, initializing the database class during the start of the server.

To do so, we need to add the following three lines in the server code before configuring the routes:

```
const db = require('./db');
const dbSetup = new db();
dbSetup.setupDb();
```

This will make sure that RethinkDB is connected and the required database and table is in place before accepting the request from the client.

Before moving ahead, let's check whether our code base is correct. Start the server using the following command:

node app.js

This will start the server and configure the RethinkDB database as shown in the following screenshot:

So we have a server ready to perform CRUD operations in the entry database. Next we need the **Polyglot agent**.

Developing the Polyglot agent

As we have discussed earlier, the job of the Polyglot agent is to find out the changes in the table and then generate an event for the synchronization process.

For finding out the changes in the table, we already have the changefeed by RethinkDB, and for generating events, we can use the inbuilt `EventEmitter` class by Node.js.

The event emitter is the class in the Node.js; thus, to use it we need to inherit all the functions and property in our class. We can do this by using the following code:

```
const events = require('events');
class Polyglot extends events {
  constructor() {
    super();
  }
}
module.exports = Polyglot;
```

Here we are using the ES6 `extends` keyword to perform the inheritance. In our constructor, we are calling the `super()` method to call the parent constructor, that is, the constructor of the event class.

Next, we need to assign a changefeed to our table and listen for the change. If there is a change in any of the data, we need to determine the type of change, such as add, update, or delete, and then generate the event.

Here is the function which does this:

```
const db = require('./db');
const userObject = new db();
assingChangeFeed() {
    let self = this;
    userObject.connectToDb(function(err,connection) {
      if(err) {
        return callback(true,"Error connecting to database");
      }
      rethinkdb.table('users').changes({"include_types":
true}).run(connection,function(err,cursor) {
        if(err) {
          console.log(err);
        }
        cursor.each(function(err,row) {
          console.log(JSON.stringify(row));
          if(Object.keys(row).length > 0) {
            if(!!row.type) {
```

```
            switch(row.type) {
              case "add": self.emit('insert',row);break;
              case "remove": self.emit('delete',row);break;
              case "change": self.emit('update',row);break;
            }
          } else {
            console.log("No type field found in the result");
          }
        }
      });
    });
  });
}
```

The function performs the following tasks:

1. Connects to the RethinkDB instance.
2. Assigns a changefeed to the table.
3. On the change, iterates over the data and broadcasts the event depending upon the type of operation.

To determine the type of operation, we have specified the `include_types` parameter in the changefeed.

To sum up the complete code, here is what it will look like:

```
const rethinkdb = require('rethinkdb');
const db = require('./db');
const userObject = new db();
const events = require('events');
class Polyglot extends events {
  constructor() {
    super();
    this.assingChangeFeed();
  }
  assingChangeFeed() {
    let self = this;
    userObject.connectToDb(function(err,connection) {
      if(err) {
        return callback(true,"Error connecting to database");
      }
      rethinkdb.table('users').changes({"include_types":
true}).run(connection,function(err,cursor) {
        if(err) {
          console.log(err);
        }
        cursor.each(function(err,row) {
```

```
                console.log(JSON.stringify(row));
                if(Object.keys(row).length > 0) {
                  if(!!row.type) {
                    switch(row.type) {
                      case "add": self.emit('insert',row);break;
                      case "remove": self.emit('delete',row);break;
                      case "change": self.emit('update',row);break;
                    }
                  } else {
                    console.log("No type field found in the result");
                  }
                }
              });
            });
          });
        }
      }
      module.exports = Polyglot;
```

However, this class is of no use if we don't hook it in our server. Here is the code added in the server file to start the Polyglot agent:

```
const polyglot = require('./polyglot');
new polyglot();
```

We are creating a new instance of the preceding code in our server. This will look for any changes in the table and generate an event when any data manipulation happens.

Feeling relaxed? Well, we still have a job to do. Yes, we have the Polyglot agent which will notify the change via events but what's the use if no one is listening? Right. So in the next section, we are going to do same.

Developing event consumers

As I have mentioned earlier, we are going to use MySQL and MongoDB to perform the synchronization. We have the data model ready for both of them, so all we need is to listen for events and, depending upon the type, perform database-related operations.

Before starting with the code, I would like to mention a little bit about the **Observer** design pattern because we are going to use it in the next section.

Observer pattern

The Observer pattern is a design pattern in which a subject maintains a list of its dependents or listeners and notifies them about any change. We can implement this pattern using Node.js by using the `EventEmitter` class.

Consider the following example:

```
const EventEmitter = require('events');
class MyStream extends EventEmitter {
  constructor() {
    super();
    this.files = [];
  }
  read(file) {
    this.files.push(file);
    this.emit('fileadded',file);
  }
  write() {
    var self = this;
    this.files.map(function(files) {
      self.emit('data', files);
    });
  }
}
```

We have created a class and extended the `EventEmitter` function using the ES6 `extends` keyword. Here we have two functions, `read` and `write`, which eventually manipulate an array defined in the constructor.

On addition of new value in the array, we are emitting the event. On reading the values in the array, we are emitting the event too.

Here is how we can consume the events:

```
// creating new instance of the class
const stream = new MyStream();
// Events class provides us on function to listen for events.
stream.on('data', (data) => {
  console.log(`Received data: "${data}"`);
});
stream.on('fileadded',(fileName) => {
  console.log("New file added",fileName);
});
stream.read("abc.txt");
stream.read("pqr.txt");
stream.read("eee.txt");
stream.write();
```

If you run the preceding code, you will get the output as shown in the following screenshot:

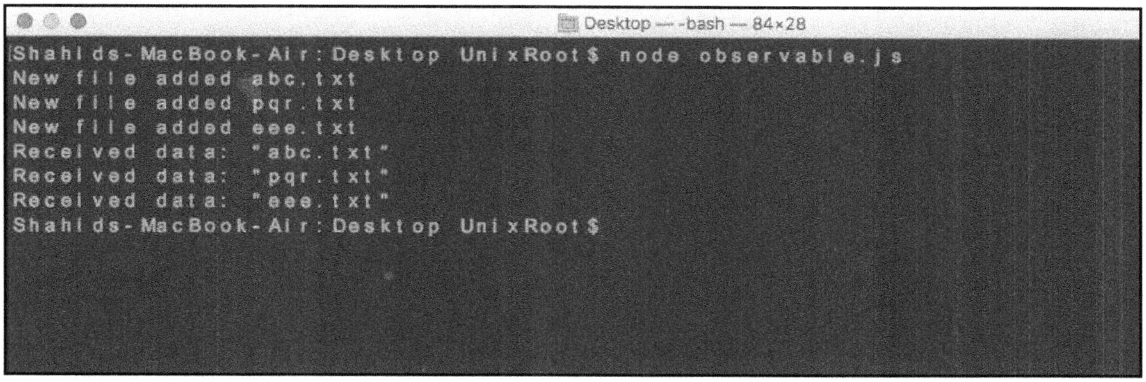

As you can see in the preceding output, we are controlling the flow of the code execution using events that are best suited for large complex systems.

Now, coming to our task, our Polyglot class is actually the Observer class so we can inherit the class and listen to each event. We have following events to listen to:

- insert
- update
- delete

We will listen to these events and then perform the database-related task. For example, for MySQL with an insert event, we need to run the INSERT SQL query and for MongoDB we need to run the save() method, and so on.

So to make it clear, we will cover each database listener in different code bases and in different sections.

Let's begin with MySQL.

MySQL consumer

Our first consumer is MySQL. We need to write a code base which listens to these events and then performs the following:

- On the insert event, run the INSERT SQL query
- On the update event, run the UPDATE SQL query
- On the delete event, run the DELETE SQL query

So let's code our consumer. Here is the skeleton class that contains code to connect and listeners for the events:

```
const mysql = require('mysql');
const polyglot = require('./polyglot');
class syncMysql {
  constructor() {
    // connect to mysql
    var connection = mysql.createConnection({
      host     : 'localhost',
      user     : 'root',
      password : '',
      database : 'codeforgeek'
    });
    connection.connect();
    this.handleOperation(connection);
  }
  handleOperation(connection) {
    let self = this;
    let sync = new polyglot();
    sync.on('insert',function(data) {
// Perform the INSERT query.
    });
    sync.on('update',function(data) {
// Perform the UPDATE query.
    });
```

```
    sync.on('delete',function(data) {
  // Perform the DELETE query.
    });
  }
}
module.exports = syncMysql;
```

In the preceding code, we are first making a connection to MySQL and then passing the connection to the next function, which in turn creates the instance of the `Polyglot` class and listens to each event.

 For more information about the MySQL node module, visit this link: `http s://github.com/mysqljs/mysql`.

We have an event listener in place, so all we need to do now is to perform an SQL query on each event. So let's begin with the `INSERT` query. I will be showing the code of each listener instead of the complete function.

Here is the SQL query for, insert event:

```
    sync.on('insert',function(data) {
        let query = "INSERT INTO ?? (??,??,??,??,??) VALUES (?,?,?,?,?)";
        query = mysql.format(query,
['users','rethinkid','name','dob','gender','location',
data.new_val.id,data.new_val.name,data.new_val.dob,
data.new_val.gender,data.new_val.location]);
// making the query.
        connection.query(query,function(err,result) {
          if(err) {
            console.log(err);
          } else {
            console.log("Synced to MySQL");
          }
        });
      });
```

If you remember, we are already passing the changefeed data from our `Polyglot` class in the events. This data looks like this:

```
{
 new_val : {},
 old_val: {},
 type: ""
}
```

For the INSERT query, you will always get the value in the new_val key.

For UPDATE and DELETE, you will get the values in the old_val key too.

OK then, we are preparing our query using the format() function of the mysql module and then simply running the query to sync the data in the MySQL table.

Similarly, we are doing the UPDATE operation. Here is the code:

```
sync.on('update',function(data) {
    let query = "UPDATE ?? SET ?? = ?,?? = ?, ?? = ?, ?? = ? WHERE ?? =
?";
    query = mysql.format(query,["users","name",data.new_val.name,"dob",
new Date(data.new_val.date),"gender",data.new_val.gender,
"location",data.new_val.location,"rethinkid",data.new_val.id]);
// running the query
    connection.query(query,function(err,result) {
      if(err) {
        console.log(err);
      } else {
        console.log("Synced to MySQL");
      }
    });
  });
```

We are preparing our query and updating each value. You can also perform the pre-check, finding out which values have changed and then updating them only, but that would require one additional query to MySQL to fetch the existing data and then comparison logic.

Notice here that we are using our rethinkId column in the WHERE class to update the data.

Let's see how we are doing the DELETE operation. Here is the code:

```
sync.on('delete',function(data) {
  let query = "DELETE FROM ?? WHERE ?? = ?";
  query = mysql.format(query,["users","rethinkid",data.old_val.id]);
  connection.query(query,function(err,result) {
    if(err) {
      console.log(err);
    } else {
      console.log("Synced to MySQL");
    }
  });
});
```

Here I would like to mention that we are using the `old_val` key to retrieve the ID of the original document in order to delete it from MySQL. The rest of the code is self-explanatory.

This completes the consumer part of MySQL. Let's move ahead to the MongoDB consumer.

MongoDB consumer

The structure of the code base for MongoDB is the same as the MySQL one but with different query syntaxes. Here is the structure code with the MongoDB collection using the `mongoose node` module:

```
const mongoose = require('mongoose');
const polyglot = require('./polyglot');
class mongoSync {
  constructor() {
    mongoose.connect('mongodb://localhost:27017/codeforgeek');
    var userSchema = mongoose.Schema({
      "rethinkId" : String,
      "name" : String,
      "dob": Date,
      "gender": String,
      "location": String
    });
    let model = mongoose.model('users',userSchema);
    this.handleOperation(model);
  }
  handleOperation(model) {
    let self = this;
    let sync = new polyglot();
    sync.on('insert',function(data) {
      // Perform insert operation.
    });
    sync.on('update',function(data) {
      // Perform update operation.
    });
    sync.on('delete',function(data) {
      // Perform delete operation.
    });
  }
}
module.exports = mongoSync;
```

For more information about mongoose, visit their official site at http://ww w.mongoosejs.com.

In the constructor of the class we are connecting to our MongoDB database, if the database doesn't exist, mongoose will create it for you. In the next line, we are defining the schema, that is, how the data should be stored in MongoDB.

Then, we are creating a mongoose model, a collection using the model() function, and passing it to the next function for further operations.

In the handleOperation() function, we are creating a new instance of our Polyglot class and listening to the events.

Here is the code for each of the events.

First, we need to add the document if an insert event occurs:

```
sync.on('insert',function(data) {
  let mongoOp = new model();
  mongoOp.rethinkId = data.new_val.id;
  mongoOp.name = data.new_val.name;
  mongoOp.dob = new Date(data.new_val.dob);
  mongoOp.gender = data.new_val.gender;
  mongoOp.location = data.new_val.location;
  mongoOp.save(function(err) {
    if(err) {
      console.log("Error creating mongo data\n",err);
    } else {
      console.log("Synced to MongoDB");
    }
  });
});
```

In the preceding code base, we are creating a new instance of the mongoose model object and mapping the schema to the values. At the end, we are using the save() method of mongoose to create a new document in MongoDB.

Next, we need to update the document if an update event occurs:

```
sync.on('update',function(data) {
  model.findOne({"rethinkId": data.old_val.id},function(err,mongoData) {
    mongoData.name = data.new_val.name;
    mongoData.dob = new Date(data.new_val.dob);
    mongoData.gender = data.new_val.gender;
```

```
      mongoData.location = data.new_val.location;
      mongoData.save(function(err) {
        if(err) {
          console.log("Error updating mongo data\n",err);
        } else {
          console.log("Synced to MongoDB");
        }
      });
    });
  });
```

In the preceding code, we are first finding out whether any document exists with this ID. Again, we are using our `rethinkId` field to find the document.

If the document is found, we are again remapping the schema to new values received from the RethinkDB changefeed.

At the end, we are using the `save()` method to update the existing document with the new data.

Next we need to delete the document if a `delete` event occurs. Here is the code:

```
sync.on('delete',function(data) {
  model.find({"rethinkId": data.old_val.id},function(err,mongoData) {
    mongoData = data;
    model.remove({"rethinkId": data.old_val.id},function(err) {
      if(err) {
        console.log("Error deleting mongo data\n",err);
      } else {
        console.log("Synced to MongoDB");
      }
    });
  });
});
```

Again, we are using our `rethinkId` field to find out whether such a document exists or not and if it does then removing it using the `remove()` method of mongoose. We are using the `old_val` key here because there won't be any value in the `new_val` key, since it is in the DELETE operation.

This completes the consumers for MySQL and MongoDB. All we need now is to execute this class as soon as the server starts. Here is the code added in the server file to create an instance for the consumers:

```
// loading the module
const mysql = require('./mysql');
const mongodb = require('./mongo');
// creating instance
new mysql();
new mongodb();
```

And that's it for the development part. To summarize, we have done the following:

- Developed a model for each database
- Developed a Polyglot agent to generate events on changes using changefeed
- Learned the Observer pattern
- Developed consumers for MySQL and MongoDB

All we need to do now is to run the application and perform the CRUD operation and see whether it's working or not. We will do this in the next section.

Running the app

So far, we have done lots of coding. It's time to test it. Before running the code, start all the databases: RethinkDB, MySQL, and MongoDB.

To run the code, go to the project directory and execute the following command from the terminal:

```
node app.js
```

It will start the Node.js server and you should be able to see a similar screen to the following:

```
● ● ●                    polyglot-rethinkdb — node app.js — 84×28
Shahids-MacBook-Air:polyglot-rethinkdb UnixRoot$ node app.js
Listening to port 4000
Database already created
table already created
Database is setup successfully
```

If you are running the code base in a local machine then you need to call these APIs using CURL or any API simulator:

```
GET /users - to retrieve all users data
POST /users - to create new user
PUT /users - to edit the user detail.
DELETE /users - to delete the user.
```

Let's begin by creating a new user. We have already used the API simulator in previous chapters so let's use CURL to make the API request.

Execute the following command from the terminal to make the request:

```
curl -H "Content-Type: application/json"
-X POST
-d '{ "name": "Shahid", "dob": "03/18/1992", "gender": "male", "location":
"mumbai" }' http://localhost:4000
```

This will return you the following output in the terminal:

```
{
    "responseCode":0,
    "responseDesc":"Success",
    "data":{
        "deleted":0,
        "errors":0,
        "generated_keys":[
            "d98b3e23-58a2-44b3-bb40-6c950a33dad5"
        ],
        "inserted":1,
        "replaced":0,
        "skipped":0,
        "unchanged":0
    }
}
```

Awesome. Let's observe the terminal where our server is running. You should see a similar screen to the following:

Observe the last line in the screen. It says the data is synced to MySQL and MongoDB. Let's do a cross-check. Log in to the Mongo shell and run the following commands in order:

```
use codeforgeek;
db.users.find().pretty();
```

This will print the output as shown in the following screenshot:

```
> use codeforgeek;
switched to db codeforgeek
> db.users.find().pretty();
{
        "_id" :  ObjectId("581a28a1d44f8b3758d5a2f6"),
        "location" :  "mumbai",
        "gender" :  "male",
        "dob" :  ISODate("1992-03-17T18:30:00Z"),
        "name" :  "Shahid",
        "rethinkId" :  "d98b3e23-58a2-44b3-bb40-6c950a33dad5",
        "__v" :  0
}
>
```

So we have seen the data in MongoDB. Let's check it in MySQL. Open phpMyAdmin and go to the database. In my case, the database name is codeforgeek, which you are welcome to change at your end.

Refer to the following screenshot showing the data in MySQL:

Awesome. It's working.

To do the update, execute the following CURL command:

```
curl -H "Content-Type: application/json"
-X PUT
-d '{
 "id": "d98b3e23-58a2-44b3-bb40-6c950a33dad5",
"name": "Shahid Shaikh",
"dob": "03/18/1992",
"gender": "male",
"location": "mumbai" }'
http://localhost:4000
```

Here we have updated the name. It will first update RethinkDB and then update it on other databases.

To delete the user, hit the following request:

```
curl -H "Content-Type: application/json"
-X DELETE
-d '{ "id": "d98b3e23-58a2-44b3-bb40-6c950a33dad5"}'
 http://localhost:4000
```

Yup, we just need the ID of the user to perform the delete operation. And of course, to read, just hit the GET request using following command:

```
curl http://localhost:4000
```

This should return all the users from the RethinkDB table.

This sums up the execution part of the program. I hope it feels like it's been worth reading and developing the code base and seeing how it works.

In the next section, we are going to talk about further improvements, which, if you like, you can do on your side.

Further improvements

There are two key improvements which you can do:

- Integrating the message broker
- Developing a distributed transaction

Let's discuss each one in brief.

Integrating the message broker

For now, we are using the `EventEmitter` class of Node.js to emit and receive events. You can hook advanced message brokers such as RabbitMQ or Apache Kafka. All you need to do is, instead of emitting the event in the `Polyglot` class, just push the changes in the message broker.

At the consumer end, any program can read it and use it for their use. This way, there will be high cohesion and less tight coupling.

If you are going to do it using RabbitMQ then we have already covered the integration part in `Chapter 7`, *Extending RethinkDB*.

Moving right along to the next improvement.

Developing a distributed transaction

For now, we are not using any transaction in between the databases to perform the CRUD operation. Since our databases can be SQL, NoSQL, key-value, graph-based, and so on, and not all databases provide transaction support, we need to develop one on our own.

The topic is still open for debate as to whether we should have the transaction in such heterogeneous databases, but if you want to then I believe it can be developed using batch operations.

Upon insertion, updating, and deletion of documents, you need to run the batch operations that take the query, status, and fallback query (the query to execute in case of an error and push it in some sort of queue). When the last database gets updated, you need to send the response to the client that the operation is completed.

In case of an error, start the process and execute the fallback query on each database and return the error to the client.

You are welcome to suggest and use the approach in a better way than this, but this is what I can think of to the best of my knowledge.

Summary

This chapter is indeed full of concepts, code, and execution. I am sure if you are reading this summary, you have got something out of this chapter. We have learned the concept of Polyglot Persistence and how we can develop it using RethinkDB. I hope it's helpful to you.

In next and last chapter, we are going to learn an amazing framework made by the RethinkDB team called Horizon. Horizon is the framework which gives you a ready-made middle-layer along with the database so that you can code your web/mobile app in blazing fast speed.

10
Using RethinkDB and Horizon

In the last two chapters, we focused on development and we are going to continue the same in our last chapter. Generally, there are three main layers of a web application development stack:

- Frontend
- Middle layer
- Backend

Even though Node.js fills the gap by using the same language, that is, JavaScript, across all three layers, there is still a need from some developers out there who just want to design their frontend application instead of writing backend logic.

Here comes **Horizon - Open source backend for JavaScript.** In one line, **Horizon** allows you to write web or mobile apps without writing backend code. Horizon uses RethinkDB as its data store and provides you with the backend logic ready to use.

In this chapter, we are going to learn topics related to Horizon:

- How Horizon works
- Installing and configuring Horizon
- Developing simple web application using Horizon

We will also look over some of the useful API's provided by Horizon.

Horizon seems really interesting with its concept and idea. It is community supported as well as supported by core founders of RethinkDB.

So let's dive in.

Workings of Horizon

Horizon is an open-source platform for building real-time, scalable web/mobile apps. It is built on top of RethinkDB, and allows the developer to get started with building modern, real-time apps without writing any backend code.

Horizon is assembled with three major components:

- **Horizon server**: A middleware server written on Node.js that works on RethinkDB and exposes simple API/functions to front-end applications
- **Horizon client**: A JavaScript client library that provides the front-end developer with access to RethinkDB with API/functions
- **Horizon CLI**: A command line tool that helps you in bootstrapping, development, and deployment

These three components work together to provide the front-end developer with a ready-made backend server.

Horizon client library provides functions such as for CRUD operations and can be directly called, which in turns asks the Horizon server to deal with the RethinkDB database. Please note that any API call from UI won't directly go to the database, it will go via the Horizon server.

Horizon CLI in turn provides you with a developer-friendly command line tool to create a new Horizon project, run and deploy it.

In the next section, we are going to learn more about how to install and configure Horizon in your machine.

Installing and configuring Horizon

Horizon is built on top of RethinkDB, so a RethinkDB server is mandatory before using Horizon. You will also need to install the latest Node.js and NPM (node package manager).

Download and install Node.js from here `https://nodejs.org/en/download/`.

To install Horizon, run the following command in the terminal:

```
sudo npm install -g horizon
```

This will install Horizon as a global node module package. You should be seeing a similar screen as shown here:

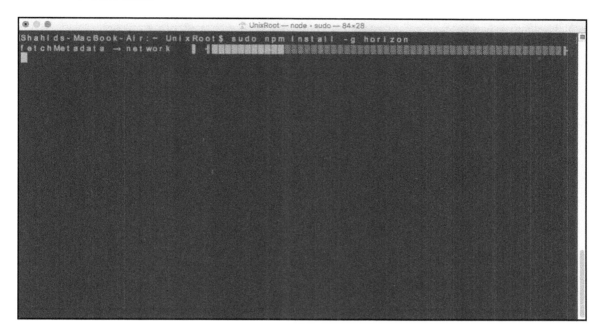

Once the installation is complete, you can access Horizon from the terminal using the hz command.

To create a new Horizon project, the CLI provides the hz init command. Here is how to create a new project using Horizon:

```
hz init horizonDemo
```

The third parameter is the project name and the directory name of the project. Horizon CLI will create the directory if it doesn't exist.

Once the project is created, it will show the files created on the terminal, something similar to the following screenshot:

As you can see in the preeceding screenshot, Horizon has created various files. Let's see what these are:

- `dist`: This directory contains static files. You can create code files directly here, or use it as the output directory for a build system such as gulp or grunt
- `src`: As the name implies, this contains the source code for your build system
- `dist/index.html`: This is a sample file to demonstrate the creation of the project. You can of course replace it with your own custom file, which we will discuss in a later section
- `.hz/config.toml`: This is the configuration file for the Horizon server
- `.hz/schema.toml`: This is the default schema file for your application
- `.hz/secrets.toml`: This contains the authentication details of the application

Since we now know what these files are, let's test out the sample application. Run the following command from the project directory to start the Horizon server. If your RethinkDB Server is up and running, it will connect to it automatically, and if it doesn't, it will also start the RethinkDB Server:

```
hz serve --dev
```

This will boot up the RethinkDB if it's not already started, and you can access your application at `http://localhost:8181/`. You should see a success message on screen similar to that shown in the following screenshot:

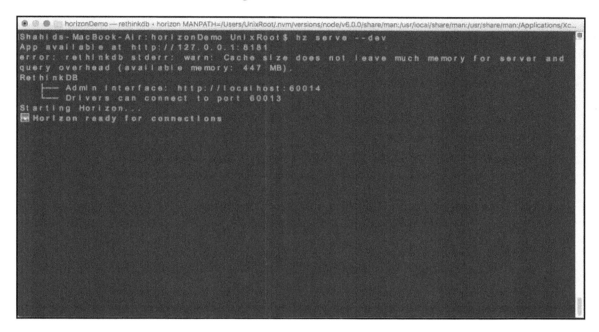

Now, go to `http://localhost:8181` to view your app. It will show you a message with your application name as shown in the following screenshot:

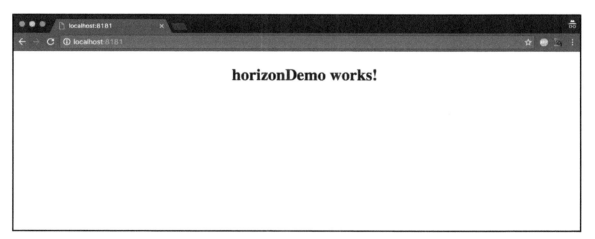

Upon execution of the `serve` command, Horizon does the following:

1. Starts the Horizon API server, written in Node.js.
2. Starts an HTTP server to serve the Horizon client library.

The `--dev` flag tells Horizon to start the application in development mode and do the following:

1. Start RethinkDB Server if it's not already started, and store the data in the `rethinkdb_data` folder inside the Horizon app.
2. Start the server in insecure mode.
3. Disable the permission system.
4. Automatically create the tables and indexes if they don't exist.
5. Serve static files from the `dist` directory.

If you don't pass these flags, none of these things will be done by Horizon. You should not use this flag in production applications, instead define the settings in the configuration file that is, `config.toml`.

 For a complete set of command line options, visit this link `http://horizo n.io/docs/cli`.

Horizon contains two APIs, which are the heart of the framework:

- **Horizon**: The class to manage the connection
- **Collection:** The class to manage data

Let's look over each in detail.

Class Horizon

The Horizon class provides us with the constructor, methods, and events to manage the connection with RethinkDB. Let's look over it in detail.

To create a new instance of this class, you can execute the following code in the client side:

```
<script>
const hz = new Horizon();
</script>
```

`Horizon()` constructor accepts various arguments, which are all optional; if you don't pass them it will use the default values.

Here are the constructor options:

- `host`: The hostname where the application is running, by default it is `window.location`, which is the native JavaScript way to determine the base URL of the application.
- `secure`: A boolean value to define whether to use a secure channel to exchange websocket messages. Default value is `true`.
- `path`: Path of the Horizon application running under the `host`. Default is `horizon`.
- `lazyWrites`: A boolean value to define whether the `write` operation should be executed in lazy manner, that is, when you execute the query in `lazy` mode, it doesn't reflect the changes in the database unless you iterate over the function returns with the write operation. Default is `false`.
- `authType`: Accept strings to determine which authentication method to use. The following are the options:
  - `unauthenticated`: No authentication required.
  - `anonymous`: Use anonymous details.
  - `token`: An object representing JWT tokens.

```
{                token: <value>,
                 storeLocally: true|false
}
```

If `storeLocally` is true, Horizon stores the authentication tokens on local storage of the browser, otherwise the user needs to authenticate the token every time he/she makes a request to the application.

Horizon also provides various methods that can help you to manage the connection. Here are some important methods.

Connect()

The Horizon connect method establishes the connection with Horizon. Although this method is optional, when you start using the collection, Horizon automatically creates the connection if it doesn't exist already.

Here is the code to demonstrate the connection:

```
<script>
const hz = new Horizon(); // Get access to the messages collection const
users = hz('users'); // Start establishing the Horizon connection.
hz.connect(); // Start using the collection
// if you skip the above step, Horizon will make connection for you
automatically.
  users.store({ name: 'John' });
</script>
```

This function returns various events related to the connection, which are as follows:

- `onReady()`: Emits when the Horizon server is ready
- `onDisconnected()`: Emits when the connection is ended
- `onSocketError()`: Emits when error occurred

You can also disconnect the connection using the `disconnect()` method.

During the application flow, you can also check the status of the connection using the `status` method.

`Horizon.status` method returns you the object containing the `type` key. The `type` key can have the following values:

- unconnected
- connected
- ready
- error
- disconnected

I think the values are self explanatory.

To check whether the logged in user is valid, you can use the `hasAuthToken()` method. You can also retrieve the user who is currently using the system by calling the `currentUser()` method. You need read access to the users collection to execute this function.

Horizon provides you with an aggregation function, which you can use in the frontend application to execute multiple queries and combine their results in one set. You can also pass this result to a `model()` function to create a new model in the RethinkDB, on which you can perform any CRUD operation.

The Horizon class does provide us with lots of functionality to manage the connection with RethinkDB. And more surprisingly, it's all happening at the frontend.

Let's move ahead and learn the next class, `Collections`.

Collection class

The `Collection` class provides us with a group of methods related to documents, and is backed by a RethinkDB table. Every document in a `Collection` is identified by a unique key stored in the id field.

To create a new collection, you can pass the name in the Horizon instance as shown here:

```
<script>
const hz = new Horizon(); // get a handle to a Collection const users =
hz("users");
</script>
```

`Collections` will be automatically created if they do not exist in development mode, or in production if the `auto-create-collection` option is set.

Methods on a `Collection` object allow you to perform CRUD, that is, create, read, update, and delete operation on documents. You can read documents by performing a match on any field by passing an object to match against.

Consider the following code snippet to understand how to perform the CRUD operations using the method returned by the `Collection` class:

```
// Store a user
 users.store({     id: 1,      name: "John" });
 // find the user "John" messages.find({name:
"John"}).fetch().subscribe(msg => console.log(msg));
 // the same, using a Horizon object directly hz("users").find({name:
"John"}).fetch().subscribe(msg => console.log(msg)); // get the message
with ID 1
 users.find(1).fetch().subscribe(msg => console.log(msg));
// Update user detail
users.update([
  {
    id: 1,
    name: "John doe"
  }
])
// get all users named John, ordered by ID
messages.order("id").findAll({name: "John"}).fetch().subscribe(msg =>
```

```
console.log(msg));
// remove user
users.remove({id: 1});
//OR
users.remove(1);
```

As you can see in the preceding code, we have demonstrated CRUD operations using the Horizon `Collection` methods.

The Horizon collection class contains lots of methods to query the data. For a complete list, please visit the following link `http://horizon.io/api/collection/`.

We are going to learn some important functions out of all in the next section.

Method subscribe()

RethinkDB results in a cursor, which we have to retrieve over to extract the data. The `Collection.subscribe()` function provides us with the same thing: it returns us a function to iterate over the cursor returned by the selection query.

This method, when attached to the `read()` query, will return three callback functions:

- `next(result)`: Returns a single document on each iteration
- `error(error)`: Returns error information
- `complete()`: This function is executed when the iteration over the cursor is finished

Consider the following sample code:

```
const hz = new Horizon();
hz("users").fetch().subscribe(
    result => console.log(Users:', result),
    err => console.error(err),
    () => console.log('All users fetched')
);
```

In the previous function, we are fetching all the users from the collection, traversing over the cursor using our `subscribe()` method, and printing the result.

 Note that when the `subscribe()` method is attached to the `fetch()` method, then the result callback contains the values in an array.

You can also attach `subscribe()` to the write functions. In the write case, it will return the `id` of the document or an error. Consider the following code:

```
hz("users").store([
    {
        id: 10,
        name: "John doe"
    },
    {
        id: 11,
        name: "Mary"
    }
]).subscribe(
    (id) => console.log("id: ", id),
    (err) => console.error(err)
);
```

You can also attach this method to changefeed, which is called watch in Horizon. In the next section, we are going to learn the watch method.

Watch method

This method converts a query into changefeed and return us a stream, which again can be hooked to the `subscribe()` method.

Refer to the following code to attach a changefeed to the collection:

```
const hz = new Horizon();
const users = hz("users");
 // triggers when user is added, deleted or changed
users.watch().subscribe(userData => {
    console.log(users: ', userData);
});
```

This will return you the exact values of the collection. Check the output:

```
users: []
users: [{id: 1, name: 'shahid'}]
```

If you would like to receive it in same way as in the backend server, pass the following parameter in it:

```
{
    rawChanges: true
}
```

And it will return the information in following format:

```
users: {type: 'state', state: 'synced'}
users: {type: 'add', new_val: {id: 1, name: shahid},
old_val: null}
```

In the next section, let's learn the methods used to perform the CRUD operations.

CRUD methods

To create one or more documents, use the `insert()` method. Consider the following code:

```
const hz = new Horizon();
const messages = hz("users");
// Insert a single document. There must not be a document with an id of 1
in // the messages collection.
messages.insert
({
    id: 1,
    name: "John"
});
// Insert multiple documents at once. All documents must be new.
messages.insert([
    {
      id: 2,
      name: "Mary"
    },
    {
      id: 3,
      name: "Jane"
    }
]);
```

Next, to read the document from a collection, you can use the `find()`,`findAll()` method. I am going to mention `find()` here. Consider the following code:

```
const hz = new Horizon();
const users = hz("users");
// get the message with ID 10
messages.find({name: "John"}).fetch();
```

As shown previously, `find()` returns the handle, which you can iterate using the `subscribe()` method.

Next, we are going to use the `update()` method to update an existing document.

To update a document, you can use the `update()` and `replace()` method. While replace will overwrite the existing document with a new one by keeping the same ID, in `update()` you can modify individual values.

Again, you can update single or multiple documents at once. Consider the following code:

```
const hz = new Horizon(); const users = hz("users");
// Updating the single document
users.update({
    id: 1,
    name: "John doe" });
// Updating multiple document
users.update([
    {
        id: 1,
        name: "John doe"
    },
    {
        id: 2,
        name: "Jane desouza"
    }
]);
```

Now, to delete a document, you can use the `remove()` method by passing the ID or JSON containing the search criteria. You can also use the `removeAll()` method to delete all documents from the table. Refer to the following code:

```
const hz = new Horizon(); const users = hz("users");
// to remove all docs
users.removeAll();
// to remove using ID
users.remove(1);
// to remove using other keys than ID
users.remove({name: "John"});
```

For information on the Collection methods, please refer to the official documentation here `http://horizon.io/api/collection/`.

In the next section, we are going to learn how to develop a simple application, using Horizon.

Developing a simple web application using Horizon

We have learned the basics of Horizon, installation and its APIs. Now it's time to combine our knowledge and build something out of it. In this section, we are going to develop a simple application that lets the user manage a TODO list. The end output will look like this:

The user can perform the following operation:

1. Add todo.
2. Update the status of todo.
3. Remove todo.

The codebase is provided by an awesome contributor, **Daniel Allan**, and the base style is forked from TodoMVC `http://todomvc.com/`.

Really amazing job, guys.

Let's move ahead to setting up the project.

Setting up the project

Start the project by creating a Horizon project using the Horizon CLI:

```
hz init todoHorizon
```

Now switch to the project directory and go to the `dist` folder. Refer to the following command:

```
cd todoHorizon && cd dist
```

Remove the existing `index.html` file and create `package.json` using the following command as shown here :

```
npm init --y
```

Now, let's install the required dependencies: in this project we are using `vue.js`, which is a lightweight JavaScript framework for app development. Refer to the following command to install the dependencies:

```
sudo npm i --S vue director todomvc-common todomvc-app-css
```

We are using the `director` module for routing purposes and the remaining two modules are for css and js from `http://todomvc.com/`.

Once the installation is complete, we can move ahead with development. We will start our development from Horizon functions to vue.js code. Obviously we need to perform a CRUD operations to manage the todo lists.

Developing the JavaScript code

Here is the codebase that manages the CRUD operation for todos:

```
(function(exports) {
 const horizon = Horizon();
 const todos = horizon("vuejs_todos");
 exports.todoStorage = {
   todos: todos,
   save: function(newVal) {
     todos.store(newVal);
   },
   update: function(todo) {
     todos.replace({
       id: todo.id,
       title: todo.title,
       completed: todo.completed,
       datetime: todo.datetime,
     })
   },
   remove: function(todo) {
     todos.remove(todo);
   },
   changes: function() {
     return todos.watch()
   }
 };
}) (window);
```

In the first two lines, we are creating a new **Horizon** instance and collection. In the next line, we are creating a function that in turn contains functions to perform the CRUD operations.

The save() function accepts the document as a parameter and will use the store method to save it in a RethinkDB table. Since we are not passing ID, RethinkDB will generate a random unique ID for the documents.

The remove() function takes the document as a parameter and removes it from the RethinkDB table.

The update() function takes the document as a parameter and replaces it with an existing document.

We are also assigning the changefeed to the table to constantly read changed values from the table and we are doing this in the changes() function.

We are going to consume these functions in our vue.js code.

Before going to `vue.js` code, let's configure our router. Here is the code to handle the routes:

```
(function (app, Router) {
    var router = new Router();
    ['all', 'active', 'completed'].forEach(function (visibility) {
        router.on(visibility, function () {
            app.visibility = visibility;
        });
    });
    router.configure({
        notfound: function () {
            window.location.hash = '';
            app.visibility = 'all';
        }
    });
    router.init();
})(app, Router);
```

In this function, we are creating a new instance of `Router` and then assigning the values to each route. These values are `all`, `active` and `completed`, and depending upon these values we will hide and show elements from the web page in `vue.js` code.

For invalid URLs, we are redirecting the user to the home page and setting the route to `all` that is, show all todos on screen. We are doing this in the `notfound()` function.

Now let's dive into `vue.js` code.

`Vue.js` encourages the developer to separate the business logic from the application logic as much as possible. `Vue.js` code is generally made up of the following:

- **Directives**: Code to extend the HTML functionality
- **Methods**: Custom functions
- **Computed**: An extension of the template to separate complex application logic from business logic

Our code also consists of directives, methods, and computed. Let's look over these one by one. Here is the code for computed logic:

```
(function (exports) {
    var filters = {
        all: function (todos) {
            return todos;
        },
        active: function (todos) {
            return todos.filter(function (todo) {
                return !todo.completed;
            });
        },
        completed: function (todos) {
            return todos.filter(function (todo) {
                return todo.completed;
            });
        }
    };
    exports.app = new Vue({
        el: '.todoapp',
        debug: true,
        // app initial state
        data: {
            todos: [],
            newTodo: '',
            editedTodo: null,
            visibility: 'all'
        },
        computed: {
            filteredTodos: function () {
                return filters[this.visibility]
                (this.todos);
            },
            remaining: function () {
                return
                filters.active(this.todos).length;
            },
            allDone: {
                get: function () {
                    return this.remaining === 0;
                },
                set: function (value) {
                    this.todos.forEach(function
                    (todo) {
                        todo.completed = value;
                        this.updateTodo(todo);
                    }.bind(this));
```

```
                                                 }
                                   },
                         }
          });

          todoStorage.changes().subscribe(todos => exports.app.todos =
          todos)

   })(window);
```

First, we wrote some functions which our computed is going to need. These functions returns all todos, active todos, and completed todos from the RethinkDB. The reason for having these functions is that they are not directly inside the completed, but it is used to practice the separation of logic.

Next, we have defined our `computed` functions; there are three functions that are going to return the todo lists from the RethinkDB.

The `filteredTodos()` function calls the filter function, depending upon the route. If the route is `all`, it will call the `all` function of the filters, and so on.

The `remaining()` function returns the todos lists that are not completed.

The `allDone()` function performs two tasks: first, it returns whether all todos are done or not in boolean and next, it marks all todos as completed and reflects it on UI.

Next we are using our `changes()` function to iterate over the changed data and assign it to the todos array, which we defined at the beginning of the `Vue.js` function.

Next we need to define the methods: we need methods to call from the UI to create the todos, and do the updating and deleting.

Here is the code for the methods:

```
methods: {
      addTodo: function () {
            const value = this.newTodo && this.newTodo.trim();
            if (!value) {
                  return;
            }
            const todo = {
                  title: value,
                  completed: false,
                  datetime: new Date(),
            };
            todoStorage.save(todo);
```

```
                        this.newTodo = '';
        },
        removeTodo: function (todo){
                todoStorage.remove(todo);
        },
        editTodo: function (todo) {
                this.beforeEditCache = todo.title;
                this.editedTodo = todo;
                this.updateTodo(todo);
        },
        doneEdit: function (todo) {
                if (!this.editedTodo) {
                        return;
                }
                this.editedTodo = null;
                todo.title = todo.title.trim();
                if (!todo.title) {
                        this.removeTodo(todo);
                }
        },
        updateTodo: function(todo){
                todoStorage.update(todo);
        },
        cancelEdit: function (todo) {
                this.editedTodo = null;
                todo.title = this.beforeEditCache;
        },
        removeCompleted: function () {
                filters.completed(this.todos).forEach(this.removeTodo);
        },
}
```

The first function is going to take the todo entered by the user and form the JSON document. Then it will call the function that we developed earlier to save the todo in the RethinkDB table.

The next function is going to take the value of todo as a parameter and remove it from the RethinkDB table using the function we developed in the earlier section.

While editing the todo, the user can either save the edited todo or just change his/her mind and leave it. If users leave the todo while editing, the application should undo the change and show the actual todo.

In the editTodo() function, we are dealing with this scenario by setting the flag variable called beforeEditCache , which stores the old todo name, and in the updateTodo() function we are updating the todo in our RethinkDB table.

If the user chooses to cancel the editing, we just replace the todo name with the value saved in our beforeEditCache variable. We are doing this in cancleEdit() function.

We remove all completed todos in our removeCompleted() method.

This covers the JavaScript code part for the application. In the next section, we will develop our frontend for the todo app.

Developing the frontend

We are going to use vue.js and director in our frontend code, so we need to first include them using the <script> tag. Here is the basic skeleton of the HTML code:

```
<!doctype html>
<html data-framework="vue">
    <head>
            <meta charset="utf-8">
            <title>Todo app using Horizon</title>
            <link rel="stylesheet" href="node_modules/todomvc-
common/base.css">
            <link rel="stylesheet" href="node_modules/todomvc-app-
css/index.css">
            <style> [v-cloak] { display: none; } </style>
    </head>
    <body>
        // custom code
            <script src="node_modules/todomvc-common/base.js"></script>
            <script src="node_modules/director/build/director.js"></script>
            <script src="node_modules/vue/dist/vue.js"></script>
            <script src="/horizon/horizon.js"></script>
            <script src="js/store.js"></script>
            <script src="js/app.js"></script>
            <script src="js/routes.js"></script>
    </body>
</html>
```

As you can see in the code, we have included all of the JS code after the body tag completion. This is called the **off the fold** technique to speed up the rendering of the page in the browser.

Next, we need to create the HTML code to make the UI where the user can enter the todo, and edit and delete them. Here is the code that goes right after the body tag:

```
<section class="todoapp">
  <header class="header">
    <h1>Todos</h1>
    <input class="new-todo" autofocus autocomplete="off" placeholder="What
needs to be done?" v-model="newTodo" @keyup.enter="addTodo">
  </header>
  <section class="main" v-show="todos.length" v-cloak>
    <input class="toggle-all" type="checkbox" v-model="allDone">
    <ul class="todo-list">
      <li class="todo" v-for="todo in filteredTodos | orderBy 'datetime'
-1" :class="{completed: todo.completed, editing: todo == editedTodo}">
        <div class="view">
          <input class="toggle" type="checkbox" v-model="todo.completed" v-
on:change="updateTodo(todo)">
          <label @dblclick="editTodo(todo)">{{todo.title}}</label>
          <button class="destroy" @click="removeTodo(todo)"></button>
        </div>
        <input class="edit" type="text" v-model="todo.title" v-todo-
focus="todo == editedTodo" @blur="doneEdit(todo)"
@keyup.enter="doneEdit(todo)" @keyup.esc="cancelEdit(todo)">
      </li>
    </ul>
  </section>
  <footer class="footer" v-show="todos.length" v-cloak>
    <span class="todo-count">
      <strong v-text="remaining"></strong> {{remaining | pluralize 'item'}}
left
    </span>
    <ul class="filters">
      <li><a href="#/all" :class="{selected: visibility ==
'all'}">All</a></li>
      <li><a href="#/active" :class="{selected: visibility ==
'active'}">Active</a></li>
      <li><a href="#/completed" :class="{selected: visibility ==
'completed'}">Completed</a></li>
    </ul>
    <button class="clear-completed" @click="removeCompleted" v-
show="todos.length > remaining">
    Clear completed
    </button>
  </footer>
</section>
```

Let's understand this code.

First we have created a textbox using the `input` tag and assigned our CSS classes to it, and once the user hits enter by typing something in it, we call our `addTodo` function:

```
<input class="new-todo" autofocus autocomplete="off" placeholder="What
needs to be done?" v-model="newTodo" @keyup.enter="addTodo">
```

Next, we list all the todos that are remaining and not completed yet. Here, we use our `computed` function to render the todos' data directly.

We use the `filteredTodos computed` function to retrieve all todos based upon the route. Each todo has a checkbox, and upon clicking on that, the user can update the todos.

Next, in the `footer`, we use the `computed` function again to fetch the count of todos. Finally, we call the `removeCompleted` function when the user is trying to clear all the completed todos.

This completes our codebase. Let's try to run it and see how it works. To run the application, switch to project directory and run following command:

```
hz serve --dev
```

This will start the RethinkDB and Horizon server; you should see the message in the terminal as shown here once the application is ready:

Now visit `http://localhost:8181` to view the application and start creating todos. Here is the main screen with the todos:

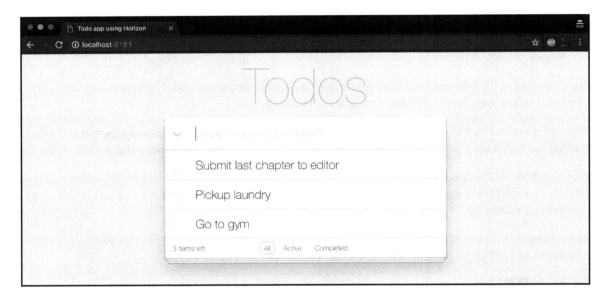

Now you can mark the items as completed by clicking on the checkbox placed on the left hand side with each todo; refer to the following screenshot for this:

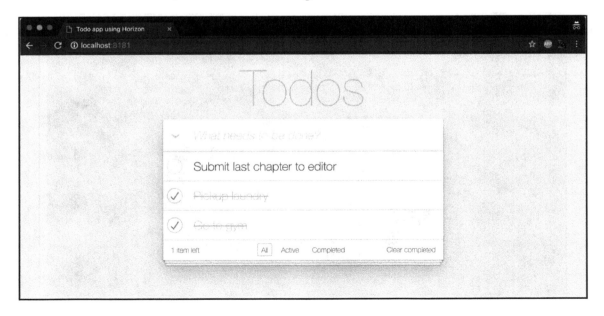

You can view the active and completed todos using the button on the footer. Click on the button placed on the right side of the footer to clear all the completed routes.

This completes the development of the web application using Horizon. In the next section, we are going to learn about the Horizon user management system.

Horizon user management

If you are using Horizon's Authentication system and not any third party authentication, such as Facebook, Twitter, and so on, user information is stored in a special Horizon collection called **users**.

You can use the user's collection either by loading it similarly to other collections, or access it directly as shown in the following code:

```
const horizon = Horizon();
// Access as a standard collection
const users = horizon('users');
// Access through the shortcut
const users = horizon.users;
```

 Note: Third-party authentication is not in the scope of this chapter, however you can learn about it here http://horizon.io/docs/auth/.

When a new user is created, Horizon assigns it two user groups, which are:

- **Default**: Rules for all the users
- **Authenticated**: Rules for those users who are authenticated by the system

These user groups are used to assign permission to the user. A typical document in the **users** collections looks like this:

```
{
    "id": "D6B8E9D0-CD96-4C01-BFD6-2AF43141F2A7",
    "groups": [ "default", "authenticated" ]
}
```

You can make changes to the document in the **users** collection, but not to the collection itself. No user is allowed to perform any change in the collection.

This covers the user's authentication in Horizon. To learn more about the permission system, please visit the official link `http://horizon.io/docs/permissions/`.

Summary

We started with the basics of Horizon and then moved to its installation and project configuration. We learned about two important APIs that are the heart of the Horizon framework. We also developed a web application using Horizon and `vue.js` and then learned about the user management system in Horizon.

I hope you have got something out of this chapter as well as this book, since this is our last chapter, and if you are reading this summary then I would like to thank you and wish you a great life ahead.

Index

Credits

Author

Shahid Shaikh

Reviewer

Rafael Ferreira dos Santos

Commissioning Editor

Amey Varangaonkar

Acquisition Editor

Vinay Argekar

Content Development Editor

Amrita Noronha

Technical Editor

Akash Patel

Copy Editor

Vikrant Phadkay

Project Coordinator

Shweta H Birwatkar

Proofreader

Safis Editing

Indexer

Mariammal Chettiyar

Graphics

Disha Haria

Production Coordinator

Arvindkumar Gupta

About the Author

Shahid Shaikh is an engineer, blogger, and author living in Mumbai, India. He is a full-time professional and a part-time blogger. He loves solving programming problems and he is, expert in software backend design and development.

Shahid has been blogging and teaching programming in practical way for more than two years on his blog. His blog is quite famous in the developer zone and people all around the world take advantage of his expertise in various programming problems related to backend development.

Shahid has also authored a book on Sails.js – MVC framework for Node.js published by Packt.

I would like to thank my parents, my family, and my friends for being kind and supportive during the book development period. I would like to thank my friends, who changed their plans according to my schedule for various occasions. I would also like to thank the RethinkDB team for helping me out with various architectural questions. You guys are awesome!